Golden Boy
—— THE ——
HAROLD SIMMONS STORY

John J. Nance

Co-Produced by Patricia A. Davenport

EAKIN PRESS ᴇᴘ Austin, Texas

FIRST EDITION
Copyright © 2003
By John J. Nance
Published in the United States of America
By Eakin Press
A Division of Sunbelt Media, Inc.
P.O. Drawer 90159 ☞ Austin, Texas 78709-0159
email: sales@eakinpress.com
💻 website: www.eakinpress.com 💻
ALL RIGHTS RESERVED.
1   2   3   4   5   6   7   8   9
1-57168-747-5

Library of Congress Cataloging-in-Publication Data

Nance, John J.
  The Harold Simmons story / by John J. Nance.– 1st ed.
    p.   cm.
    ISBN 1-57168-747-5 (hb)
  1. Simmons, Harold (Harold C.) 2. Businessmen–United
States–Biography. I. Title
HC102.5.S42N36 2002
338.092–dc21   2003000433

Introduction

*E*ast Texas in the spring can be beautiful beyond reason. In the throes of a mild, windy day with clouds gliding by urgently overhead, there is an inspiring majesty to the place, a living canvas of color, as the fields explode into an endless carpet of wildflowers. Never mind that, when in the jaws of summer, the same place feels like a construct of Dante. Never mind that in July the amber waves of grain are replaced by wavering columns of rising heat from the parched fields.

It was on such a day that I began the field research for this book, eager to see the tiny place called Golden and find the true roots of a man I'd known off and on since the sixties. With the gentle wind and the restless clouds as my accompaniment, it seemed logical that the Golden, Texas, of today must be light years away from the wide-spot-in-the-road community that had launched Harold Clark Simmons on a journey to amazing wealth and success. I recall saying as much to my editor and business partner, Patricia Davenport, as she took notes and pictures that day to catalogue what would presage a voluminous collection of research.

Change is always a constant, and I recall postulating that there had probably been vast changes in Harold Simmons since his Golden days. Whatever forces had shaped him, I thought, a man who had lived the American dream to the extent he had, building a rock solid collection of companies and wealth through intellect and perseverance, probably wondered himself where that little boy from Golden had gone. Indeed, how could he be the same? Billionaires, American mythology holds, are not like ordinary people. A billionaire could never have retained those basic traits of honesty and integrity that were the bedrock of teaching in the Simmons household. Aren't we told to win by intimidation, adopt the management methods of Attila the Hun, or otherwise approach business as mortal combat in which there are no rules of civility and humanity? If true, then I would find a wide gulf between the boy and the man, and there the postulation began to falter, because I already knew that Harold Simmons was no heartless Attila.

But certainly the steely determination and quiet self-assurance demonstrated so effectively in his business dealings had to be traits acquired along the way, though some of the seeds might have been sown in Golden. Changes and forces yet undiscovered, in other words, had to have separated the man and the boy in the ways that always excite writers.

But I was wrong.

The Harold Simmons I knew contemporarily as chairman of the board, billionaire, and philanthropist is the very same person as the little boy I'd envisioned standing in those fields wondering about an unknowable future. The traits, the self-assurance, the integrity, and the sly, almost stealthy sense of humor described in the many interviews to follow tracked with unwavering consistency from the Golden years to the present day. Perhaps that was the greatest surprise. I was a sophomore at Southern Methodist University when I first met Harold in the drugstore he'd purchased across the street from the campus. He was in his thirties, quiet and friendly and obviously a hard-working man who happened to employ a lady named Ruth Priest, the mother of my future wife, Bunny. Where your girlfriend (and later fiancée) spends a lot of time, so do you, and I found myself an unofficial member of the University Pharmacy crowd, spending too much time in the booths of the coffee shop Ruth managed, and spending too much money on hamburgers and coffee. But it also qualified me as an early observer of Harold Simmons, and he was a study in responsibility and dedication, a young employer who took good care of his employees, and for whom no job in the store was too menial.

I suppose I knew Harold Simmons would end up owning more than one store, but as the years progressed and I flew through Vietnam and an airline career living a long way from Dallas, the newspaper clippings from the home front told of the rise of Harold Simmons from corporate entrepreneur to investor to empire builder. And throughout, my family and I were cheerleaders in absentia for the success of a man we all knew richly deserved his success.

What I did not know, until the opportunity to write his biography came about, was how much of a struggle his life and career have been at times, and correspondingly, how stoically and steadily he's guided his companies and his family through personal and professional storms that would have sunk a lesser man.

Later in life than should have been the case, Harold met and married the woman so many of his friends wish he'd found decades earlier. Annette Simmons, a bright and beautiful, capable and equally determined Texas girl with a degree from SMU, gently and firmly opened up new worlds for Harold, though there is much about their remarkable years together I was unable to chronicle in these pages. I'm sorry, for instance, that the difficulties of marrying into a diverse family with young girls in teenage crisis—a difficult circumstance for any new wife—could not have been more thoroughly illuminated. Suffice it to say that I am somewhat in awe of Annette's above and beyond history of patience and resilience in trying to build bridges of love and caring to Harold's daughters, two of whom rejected her as viciously and wantonly as they rejected their father years later when they launched a heartbreaking attempt to destroy him.

Overall, however, this book is Harold's journey in the world of business, and the underlying strength of that remarkable story is a constant quality and axiom: Good people do finish first, and the American dream can be won by decent men and women who care about others, regard their word as their bond and honesty as their responsibility, and who regard the wealth they may achieve as a God-given responsibility, not a jackpot.

JOHN J. NANCE
University Place,
Washington
March 1, 2003

BOOK ONE

The Golden Years

CHAPTER 1

GOLDEN, TEXAS: 1947

*J*ohnny Dowell shook his head and groaned, the protest coming too late as his companion across the checkerboard grinned and plucked several pieces from the rickety table balanced on the front platform of the icehouse.

"Game!" Harold Simmons said.

"*What?*" Johnny answered in mock pain.

"I figure that's about as much a beating as you can take, Johnny."

"Pure luck! You took advantage. I was distracted."

"Sure you were."

"I was. I was thinking about that little redhead I was telling you about. Come on, Harold. One more."

Harold was already on his feet and stretching, his arms high over his head, his lanky six-foot frame looking thoroughly suited to the high school basketball court he'd been practicing on an hour before. He finished the stretch and held his hands behind his head a few seconds as he studied a passing flatbed, a barely animated old Ford chugging along toward Mineola with a single bale of hay on the back. He could hear grousing as Johnny Ray Dowell replaced the checkers and pushed back his chair in resignation, regarding his slightly older friend with a cock-eyed expression.

"What are you thinking, Harold?"

"Thinking about the next basketball game."

"Yeah, and you're gettin' a big head, 'cause the only strategy the coach could come up with last week was 'Everyone pass the ball to Harold.'"

"Good advice."

Johnny shook his head again, noticing that Harold's eyes were on the western horizon and tracking the Saturday afternoon shadows thrown by a huge live oak across the road. The sun popped out once more from behind a passing cumulus cloud, the downbeat to a sensory symphony of light cascading in on a freshening northwest breeze. The wind carried the aroma of freshly cut hay and the sweet perfume of the surrounding woods exploding into springtime in the wake of a hard winter, and Harold loved every bit of it.

The skyline was full of leaves. Big leaves, small leaves, all of them urgently green and wearing mistletoe capes. Everywhere he looked, the boisterous color of the sweet gums, elms, and post oaks once again eclipsed the wispiness of the steadfast loblolly pines whose faithful long-needled branches always kept the East Texas woods supplied with a lifeline of color through the otherwise monochromatic winters.

In the distance, a mockingbird suddenly belted out an impassioned coda as wildly unprincipled and enthusiastic as Harold knew he should feel at sixteen. The breeze stiffened, tousling his dark and full hair, which framed clean-cut features that had never escaped the notice of the local girls.

"See you later," Harold said as he stepped down from the front stoop of the icehouse and turned south without looking back, aware that Johnny was following and coming up beside him, his own six-foot-one frame an easy match.

The two friends walked in silence for a while, kicking through the new grass and across a red dirt road toward the small creek bordering the south end of town.

"You remember when I first met you, Harold?" Johnny said at last, once again unable to make heads or tails out of his friend's expression.

"Yeah. I punched you in the nose."

"You were six, and I came up to you in church and showed you my muscles, Popeye style."

"I remember. You had it coming."

"Probably did. I always respected you after that."

A passing cloud swallowed the sun again, softening the intense colors in the field ahead, a carpet of Indian paintbrushes and black-eyed Susans sprouting among the Johnson grass. Something slithered urgently away from the sound of thier footsteps, but neither of them took notice as they approached the bank of the creek and found a place to sit.

"So, you going on to Austin?" Johnny asked, running the few images he had of the University of Texas around in his head as he scratched his chin.

Harold nodded.

"You lookin' forward to it?"

The senior basketball star of Golden High School shook his head in silence, his eyes on the opposite bank, his mind racing through the conflicting thoughts the question had triggered. He was graduating. He had a 97 average and a family that would settle for nothing less than a four-year degree. His father, Reuben Leon Simmons, was the school superintendent of the Golden School District, his mother, Fairess Clark Simmons, a well-educated English teacher and pianist.

"I hear Glenn Reuben's doing okay," Johnny offered, thinking about Harold's older brother, and remembering one of Mr. Simmons' serious lectures on the importance of education. He shivered slightly at the thought of ever being disciplined by the "Fessor," as everyone called Harold's father. One year left, and so far Johnny had avoided being sent to the office.

"Glenn's doing fine."

"How're you doing?"

"Meaning?"

"Something's eating you."

"Probably chiggers."

"No . . . you've been real quiet-like this last week. We've all noticed."

Johnny lobbed a small pebble into the water, his eyes following the ripples as they moved lazily downstream. He didn't expect an answer. It was just a fact most everyone knew. Harold Simmons was not keen on leaving Golden, Texas.

■   ■   ■

There was a world out there, of course, Harold knew. His father and mother's school might have been small, but the academics were thorough, and he had learned enough of history and geography and science and languages and even politics to know that Golden was neither the center of the known universe nor his ultimate destination.

But it was more than home.

Glenn Reuben, his brother—now away at college himself—had called his younger brother a smarter bear once. Maybe he was. Grades came easier to Harold than to Glenn, but Glenn never seemed to be upset by that. Harold could just figure things out a bit easier. Even things he really detested, like having to speak or perform in front of others.

Harold thought back to the years of growing up in the Baptist church. It had been built in 1912, and was well worn when Harold came along and his mother started playing the piano in the Sunday service. He couldn't remember when he wasn't a member of the Baptist Youth Fellowship Union, though he'd tried to forget the times he had parts to perform during the meetings. His friends would give him a hard time for memorizing his lines, while they had to stumble and read theirs, but the thought of messing up in public was not pleasant. At least if it was memorized, he'd explain, you'd get that part of it right.

He let the past sixteen years sweep like a wave through his memory, a warm cascade of images such as movies at the Select Theater in Mineola, riding the mare he'd owned until age thirteen, getting his driver's license at age fourteen, and singing in church next to his mother at the piano. So many memories, and so many people, such as his mother's half brother, Shelton Clark. Uncle Shelton was fat as a hog with manners to match and abysmally unaware of it, but generous to a fault—though there were times when Harold thought the old '37 Chevrolet Uncle Shelton let him drive had probably been a thinly disguised murder attempt. The steering was so loose he could barely control it. Shelton had warned he had to keep it in the middle of the road, regardless of who or what was coming. The old Chevy had achieved a local status equal to the Ancient Mariner's albatross: all but dead, but still a dangerous ornament around that neck of the woods.

He thought of his father rolling his eyes at the sight of that car lurching to a halt in front of the house and his uncle lifting his huge stomach out of the car to amble up to their front door for dinner—an all-too-regular occurrence.

"Oh, Lord, here he comes again!" the senior Simmons would mutter, causing them to chuckle.

Harold had seldom seen his father laugh at anything. An orphan at the age of fourteen in 1904, Professor Simmons had sculpted himself into the image and substance of a serious educator without the help of formal education. With little more than the second grade behind him, he had studied on his own through a young life of hard work on various farms and had taken many tests to earn his college degree and teaching credentials, and later a master's degree. He was the professor of Golden—the "Fessor"—respected, stern, serious, and determined. He was devoted to his boys and his wife, but was not the sort of man to take his sons hunting or fishing. His one indulgence, Harold knew, was walking the 160 acres he had purchased across the road, looking at their small herd of cattle, and presumably ruminating over important things. Harold had never thought about loving his father, any more than it would have occurred to the elder Simmons to announce to his son that his father loved him. It was simply an understood fact, reflected in their mutual pride and respect for each other. And Harold was immensely proud of being the Fessor's son.

Now his father was thinking of moving the family to Austin and changing jobs so that Harold could go to UT and still live at home. That was disturbing, somehow, even though it was a selfless intention and might mean a better house than the small clapboard superintendent's residence the school district had provided for fourteen years. The house was conveniently located only a hundred yards or so from the school. It had been electrified only two years before, and everything now looked different in the harsh light of the naked bulbs hanging over the rough pine-board floors. Gone were the flickering kerosene lamps that had been their only illumination before electric-powered lights had been installed. There was a cold water pump now on the screened-in back porch, which ended the daily water draws, and a butane-powered stove for heat. Since his sophomore year, Harold had luxuriated in the warmth of a kitchen heated by a butane stove instead of the ancient wood-burning variety he'd stoked for his mother almost every morning of his life. Of course, an indoor bathroom was still someone else's luxury—one of those things you knew they had in Dallas, and maybe in a few homes in Mineola. Harold considered that a future luxury, the absence of which would never justify leaving the good life in Golden.

At least Johnny hadn't asked what he wanted to do with himself after college, Harold thought. It was something he didn't want to think about. The prospect of moving was jarring enough. There was a tiny ache to get on with life, but a bigger ache about leaving friends like Johnny Dowell, or girlfriends like Thomasene Champion, Johnny Bill Gilbert, Cleta Worley, and Bobbie Nell Cathey. His gang. His lifelong companions, most of whom were equally puzzled at what they should do and why they should leave their little corner of paradise at all. The girls, of course, would probably be teachers if they did anything before marrying. But the guys had bigger choices, especially now that the war was over and America had won and there were no limits. Of that Harold was sure. He could be a farmer or a lawyer or anything he wanted to be.

If he had any idea what he wanted to be.

Harold shuddered a bit, remembering the inscription his father had written in a small autograph book at the end of third grade. "I expect, Harold," the senior Simmons had said, "that you're going to make a fine lawyer, and maybe a judge. So I'm going to be sorely disappointed if you're not on the United States Supreme Court by the time you're sixty."

So it would be pre-law courses at the University of Texas in the fall, although the idea of being a lawyer someday and trying cases and having to speak in front of a courtroom full of people was chilling. Any form of public speaking was a nauseating experience for him.

Harold got to his feet suddenly and shoved his hands deep in the pockets of his dark pants as Johnny looked up, thinking how well dressed his pal always looked.

"That new movie starts tonight in Mineola, Harold. You goin'?"

"Which one?"

"That Betty Grable movie. Mother ... wore something."

"*Mother Wore Tights*. I saw the billboard last week."

"Yeah. You goin'?"

"Don't know."

"It's Saturday *night,* Harold."

"Yeah, I know. Happens every week about this time."

"Very funny. So you goin'? Or are you still sore because they raised the price?"

"Used to be a dime and now it's a quarter. I'm trying to save my money."

Johnny shook his head sadly. "Well, look ... I'll come by later. See if you've loosened up some."

■   ■   ■

It was a short walk back to the house, and dinner would be on the table soon, Harold knew. He could hear the voice of his five-year-old brother, Douglas MacArthur Simmons, echoing from the front yard, accompanied by the distant sound of a car rumbling down the road and someone shouting a "howdy" back in the tiny town. Tomorrow was Sunday, he thought, which meant the young preacher they often hosted for Sunday dinner and overnight lodging would be back. He looked forward to that. Foy Valentine drove to the Golden Baptist Church twice a month from the seminary in Fort Worth. He was still training to be a pastor, but he was already their preacher.

But that was tomorrow. Tonight, it would be just the family, and maybe the radio, unless he decided to go to Mineola after all. Or maybe he should go down the road and see Thomasene. He'd seen too little of her lately, and he knew she was a bit confused by graduation, too.

The sun was hanging low in the west, the warm, rosy hues of evening softening the red dirt of the road, igniting the glow of the grassy fields and painting a towering cumulus to the north with stratospheric brush strokes of pink and red some 30,000 feet high. The distant thunderstorm had muttered and grumbled with faraway thunder. It trundled past as if irritated that Golden was to be left untouched by anything but the conflicting emotions of one of its native sons.

Somehow it seemed to Harold that he was seeing his hometown for the first time.

He drifted across the road and behind the house and sat on an old stump just north of the detached garage, listening to the scurrying and cackling of the chickens penned up just beyond. How many times, he wondered, had he and Glenn fought to get out of plucking a chicken after their mother had picked one up and wrung its neck with perfunctory ease? He hated that job. Both of them did. And she was never happy with the results, since the brothers would always leave some of the tiny pinfeathers and she'd have to singe them away over the gas flame. He loved the results, though, since Mrs. Simmons made the best fried chicken in town. Probably in the known world.

In his peripheral vision, Harold saw movement around the corner of the house, where he had seen Glenn come into view so many times. But it was only Mackey, as Johnny and the others called his baby brother. He missed his big brother a little, but that, too, was something he never really thought about. Glenn was doing what Glenn had to do: going on with life. And life, the way Harold had always defined it, when he thought about it at all, was an endless procession of steady activity— much of it interesting, some of it a little exciting, and all of it satisfying.

Life centered around the Baptist church and the school and his family and friends.

Life was stacking watermelons in the summer for money, and doing it better than anyone else. It was delivering his brother's *Dallas Morning News* route after Glenn left for college, and being on time and reliable. It was riding his mare and being the school's best basketball player in his senior year.

Life was being the responsible son of a very respected family, and being lucky enough to be better off than some of the folks around East Texas who could barely afford shoes and food.

And life was having an amazing mother who could cook, sew, teach, manage, and inspire love.

Harold let his gaze wander from the house to the town, past the Gilberts' place and the undulating tracks of the pathetic little railroad which operated occasional trains, to the post office where their box, number 325, was located. This was Harold Simmons' home, that number seemed to say. Always had been. What was waiting down there in Austin at the University of Texas might prove exciting, but it couldn't get any better than this.

CHAPTER 2

*T*he mental concentration of shaping a two-page history paper into "A" work for a tough professor had muted the mundane sounds of life in Harold Simmons' consciousness. Even the ringing of the single telephone in the family's new home hadn't yanked him back to the present—until now.

Slightly disgusted with the phone's shrill ringing and the fact that he was the only one home to answer it, he let his pencil drop to the table as he launched himself toward the offending instrument.

The voice on the other end was cloyingly cheerful. A radio announcer, sponsored by the local red-and-white grocery chain. "You're on the air!" the announcer proclaimed, as if that fact would fulfill some lifelong dream. "Are you ready to answer our three-part question?"

Harold glanced back at the table, where the unfinished report lay amidst a minor explosion of textbooks and notes, the half-empty pages mocking his break in concentration. He recognized the radio show. It was on every day, but a forgettable program. He preferred music, something on the order of Hank Williams or maybe something by Bob Wills and His Texas Playboys.

"Okay, what question?" Harold asked.

"Name three departments in a grocery store."

"That's the question?"

"Yes, sir! For one hundred fifty bucks, can you name three departments you might find in a grocery?"

Harold snorted and shook his head. Who couldn't?

"Bakery, produce, and meat," Harold said.

"That's RIGHT!" the announcer yelped, seemingly overjoyed to the depth of his being.

When enough information had been exchanged for Harold to pick up the money at the station the next day, he returned to the table and sat down, his thoughts a million miles away from the half-finished assignment.

Of course, $150 wasn't a fortune, but for a college junior with a monthly allowance of $25, it was a nice surprise. If that sort of windfall could be replicated at will, it might add up to some real money.

Harold picked up his pencil again, the traffic outside on Airport Boulevard competing with the sound of the deep-throated engines of a departing DC-4 accelerating less than half a mile away at Austin's municipal airport. The small sounds and stimuli that had been inaudible and undetectable earlier against his considerable powers of concentration now roared in his ears.

A contest. They had called him. Were there other contests out there with such unbelievably easy answers, and money attached?

A heavy truck rumbled by, and suddenly the room seemed a little warm—luxuriously warm, compared to the drafty old house they'd left in Manor, Texas, twelve miles to the east. He got to his feet again and ambled absently toward the back door.

In the summer of 1947 his father had accepted the position of Manor's school superintendent. Leon Simmons had moved his family from Golden before classes started in the fall, taking over the small 1890s house that the school district had refurbished. For the first time, there was an indoor bathroom, though only cold water poured from the pipes. No matter. The house was comfortable and close to Austin, and by October, Harold had perfected the fine art of hitchhiking back and forth to the university as his father and mother settled into their new scholastic duties at Manor.

A hundred and fifty dollars! Six months' allowance! Harold suddenly smiled at the fact his mother hadn't been around that afternoon to hear about the win. A little private mad money was a good idea.

He cracked open the door, letting the cold outdoor air spill inside, bracing and sharp. Under the expanse of a winter-gray sky, the small patch of Bermuda grass they'd planted was still brown, but the yard was the nicest they had ever had. It surrounded the new Austin stone residence, which had been built by his father on the lot he'd purchased a year ago. The house was a prideful investment for the elder Simmons, a tangible icon of his success as a school superintendent who could now afford to build his family a comfortable home with all the modern amenities: indoor plumbing, hot water, central heat, a gas kitchen. While nothing they'd had before had amounted to hardship, this was truly nice. Complete luxury. And what had pleased his father even more was the prominent location, since a little display of success was within the value system of Professor Simmons.

There was a young magnolia tree in the backyard. When the weather warmed, Harold thought, that tree should explode in fragrant blossoms. Spring would bring a collage of colors and aromas of magnolias and jonquils and hyacinths and maybe even the heavy, sweet essence of gardenias—as well as freshly mown grass.

He remembered the little lawns of Golden. More patches of grass than lawns, really, but he had been the best grass cutter in town. A quarter per yard had paid for many a movie. And the smell of freshly cut grass on a warm morning was like nothing else on earth.

Duty scratched at the back of his consciousness and he closed the door, forcing himself to return to the table. His mind, however, remained focused on how to replicate the sudden little coup of found cash.

■　　■　　■

Not even the weighty requirements of the University of Texas had been able to lessen Harold Simmons' academic progress. He'd achieved perfect straight A's in high school, and he easily made the dean's list in his first year of collegiate courses; however, his major changed from law to economics with the confirmation that lawyers were, indeed, required to speak in front of others. Basketball and the challenge of winning a letter on the varsity team had occupied some of his extra time in the first two years, but once that had been achieved, the lure of the game began to pale against the ever-interesting pursuit of girls and the widening possibilities of life in general.

There was a troubled world out there, even in the midst of the postwar euphoria, but while the endless reports of daily disasters and periodic progress failed to hold his rapt attention, the drumbeat of news was not lost on him. In many ways he had grown up with newspapers and their messages. Somehow newspapers and a cherished collection of Classic Comics helped prepare him to understand more easily the world beyond Golden and Mineola, and even Austin.

■   ■   ■

The growing threat of world communism loomed like an approaching line of Texas thunderstorms as 1950 dawned. China had fallen to the communists. A presumed turncoat named Alger Hiss was going to prison for being a communist in the State Department. The rise of a communist government under someone named Ho Chi Minh in an incomprehensibly distant place called Vietnam was being reported. And, though few saw it coming, the Korean peninsula was about to explode in a communist-driven war that would suck in the United States and make the draft even more of a clear and present danger to those who drifted academically.

There were weighty personal decisions pending just around the corner for Harold, decisions about advanced degrees and the eventual direction his working life should take. But those could wait. Classes and studying and dating were satisfying enough, along with the occasional trip to a dance hall like the sawdust-on-the-floor establishment north of Austin in the tiny community of Dessau.

Cleta Worley had taught him and Johnny Dowell to dance back in Golden, and Harold had taken to it right away. He liked the movement and the music and the general feeling of enjoyment all around.

"You've heard of Dessau Hall, haven't you, Harold?" a UT friend had asked one afternoon.

"Sure have. Why?"

"You know about that professor who holds a contest every Wednesday?"

"No. I've seen Tex Ritter there, and the band named Amarillo. They're really great."

"Well, Wednesday nights one of our psychology profs is out there asking twenty questions on computer punch cards, and every time he can't find a winner, the jackpot goes up."

"Really? I may have to look into that."

The memory of his $150 radio win and the challenge of questions which, if answered correctly, could bring cash prompted a series of Wednesday nights at Dessau Hall. Harold enjoyed the music and dancing, but the main attraction was trying to figure out how the contest could be won. Each week the jackpot climbed a little higher as the contestants failed, but by the third visit, Harold Simmons had spotted something no one else had detected: There was a pattern to the answers. They were predictably counterintuitive.

"Look here," he said to his date, Norma Jean Fairchild, on the way to Dessau one Wednesday evening, "that guy asks who invented chop suey, for instance, and then gives you a choice of answers with two Chinese names, an American name, and one very Irish name, right?"

"Uh-huh."

"Okay, there're two logical choices—the Chinese names—so it can't be one of those. Understand? Too obvious."

"I suppose."

"Then there's one semi-illogical choice, which would be the American name. But then there's this far-out, highly unlikely choice, and it's always that highly unlikely one. Week after week."

"If you say so."

■   ■   ■

The jackpot topped $325 the following Wednesday evening when Harold answered all the remaining questions correctly and won the prize. Walking away with the money felt very good. After all, Glenn had said he was the smarter bear, and he was. He'd figured it out, even though the questions weren't things anyone would have necessarily learned in a classroom. There had been a system there, a method, and he'd solved the puzzle by deciphering the system.

The call the following week wasn't entirely a surprise. Hub Sutter was the half-blind leader of Hub Sutter and the Hub Cats, the group that had been holding forth the night of the big win. Hub had a local radio show. Would Harold mind "a'coming on down and doin' the show," as the big, smart college boy winner?

"Sure," Harold agreed. Hub might have a vision problem, but he was one heck of a clarinet player, and Harold liked his music.

The experience of answering a few questions in front of a microphone didn't go badly, and Harold might have admitted to enjoying the process if a family friend hadn't heard the radio broadcast and phoned Professor and Mrs. Simmons to congratulate them on their boy's windfall.

"How much was that windfall?" the senior Simmons had apparently asked the well-meaning witness. "Three hundred twenty-five dollars!" came the impressed reply—which revelation was followed by the immediate cessation of the not inconsiderable allowance provided by the family since his freshman year. Suddenly, Harold found his expertise in winning had also won him the right to pay his *own* tuition, as well as the opportunity to practice some accelerated diplomacy by smoothing a few ruffled feathers at home about the unannounced win.

But—the thought kept occurring to him—*he'd figured it out!* And if you could figure out things and make legitimate money doing so, there was a lesson there.

Somewhere.

CHAPTER 3

AUSTIN, TEXAS: 1951

"*A*nother roadrunner!"

A startled chaparral cock suddenly coalesced from the heat-driven mirage on the griddle of a blacktop road ahead, racing for its life to get out of the way as the big '47 Dodge roared past, its driver smoothly pulling the wheel to the right to follow the next curve. With the sun beating down and the mercury somewhere above ninety-five, the open windows scooped in a blast of heavy, humid summer air, but the two young Texans inside the car were used to it. Stifling heat and the sight of Lake Austin's blue waters to the west and a thousand feet below the road were ritual elements of spending summer in the sleepy university town of Austin in 1951.

"So what *are* you planning to do?" the young man in the passenger seat asked the driver.

"What do *you* think I should do?" Harold Simmons asked evenly in return.

"You in love with her?"

Harold glanced right and grinned slightly. "Penny, you mean?"

"No, your damned car. Of course Penny! You in love with her?"

"Yep. She's . . . incredible. I can't imagine being without her. And she really needs me, you know? She didn't have much of a childhood."

"So where is she today?"

"Belton, with her folks."

"What's her daddy do there?"

"He's a barber, I think. Part-time."

"You *think?* You don't *know?*"

"Well ... he moves between jobs a lot."

"Harold, I don't think I've seen you anywhere without her in months. It's as if she's attached at the hip. I'm surprised she lets you out of her sight."

"Yeah, she's a bit clingy, but I like that," Harold said, a smile playing around the edges of his mouth. "She's a honey, and she's all mine."

"Marry her. That's my opinion. Saves money in the long run." He glanced around at the lake far below as the car once again rolled perilously close to the razor-thin shoulder. "You planning to get us back to the campus in time for class? Alive, that is?"

Harold nodded as he slowed the big Dodge for another curve, then glanced over at his friend with raised eyebrows. "I just like to drive. Usually I like to drive without someone chattering my ear off."

"I'll ignore that insult."

"You really think I should marry her?"

"Yep."

"Well, that's good, since we've already come to the same conclusion."

"And already set the date, I expect, without telling any of your friends. When? Next month?"

"Next month," Harold nodded. "October. I may even invite you if you promise to be civil."

Norma Jean Fairchild had been known as Penny most of her life. She was three years older than her twenty-year-old graduate student fiancé, but Harold Simmons fit almost perfectly the profile of the husband she'd hoped to find at UT: steady, employable, and protective. She needed rescuing, and Harold was the appropriate knight.

Life in the Fairchild family had been tenuous at best, with a father whose grandiose, uneducated, money-making schemes had all but impoverished them, leaving her mother and three siblings to lurch from one financial crisis to another. In her desperate search for someone who could take her away and give her something resembling a stable life, little more than six months of dating the handsome young man from Golden was all she needed to seal her decision. Harold's proposal, once made, was instantly accepted.

■   ■   ■

The Texas weather had cooled considerably as Harold stood with Penny before a minister in the chapel of the UT Baptist Student Center in early October. Both sets of parents were present. Glenn Reuben served as best man, while one of Penny's girlfriends played the sole bridesmaid, and Harold's little brother Douglas stood with Glenn's wife and a handful of university friends. Penny was slim and attractive, and even though a full white wedding dress was beyond their collective means, Harold thought she looked resplendent in the informal suit she wore.

The service was brief, but before the vows had been completed, Penny swayed and tottered before falling gracefully to the floor in a dead faint. Harold barely managed to catch his bride in time, and as he sat with her on the floor of the chapel trying to bring her back to full consciousness, Pastor Blake Smith of the University Baptist Church of Austin finished the deed by pronouncing them well and truly married.

Less than a year of graduate school remained as they settled into the one-bedroom furnished apartment Harold had rented in Austin. The honeymoon consisted of a relatively expensive restaurant dinner before an initial voyage of physical surprise in their new bedroom. The intimacy of their first night together seemed enough of a celebration, since there was work to be done to finish up his degree and money was tight. The two lovers shouldered it all with cheerful equanimity: Harold graduated Phi Beta Kappa and then excelled at the task of finishing a master's in agricultural economics in record time with near-perfect grades, while Penny secured a job with the U.S. government in Austin as a clerk-typist, bringing in the type of salary typically paid to women in the postwar period. Rosie-the-Riveters were scandalizing society by wanting to work at men's jobs for equal pay: $100 or so per month.

By January 1952, their first child was on the way, and after the onset of summer brought graduation, Harold had aced the tests to qualify for a position with the U.S. Civil Service Commission as an investigator. Scoring high enough to bypass the preference given to veterans, he secured the GS-7 position with ease, aware that it would take them far away from Austin.

With Penny in the last stages of pregnancy, Harold packed the '47 Dodge his father had purchased for him in 1951, hugged his mother, shook his father's hand, and steered the car onto U.S. 81 for the five-hour trip up to Dallas, which would be his first duty station with the Civil Service. A tiny furnished duplex on Mt. Washington Street had been rented for the princely sum of $67 per month (and paid for on the first and fifteenth out of necessity), and Harold soon settled down to what would prove an interesting job, if one which failed to fully challenge his capabilities.

Scheryle Simmons entered the world in a Dallas hospital on October 5, 1952, as her young father paced a hole in the waiting room linoleum. The delivery was not particularly difficult for Scheryle's mother, but her father was a different case. Harold Simmons had given no more thought to the status of being a father than any other young man of stable background, limitless future, and new wife. In fact, he was barely conversant with the fact of *being* married, with all its implications. How could he be a father? A father towered almost larger than life: respected, stern, educated, and far older than Harold's twenty-one years. A father did things like run a school district, however small. A father was that rock of reliability you could always depend on for answers to anything.

How could a father be a freshly minted graduate with more questions than answers?

Yet, here she was—his daughter. However short his self-image might be from that of the classical father, there was no denying his new status. Little Scheryle was his, and that reality called for an indulgence seldom experienced in the Simmons clan: a celebration.

As soon as Penny felt sufficiently strong, Harold hired a babysitter and headed for one of the best restaurants in downtown Dallas, one located next to his office, and one he'd been promising to take Penny to for many months. With Harold in his suit and Penny in an attractive dress, they were seated without reservations in the plush interior, both of them feeling adventurous and special—until Harold opened the menu.

In a day when a full meal at a café might run to $2.50, the dinners lavishly described before them began at $12.00. By the time they ordered coffee and paid a tip, $20 would be gone—almost ten percent of Harold's monthly take-home paycheck. There was no way.

Chastened and somewhat embarrassed, Harold and Penny quickly left the restaurant and went down the street to Luby's Cafeteria, where they indulged in a relatively lavish steak dinner for about $3.00.

"You know," Harold said as he looked at the cash register tape and shook his head, coffee cup in hand, "I don't understand why anyone eats in a fancy restaurant like that when you can get a great meal at a place like this for normal prices. I mean, what's the point? Who needs fancy surroundings?"

"Not us," Penny agreed. "Definitely not us."

■　■　■

Diapers and highchairs and baby clothes added up, and $350 per month began to seem barely adequate to cover expenses. Though it was a good starting salary by the standards of the day, Harold realized he had to look for savings wherever he could, and soon discovered he could save almost $15 per month if they moved out of the furnished duplex and into an unfurnished one. Finding something to serve as furniture was the only challenge. Harold bought a divan, a small TV set, and a couple of $2.98 lawn chairs from a nearby drugstore to go with the bed his mother had given them. He hauled the old, flat spring and mattress bed combination all the way from Austin, lashed to the roof of his car, and bought a folding card table to use in the breakfast nook. It was anything but opulent, but it was home—and it was a beginning.

Harold's new headquarters office was in Dallas, but the constant out-of-town assignments became an immediate challenge, and one the young father resolved to handle by taking his family on the road with him whenever possible. They didn't go along on shorter field assignments, but longer ones, such as the two-month posting to the Civil Service's office in Hollywood, California, in the spring of 1953. Harold packed Penny and Scheryle in the car and headed west, immensely enjoying the unfolding vistas along U.S. 287 through Amarillo, and the famous two-lane Route 66 through New Mexico and Arizona to Southern California. The cheapest tourist courts available (the nascent versions of what would ten years later become motels) served as shelter along the way, and a rustic variety of inexpensive truck stops and cafés provided their meals. If there was hardship attached, it went unnoticed. Harold knew his salary would have to be stretched, and when they reached the exciting surroundings of Los Angeles, he felt fortunate to find a tiny, inexpensive apartment to serve as a temporary home.

The assignment was a perfect opportunity to see an exciting area, and Harold did his best to take Penny and Scheryle to see the sights, including one particular foray to Knott's Berry Farm in Orange County, not far from where Disneyland would later be built. They decided to have lunch there as well, but the fried chicken they ordered was all but inedible, and the restaurant was wholly uninterested in refunding their money. On return to their apartment, Harold wrote a letter to the head of Knott's Berry Farm describing the situation and demanding their money back. Such a bold demand was an inconceivable act to Penny, but weeks later Harold received a gracious reply from the president and a full refund, a response he would never forget.

Life in the first years of marriage seemed to require little else for Penny but the satisfaction of having four walls and a roof around her— and a supply of the Dr Pepper she drank all day long. Whether in an inelegant room in some far-flung city or back in the small house in Dallas, her security was having a husband with a steady job, regardless of what that job might be. Life could offer no greater horizon. It was the answer to the prayers Penny's mother had uttered in vain most of her married life, the goal of having a breadwinner who knew how to work hard and steadily without irresponsible thoughts of get-rich-quick schemes. Life was hard work, and the most you could expect was having a steady supply of it and a roof over your head. That was enough for Penny.

It would not, however, be enough for her husband. There was a quiet determination building in him that she did not see—could not see; did not want to see. For Harold, each new experience on the job and each new contact with the world of business pushed the vanishing point of his horizon to greater distances. His professional peripheral vision, his ability to be aware of and learn about the business world which seemed to whirl all around him (while he did the mundane things a Civil Service investigator did), was sparking increasingly broad ideas, all of which revolved around a growing recognition that while money wasn't everything (as his mother had taught him), it was apparently a lot more important than he had ever believed.

After all, he was a father now, and his little girl would one day need money for college, just as he had needed his father's financial help in his collegiate years. Someday, he and Penny and Scheryle—and perhaps a second or third child—would need a bigger house, with a larger play yard, and maybe a new car for a growing family. Such things could cost a lot of money, and government jobs, however secure, would never reap anything more than a modest income.

What had seemed perfectly acceptable from the perspective of college and graduation began to echo ominously with hollow promise.

It was late October 1953, and the last of the leaves were gone from the broadleaf trees of North Texas, leaving behind a landscape as colorless and bleak as the mere thought of a working life in midlevel jobs. A modest income would leave him forever on the backside of the money curve, always wanting more, and always depending on the largess of others as he waited for the next marginal raise.

And what if those others were not as smart as he was?

Occasionally he would drive past a small row of shabby houses somewhere along a highway, and for a second, the sameness of the dwellings would equate with a form of economic servitude. For the occupants of those apartments, that was the best they could do. But it wasn't the best *he* could do.

Harold thought back to the two-month assignment in L.A. There were beautiful estates there, many of them belonging to the film stars who had made Hollywood a glitterdome of artificial excitement. He'd spent several afternoons motoring alone through Beverly Hills after work, passing the marbled arches and gated drives of the wealthy, glimpsing the Mediterranean mansions through the opulent veil of mighty oaks, fragrant eucalyptus, and stately palms, all of them maintained by armies of gardeners surrounding the unseen staffs of servants within. It was quite a show for only a few gallons of cheap gasoline, but curiously, the magnificent vistas ignited no bonfire of desire in his gut. Opulent mansions and great wealth were not required to attain the things he wanted—merely the ability to make enough money to have what a young family would need without struggling and drowning in debt and being forever under the thumb of someone else. That and the satisfaction of proving he could do better than the average guy. How to achieve such things was just a puzzle, and puzzles could be solved.

Increasingly, such thoughts occupied his mind on the long drives to various assignments around Texas in 1953 and '54, weeklong trips he made alone, since Penny preferred to remain at home. Harold Simmons was developing a deep love of the open road. Unfolding before him on a sunny day, it offered a form of exquisite solitude, a view of life from a slightly loftier perspective. Especially the Texas roads of the fifties, which were some of the best in the nation. Texas had pioneered a network of wide, two-lane highways connecting the myriad towns and hamlets of Central and East Texas as efficiently as the arteries and vessels of the human body. They were rivers of concrete easily navigable by a driver whose mind was wandering the feathered canyons of distant skies as well as figuring out solutions to various problems. Texas roads were nothing like the monstrous, pothole-ridden, semi-paved wagon roads of Oklahoma, Arkansas, or Louisiana.

Sometimes it was just the chance to think that made the drives so enjoyable. Sometimes it was the opportunity to sing at full volume. Show tunes, popular songs, melodies from endless nights in Golden listening to country music—all of it would burst from the car through the medium of Harold's voice, the tunes wafting away into the slipstream as the band played on in his mind. The miles would melt into a pleasant blur of passing trees and houses and cotton fields, his ears full of the sound of engine and wind, his mind working away at the intriguing puzzles of commerce and personal destiny. When in the thrall of such moments, not even the popular Burma-Shave signs along the way could distract him.

■　　■　　■

In 1955 the Civil Service Commission suddenly decided to reduce their force of investigators. Veterans still had preference. Even though his high scores on the qualification exam put him ahead of the former military men in acquiring the job, the scores were meaningless in deciding who to let go. Non-veterans went first, and Harold Simmons found himself furloughed, but given the opportunity to join the Federal Deposit Insurance Corporation (FDIC) as a bank examiner. It meant less money per month, since the FDIC job was a GS-6 instead of a GS-7. It also meant being stationed in Alexandria, Louisiana, instead of Dallas. But it meant a new opportunity. If he wanted to know how to make money in reasonable quantities, banks—as the infamous John Dillinger had said—were where the money was. Perhaps spending several years looking at the books of tiny backwoods banks could unlock some more of the mystery.

News of the furlough had been a blow, but this was more than a new horizon—it was exciting! Information was the key to figuring out how things worked, and he was going to get paid for the experience, which was, all in all, a pretty fair deal.

The job had already been accepted and the plans for moving final-ized the evening Harold sat beside Penny on their small bed and tried to paint for her a verbal image of the vision he was seeing. Penny sat silently as he talked, the omnipresent Dr Pepper in her hand.

"Maybe, within a year or two," he was saying, "I can figure out how to raise the money to start or buy a small company. Something I can make grow."

"Why?"

Harold turned toward her, not noticing the flash of fear in her eyes. There was a wind blowing outside through the Dallas darkness, and rain was pelting the small duplex, chattering against the window glass with a nervous patter, as if warning of worse to come.

"Why? To make us some money. You don't want to live here the rest of your life, do you?"

"We're not anyway. We're moving to Louisiana."

Another gust of wind rocked the house ever so slightly, the power of it sending a shiver up her spine, the recognition of something else she was powerless to control.

"Penny, that's not the point," Harold was saying. "There's a lot of opportunity out there, and this is a good chance to learn how to do something with it."

"I don't care about opportunity. A good job is a good job. Just be glad you have a job."

"Well, I *am*, but I want to do something with it," he said. "I'm smarter than half those people out there who are making money build-ing good businesses. If they can do it, I can."

"And what about what *I* want?" Penny shot back.

"I don't understand."

"That's right, you don't understand! You don't understand what it's like to be a miserable little girl, ignored by her parents, nothing but white trash in a world that ignores white trash and destroys peasants like us who try to buck the system and get rich quick with grandiose schemes."

"I didn't say anything about grandiose—"

"You want to own businesses! You want to buy companies! So did my father, and they always beat him down. You don't care what I want."

"Penny, what are you talking about?"

"*Me!* I'm talking about *me!* I don't want any crazy schemes. I just want us to settle down and work. I want a little of your attention. You ... you pay more attention to the baby than you pay to me."

"Honey, look, I'm sorry ... " he reached for her, startled by the dismissive response.

"We need some sleep if we're going to drive to Louisiana tomorrow," Penny said, clearly ending the discussion.

CHAPTER 4

JARRELL, TEXAS: 1955

*H*arold nosed his 1952 Rocket Olds 88 into a parking place in front of the small, brick bank building and set the brake, thinking about the Louisiana license plate he'd just seen on the highway. He'd moved his family to San Antonio, Texas, recently, and already Alexandria, Louisiana, seemed a million miles away, as did his first days examining banks—although the job had begun only six months before.

Wait, it was eight months.

He glanced at the dashboard of the Olds. His first new car, and he'd already had it three years and put over 120,000 miles on it, along with three sets of tires. The engine was getting cranky and the suspension a bit soft. Maybe it was time to buy something else.

He looked up through the windshield at the small bank. They were all alike, Harold thought, these small-town banks. Every week, since he'd joined the FDIC, essentially the same bank building had appeared in his windshield as he parked the Olds. Different towns, different names, and slightly different fronts, to be sure, but the small-town banks of Texas and Louisiana that Bonnie Parker and Clyde Barrow had achieved folk-hero status robbing during the twenties were still in business, often owned by one person or family. Some built around 1900, some a bit later, they were square, two-story, and brick, usually occupying one corner on a town square. Some sported an elaborate square clock hanging over the door with the bank's name printed in gold leaf.

Some were too poor for even that ornamentation. The total deposits of such little institutions seldom topped more than half a million dollars, and most of them, as businesses, weren't worth more than $30,000 to $50,000.

Yet they were the backbone of the community to hard-working farmers and ranchers and small-town merchants. They kept the checking accounts and the savings accounts and issued the loans that kept the community going, sometimes with more altruism than business sense. Few such banks ever charged a fee for anything. Checking accounts were free, interest on loans was low, and, like the people they served, they were solid but unspectacular in their profit potential. A sharp businessman could improve their performance and turn a profit on such a bank. It had taken Harold Simmons less than six months on the job to become intimately familiar with the picture.

He pulled on the coat to his only business suit and closed the car door, then stood in the street alongside, stretching for a second, inhaling a potpourri of aromas: fresh bread from a bakery halfway down the same block, fragrant red mud along the gutter from a recent rain, and a whiff of gasoline from somewhere down the street.

He would be soloing this time. After a short apprenticeship traveling with a team of inspectors on a long list of other audits, it was his turn to enter a tiny bank lobby with worn pine-board floors and aged woodwork around the small tellers' cages and announce the federal examination they already knew was coming. There would be paper bands bearing the letters "FDIC"—seals, really—to place around all the ledgers, cautioning the employees not to touch. And he would have to count and total the cash in the various tills and work into the evening to learn what he needed to know to permit them to open on schedule in the morning. Then he would examine the loans and the other records that made a bank a bank, looking for things out of balance, or improper transfers of money, or whatever else might imperil the bank's ability to continue honestly serving its community—in this instance, Jarrell.

He looked up at the name of the bank just to make sure he knew where he was this time. It was on the sign, all right. Jarrell. The First State Bank of Jarrell.

When he was done, Harold thought, he'd probably leave behind a few gentle recommendations and take his leave with a smile and a handshake. He'd return, then, to the San Antonio office and file his routine paperwork before heading home to a very pregnant Penny and two-year-old Scheryle.

He closed the door to the Oldsmobile as a heavy truck rumbled by behind him and a block away the voice of a young woman bellowed from the open window of a pickup truck as she hailed a friend on the sidewalk. Harold turned to watch for a second, his attention momentarily diverted, then turned back to the bank. He would check into the hotel later, probably around 7:00, and find a café for dinner. He'd already had lunch along the highway in Austin, just a few dozen miles to the south.

He walked the few paces to the southwest corner of the bank building and pushed through a set of tall, creaking doors mounted at a forty-five-degree angle in the corner of the two-story brick structure.

Once inside, the familiar smell of aging woodwork and stale smoke greeted his senses. There was a blue haze in the place, the smoke hanging just beneath the dark-stained, embossed-tin squares which formed the ceiling. With the temperature outside in the sixties, the interior was cool, but comfortable, and he wondered why the ancient pot-bellied stove in the corner behind the teller wasn't crackling with a wood fire.

It was very quiet. As the doors shut behind him, he could hear the stately ticking of a wall clock and the clatter of an ancient adding machine somewhere toward the back.

Familiar sounds.

The only teller behind the two cages—a humorless woman in her sixties—looked up at him with a wholly puzzled expression and then a sudden flash of recognition. Behind her, he could see the bank president, a woman, who was already on her feet and coming around the side of her weathered desk, reminding herself to smile and shake the hand of the young examiner who was about to disrupt her institution. Harold could see fatigue in the woman's eyes as he approached, and knew instinctively she had probably guided the tiny bank through the depression and the war. He would find out later. He liked people like this. Solid people. Texans, like himself, who handled life even-handedly and honestly.

It was unusual for a woman to be in charge. Typically, the president was some well-worn male, often carrying a half-chewed Travis Club cigar as he guarded his tiny domain from the back side of an ancient desk.

■   ■   ■

It was 7:30 before Harold could clear the bank for reopening the following morning. One of the tills was a few pennies off, but other than that, tomorrow's work would involve looking at the loan portfolios and records, things he could do without disrupting the flow of business and conversation as the citizens of Jarrell and surrounding communities came in and out.

There was a small, two-story hotel two blocks down that had been in business since the twenties, and he walked over to get a room. The clerk was apologetic about the lack of television in the rooms, but Harold hardly understood the apology. He had a book to read, and if he got too bored, he could always drive back toward Austin to one of the dance clubs he used to frequent, or go see his mother and father. Or, better still, just get to sleep early.

There was a gentle rhythm to being on the road alone, if you didn't push it. Harold enjoyed being able to sit in a quiet room, with no one bothering him, and read until he got sleepy. And there was so much to read, and to learn, although the mystery of the banking business at this level, he thought, was no longer a mystery. He was vaguely aware it might be bravado talking, but he'd all but decided that there wasn't much more to learn from these tiny backwoods banks. Maybe, instead of examining them, he should be buying them and changing the way they did business. Strange that others weren't thinking the same thing.

Harold recalled an injudicious remark he'd made to a bank owner a few months earlier in the tiny community of Lavernia. There was a chance the bank president might have taken it as an insult, although he hadn't acted that way.

"Well," Harold had told him, "you've got a nice bank here. If you ever want to sell it, I'd sure appreciate it if you'd give me a call. I think I'd like to buy it."

The man had nodded solemnly, but he'd probably been laughing inside, and thinking, *Here's a foolish kid, hardly out of college, who wants to buy my bank? And what does he expect to use for money?*

Harold smiled to himself. He had that part figured out. It wouldn't take much to leverage the purchase of a little bank. Maybe five thousand. Ten at the most. He could probably get Glenn to help and find someone to lend him the rest. If he could get this one, he could move the family to Jarrell and show the entire banking community how to really make money by increasing the yield and efficiency of the place.

The thought of Penny stopped him. She would balk at the idea of their buying a bank.

Harold remembered the chocolate bar he'd stowed away earlier in his briefcase. Not much to eat, but it beat spending money on a sit-down dinner when he wasn't really hungry. He opened the window of the tiny hotel room and sat on the single chair, watching the deep purple of twilight still hanging in the western sky. He munched on the chocolate and calculated how he could raise enough money if the owner should happen to take him up on the offer.

After all, it was possible.

Anything was possible.

CHAPTER 5

AUSTIN, TEXAS: 1955

*T*he return drive back to the family home from his father's gravesite service was understandably difficult for Harold Simmons' mother. For Harold, married now and a father himself (as was Glenn), the continuity of the family in Austin had been an unspoken, if unrealistic, expectation. The jarring loss of that foundation in his life—the sudden, heart-wrenching sight of his mother sitting in abject confusion in the living room trying to come to grips with the task of raising her youngest son without her husband or his income—was very difficult to comprehend.

Somewhere in previous years, Harold recalled someone saying or writing that a man was never truly a man until his father had died. He had thought that a curious statement at the time. His father had always been timeless and indestructible.

But now the "Fessor" was gone, a fact which seemed impossible, even though Harold had been at his bedside just after the initial heart attack, and remained for several weeks until a second heart attack plunged his father into a coma from which he never awoke.

Through the months that followed, Harold moved Penny and Scheryle from their San Antonio apartment to the family home on Airport Boulevard in Austin to save money and to keep his mother company. He continued his weekly travels and audits around Central

Texas for the FDIC, but spent as much time as possible at home, deeply worried about his mother.

There had been no health insurance and no life insurance, and barely $7,000 in savings, all of which went to pay the hospitalization and burial. Mrs. Simmons still had her job as a schoolteacher, but the income would barely cover the cost of the home mortgage plus basic expenses, and the only way she could significantly raise her salary was to get a master's degree, something which could hardly be done overnight. While Harold urged his mother to enroll at the University of Texas in a master's course, he knew it would take her years to complete the curriculum on her own, even in night school. But the goal of earning an additional thousand dollars a year just for holding such a degree was a substantial incentive, and so, she began the course, working with her son's assistance to complete her thesis and secure the master's degree.

There was, as well, a $500 note due at the bank, one taken out by his father. On a cold day in the fall, Harold walked into the Austin bank and paid the full amount from his own savings. The payment was a very personal, heartfelt gesture of respect and thanks to the man who had worked so hard over the years to nurture and educate him. Harold walked from the bank that afternoon substantially poorer in monetary terms, but richer in so many other ways, and that recognition left him silently fighting back tears on the trip back to his house.

■　■　■

On December 15, 1955, Lisa Simmons made her debut in an Austin hospital just as her father was closing in on his first genuine business deal. Enthused and excited about both events, Harold Simmons marked the date as the real beginning of his ability to make money and control his own destiny.

The purchase involved another tiny bank he had audited, this one in Bosque County in the town of Iredell, seventy miles northwest of Waco. Unexpectedly, he'd found the bank was for sale, and he'd made an offer almost immediately as he scrambled to scrape together enough cash to make the deal work.

"This could be exactly what we've been looking for!" Harold had said to Penny with barely-contained enthusiasm. But with her thoughts fixed solely on a new baby and three-year-old Scheryle to care for,

Harold's news had sparked instead an ever-deepening indifference, if not panic. If he succeeded, they would move to Iredell, which was close enough for periodic drives back to Austin to check on his mother and Doug, but distant enough to resume their own lives—something Harold was increasingly determined to do. With monetary success could come the ability to help his mother financially. Though she had her own salary, its limitations were well understood, and those limitations had become a new motivation, however slight, to make money in greater quantity.

Harold's plans and spirits had soared as the negotiations coalesced to a series of offers and counter-offers and a road trip to Iredell. He knew the book value of the bank, around $35,000. He knew the market value was a bit higher. And he knew the bank's potential was far higher if it were managed well.

It all made sense. He'd need $5,000 to swing the deal, and that could be raised. He was sure it could.

But something felt wrong. Without a personal history of buying and selling banks, Harold knew he was at a disadvantage, but he was perplexed at his own nervousness. Returning from his last visit to Iredell with the deal almost in hand, and with a fairly good chance of scraping together the money needed, his confidence suddenly evaporated, leaving him with a shaky latticework of plans and assumptions which immediately began to totter and fall.

One of the biggest worries was the fact that Penny virtually hated the idea of moving to Iredell. In fact, she hated the idea about as much as she hated the idea of taking any financial risks in the first place. Then, too, he had to admit that Iredell was basically an impoverished farming community in a sea of rattlesnake-infested mesquite and open fields, few of which yielded anything which could be charitably called reliable agriculture. Regardless of how smart Harold was, Iredell could prove to be a turnip at the blood bank, incapable of yielding profit to even the most brilliant management ideas. And then there was an even more important question: Was this *really* the place he wanted to use to demonstrate his capabilities in business and finance? Sure, he had figured out the small banking business, but was that enough?

Any such deal would require money from Glenn, and it would drain Harold's last dollars from savings. His ability to feed his family after paying the mortgage for the loans to buy the bank would depend on his being able to pay himself a salary as the owner of the bank—all of which suddenly seemed too great a risk to take, especially with the loss of his father.

The outskirts of Austin had come into view when the last of the jury-rigged idea crashed in a heap in his mind.

"That's okay," Harold told himself. "I'll find a better deal." Besides, he rather liked what a big city had to offer. Why on earth would he want to spend years of his life in a hick town like Iredell with a wife whom he felt was already becoming obstinate and distant and discontented with his traveling? Not that he was particularly happy being on the road five days a week.

Harold steered his car into the driveway of the Simmons home and set the brake, intent on announcing his decision as soon as possible. He'd had enough of the FDIC and bank audits and traveling and delaying the true start of his business career. In fact, Harold thought, Doug and his mother could use some privacy, something they seldom got with Penny spending all her time in the house tending to the girls.

They would pull up stakes, move back to Dallas, and Harold would look for a job at one of the major banks to learn the rest of the business of banking and finance. He could help his mother from Dallas just as easily. He'd walk away from the Iredell deal. There would be something better just ahead.

He got out of the car and closed the door, whistling as he headed for the house.

BOOK TWO

Where the Money Is

CHAPTER 6

DALLAS, TEXAS: 1956

"*S*ir? Excuse me. Are you here for the next tour?"

Harold Simmons turned quickly toward the voice. A young woman wearing a white blouse and long skirt had come up behind him.

"Uh, no. I was looking for the personnel department," he replied, a bit off balance, his eyes narrowing suddenly. "You ... give tours?"

"Yes," she said brightly. "Everybody wants to see this beautiful building."

"Maybe later, I could do that," Harold replied, smiling broadly at her.

"You were just looking a bit lost," she said, smiling back. "Personnel is on the fourth floor, and the elevators are over there."

Harold thanked her and began walking in the direction of the elevator lobby, his eyes roaming the interior of the sparkling new Republic National Bank building. Somewhere in the distance, Patti Page was singing the praises of Cape Cod, her voice drifting through the interior and echoing off the marble floors which smelled of fresh polish. Outside in the cool air of early November, the gleaming stainless steel panels—each embossed with a stylized star—encased the entirety of the bank's new thirty-five-story skyscraper, making it the proudest, grandest feature of the Dallas skyline.

Republic Bank was going places, aggressively shoving open the capital markets of the Southwest with business loans and promotions aimed at pulling in more deposits and business than any other Texas bank. A huge rotating light had been added to the top of the seventy-foot metal spire, just to ensure that no one in a radius of thirty miles forgot the point, even in the dark of night.

Down the street, the First National Bank was following closely in the Republic's wake, but several blocks to the south, the occupants of the Mercantile Bank were keeping to their business-as-usual attitude of hide-bound conservative growth and careful lending. Housed in a traditional brick and mortar high-rise more at home in New York or Chicago than next to Republic's modern structure, the Mercantile was beginning to be viewed as too conservative to compete.

Which was why Harold Simmons, at the ripe age of twenty-four, had walked into the Republic's new lobby as a newly unemployed "banker," a fact he had no intention of sharing with the Republic Bank personnel department. Banking was still a business of personal recognizance and reputation, and he correctly surmised that no one in a position to award a job with Republic would want to hear that young Mr. Simmons had just walked away from a perfectly good job at the Mercantile. They were, after all, Dallas bankers, and how you behaved in one bank could foretell how you'd behave in the next.

"If you'll have a seat, I'll let someone know you'd like an interview," the receptionist in personnel said, pointing the way to a modernistic couch.

Harold sat down, grateful for a few minutes to organize his thoughts. The possibility that he might need someone to recommend him to the bank hadn't entered his thinking. Obviously, a person could get an interview just for the asking. Even without an appointment. That fact bolstered his confidence. Republic was expanding. It was inconceivable that they wouldn't need someone of his caliber and education. Certainly the Mercantile hadn't understood his capabilities.

He couldn't believe he'd missed all the signs of what the Mercantile was up to when they hired him on the spot six weeks before as a trainee. Of course he was qualified, but that wasn't the point. It had been too easy and too fast at too low a salary, and those facts should have raised his suspicions that perhaps the trainee program was not all they made it seem. Instead, he had assumed it was all just an entry-level ritual. He had to start somewhere, and within a few months—when they were ready to move him from a trainee position to a real position—it would be obvious how valuable he was. Starting as a clerk in the Loan and Discount Department was merely the first step. The sky was the limit from there.

But then he began meeting the other trainees, new hires who had been in the same position for months, even years, with no promotion, no regular assignment, and no increase to a living wage. It became painfully obvious that the Mercantile would hire any warm body that could walk and talk, and the bank was shamelessly using them as a crop of low-paid errand boys with the ruse that they were being groomed for something better.

Quitting the Mercantile after that recognition was not a difficult decision, even though Harold's savings account was being steadily depleted by the costs of maintaining a family. The money that was to have gone toward the purchase of the Iredell State Bank would keep leeching away until he secured a job.

■   ■   ■

The receptionist was motioning to him, and Harold got to his feet and followed her to an open desk at the back of the office. An expressionless woman waited there, barely acknowledging him as she motioned to a chair and began asking questions.

"How much of a salary would you require?" she asked at one point. A hopeful question, Harold figured, especially since she'd been over his master's degree and banking examiner experience.

"I have a wife and two children, so I'd need at least four hundred per month."

There was a small noise as the woman closed the notebook she'd been using and put her pen away, barely hiding the small scowl on her face. *The effrontery of an applicant wanting so much money!* she seemed to be thinking.

"I'm sorry, Mr. Simmons. Entry level jobs at the Republic do not begin at anywhere near that salary range."

She got to her feet and Harold followed reluctantly. "Well, wait a minute ..." he said, trying to keep his voice even. "I mean, what *could* you offer me?"

She stuck out her hand in a perfunctory manner. "Good day, Mr. Simmons. Thank you for coming in." The cold look in her eyes told him to forget it. She was already sitting again, pulling at other papers and expecting him to disappear.

Harold turned and headed back the way he'd come, fighting a combination of irritation and alarm, the pungent odor of purple mimeograph ink barely registering as he passed a small alcove where another employee was turning the crank handle on a duplicating machine. Maybe it had been naive to expect to just waltz into the biggest bank in town and get a job. This wasn't the Mercantile.

The receptionist barely looked up as Harold passed her desk in moderate confusion, wondering whether to go straight over to First National Bank or go home first and think out the next move.

Maybe I need a recommendation, but where . . .

"Excuse me!"

A feminine voice from behind broke through his thoughts and he turned to find an elegantly dressed woman in her thirties.

"Yes?"

She held out her hand as an accompaniment to her warm smile.

"Mr. Simmons, isn't it?"

"Yes, ma'am."

"I understand you're applying for a position with the bank?"

"I was, yes, but . . ."

She dismissed a recitation with a wave of her hand. "That's all right. There are six of us here, and we all handle recruitment for different departments. If you don't mind some of the same questions, I'd like to interview you."

"No. I mean, of course I don't mind," Harold said, following as she turned and walked to an adjacent room, and wondering where this strange turn of events would lead.

The woman's cordiality and friendliness were a stark contrast to the attitude of the first interviewer. She took it in stride without comment when he mentioned a need for $400 a month, and she seemed impressed with his background as a bank examiner.

"So, what do you think?" Harold asked.

"I think," she said, smiling, "that I'd like for you to meet with one of our vice presidents."

After a thirty-minute wait, Harold was ushered into the office of Senior Vice President Jim Cumby, who rose to shake his hand before motioning him to a chair. They talked amiably for nearly an hour before Cumby stood from behind his desk and pointed toward the ceiling.

"Well, Harold, would you care to have some lunch? You have time?"

"Sure do."

"We have an executive dining room up top of this rocket launcher, and I think you'll be impressed. We can even see Fort Worth on a clear day."

"Really?"

"Yes, sir. Now, why anyone would *want* to see Fort Worth is a different matter, but a couple of fellows I want to introduce you to will be heading up there in a few minutes. I'd like to see what they think about bringing you into our training program."

"You mentioned the program was brand new," Harold said.

Cumby was holding the office door open for him and nodding.

"It is, and if you're the right man for the job, you'd only be the second one in it. We've got high hopes for the idea, Harold. Give each man in-depth exposure to each department over a few months or so, then see where you think you'd be most happy and productive."

"Sounds like a great idea, Mr. Cumby."

"Now, understand, we've got to run you through the whole process before anyone offers you a job."

"I understand."

"But I think you might do very well."

■　　■　　■

The formal offer came two days later by phone, and Harold agreed to start immediately, quietly overjoyed that his boldness had paid off. Any thoughts that he'd been dangerously optimistic quickly evaporated.

After all, why wouldn't they hire him? He would be able to do great and profitable things for Republic Bank, once he figured it all out.

"What a way to learn the banking business!" Harold told Penny when the call had come.

"Good," she'd said. "Sounds like a place where you can settle down and have a good job for life."

"Well," Harold had replied, feeling something tighten in his stomach, "it's sure a place I can learn everything I need to know about banking. And it's the right place, too. You should've seen that dining room, Penny. Linen tablecloths, waiters, china ... everything first class. Maybe I can take you up there sometime."

"I don't need to go."

"No, but they'll want to meet my wife one day."

"That's where your job is, Harold. I'm going to be looking for my own job. Why would I want to meet your bosses?"

He'd let the matter drop and indulged himself in the memory of the elegant executive dining room and the royal treatment he'd received. Jim Cumby was a gentleman of the old school, with courtly manners to match, and the whole experience had been thrilling.

As had the view from the thirty-fifth floor. Fort Worth had, indeed, been in view in the distance, along with several small Texas communities to the north and east. Republic was planning to expand its reach in all directions, even internationally, and Texas and Dallas were merely the center of things. From such heights of power and modernity, the whole world seemed not only in view, but within reach. The lunch had proven to be more than just an overture to a job; it was also a metaphor for his own limitless horizons. With what the Republic Bank could teach him, he'd be able to master the art of making money.

CHAPTER 7

DALLAS, TEXAS: 1956

*G*lenn Simmons sat back in his chair in his Chance-Vought Aircraft office in Grand Prairie, Texas, and wondered what was going on with his younger brother. Harold seldom called him at work, and it was even rarer to hear a tightly controlled excitement in Harold's voice.

Something was up.

"Okay, Harold, 'fess up. What's going on?"

"What makes you think something's going on, Glenn? Can't I just invite you and your wife to dinner?"

"You already did. You issued the invitation last week. Now, what's up?"

"You already asked that."

"And you didn't answer."

"Well, just come on over tonight and I will."

Glenn Simmons' curiosity was getting the best of him as he pulled up to 134 Halsey Drive. The tiny house was little more than a living and dining room, two tiny bedrooms, one bathroom, and a kitchen—a floor plan used in hundreds of small homes around Dallas built just after World War II and snapped up by a small army of newlyweds, many of them returning veterans.

Harold had bought the house for $10,000 on contract directly from the builder, who had taken it in trade, although the $500 down payment had to be waived to make the purchase work.

"I didn't have it," Glenn remembered Harold saying, "but this builder, Samson is his name, had taken it back on a trade and was just getting eaten up by payments, so he let me have it for nothing down if I promised to send that five hundred dollars someday when I got it. Real nice guy."

Glenn closed the driver's door and went around to open the passenger side for his wife and two children, following them up to the compact porch where Harold was waiting with a wide grin.

"So what have you gone and done, Harold?" Glenn said after the kids were inside and Penny had brought them drinks and returned without comment to the kitchen with a Dr Pepper in her hand.

"You know that little bitty bank down in Lavernia I told you about?" Harold began.

"No. Where the heck is Lavernia?"

"Not far from San Antonio. Kind of a German community."

"Okay, Harold. What about it?"

"Several years ago I did an audit on that one and met the bank owner and mentioned I might be interested in buying if he was ever interested in selling."

"And?"

"Three weeks ago he calls and says he's ready to sell and retire."

"And you *bought* it? The bank?"

"No, I got him to give me an option to buy it for thirty thousand. Typed it up right here and sent it down there for his signature."

"All right, but where are you going to get thirty thousand? You certainly aren't thinking I've got that kind of cash in the cookie jar, are you?"

"Relax, Glenn. He gave me the option for nothing. I took out an ad in one of those banking trade papers to sell it."

"How long is that going to take you?"

"Probably not too long, since I sold it yesterday. Some guy named Keeland bought it." Harold turned and pulled something off the small mantle above the fireplace.

"What's that?" Glenn asked, getting to his feet.

"A check for the difference between the option price and what Keeland paid for the bank." He handed it to Glenn and stood back, watching the expression on his brother's face as his jaw dropped slightly.

"Seven thousand dollars?"

"That's right. Just about a year's wages for me." Harold was beaming as Glenn looked at the check and ran his index finger along the edge. "Let me make sure I understand this, Harold. You got the owner to give you an option to sell at a certain price for no money down, and then you jacked the price up by seven thousand and sold it before you owned it?"

"That's about right."

"A seven-thousand-dollar profit for just pushing paper?"

"No, for putting the right deal together. No one else had done it. What do you think?"

"What do I think?" Glenn said, chuckling. "I think, little brother, that you could sell air conditioning to Eskimos! I'm impressed. What are you going to do with it?"

"Buy a house."

"I thought you had one."

"A bigger house, with real furniture. And air conditioning."

Glenn looked around at the card table and folding chairs. The edge of the old flat spring bed Harold had hauled up from Austin could be seen through the bedroom door. There was precious little else in the way of furniture in the house.

Harold was right, Glenn thought. Scheryle was growing and a new baby had arrived. Having a few decent pieces of furniture to sit on would be nice, and another summer trying to keep the heat under control with only a swamp cooler in the window was a brutal prospect.

Glenn settled onto one of the chairs. "So now I expect you're going to be asking every bank owner in Texas for free options to sell their banks?"

"Not necessarily," Harold replied with a grin. "I may have to start charging them for the service."

"Seriously, what are you planning?"

"I don't know, Glenn. But I do know this is just the beginning. There are an awful lot of opportunities out there."

Several hours later, Glenn left his brother's house, still shaking his head. "My God, Binky," he told his wife, "I don't think I ever saw so much money in one place before in my life! If he can do something like that, then Harold's really onto something."

■　　■　　■

The act of depositing the $7,000 in his Republic savings account the next working day triggered a strange mixture of emotions for Harold. There was a definite feeling of new wealth, however contained and premature, but it was mixed up with a more profound rush of power. Between the two, the feeling of power was by far the most profound. Suddenly, the money had given him the ability to accomplish things he could not have accomplished the day before.

Penny, however, had been unimpressed and even apprehensive about the check. She'd welcomed it like a poisonous snake slithering into her home, threatening her husband's mind with the aphrodisiac of victory and the poison of ambition. Even the idea of building a new house with the money had left her unmoved, and the thought of more business deals had left her all but panicked, reactions that, to Harold, were both hurtful and predictable.

He avoided discussing it further. There was no point. He knew what they needed even if she couldn't accept it: success on a larger scale than $7,000 checks. There had to be another deal out there he could engineer. Not necessarily another option, but some way to actually purchase a bank like the one he'd walked away from in Iredell.

Evenings and weekends were spent with his daughters, taking them for walks, playing in the yard, and sometimes rubbing their backs for hours before kissing them goodnight, while Penny read her magazines, happy for any relief from child-raising duties. But regardless of what he was doing physically, Harold's fertile mind was working away quietly on the challenge of finding the right opportunities. Not even the distraction of moving the family to their new home at 1430 Summertime Lane in Oak Cliff could divert his attention from the search.

Several weeks after the move, Harold slipped behind the wheel of the family's 1957 Buick one evening and left the driveway headed south of town, motoring through the black gumbo fields of cotton and sorghum to stop on a small rise in a dirt farm road from where he could see the proud skyline of Dallas some twenty miles to the north. In the twilight, bathed by a balmy seventy-degree temperature and a slight breeze blowing his hair, he stood deep in thought with his arms folded, watching the beacon on the Republic Bank building sweep the evening sky. That beacon was an image of power and progress and determination, he thought, as well as a metaphor of supreme confidence, as if lighting the way to bigger and better things for himself and the girls and his wife.

His wife.

He let his mind wander to the growing gulf between Penny and himself, well aware he'd been avoiding the subject. She was working at another clerk-typist job for the government now, leaving the girls in the care of a housekeeper during the day, but their evenings had become increasingly strained. He had tried occasionally to take her to a movie or to enjoy some other form of entertainment, but she was seldom interested. There was a grim stoicism about her that seemed to forbid open enjoyment of anything outside the house. Two years in a row, he recalled, Penny had flatly refused to accompany him to the Republic Bank Christmas party.

The low point had been Jack Rich's party, over a year earlier. He remembered getting the invitation just after joining Republic. Jack, who had become his best friend at the bank, was a fellow officer trainee married to the daughter of the prominent merchant who was president of Sanger Brothers department store. Harold had heard about his home and wanted to see it. It was supposed to be large and beautifully furnished, and he had quickly accepted Jack's invitation.

Penny, however, had approached the evening as if preparing for a funeral. She entered the Rich home and took one look around before disappearing to a chair in a far corner of one of the rooms, where she sat in silence for the rest of the evening, refusing to move or engage anyone in conversation beyond monosyllabic answers.

"Mrs. Simmons? Penny, is it?" Jack's wife had inquired at one point.

"Yes."

"Can I get you a drink?"

"No."

The evening became an ordeal for Harold, who was acutely aware of her catatonic performance. "What on earth is the matter with you?" he whispered when he thought no one was looking.

"We don't belong in a place like this!" she whispered back through clenched jaw. "I want to go home."

Harold had never been fully comfortable himself in social settings and formal parties, but Penny's reaction was beyond even his comprehension. He could see she was genuinely petrified, and felt instinctively the reaction arose from some unfortunate self-generated idea that they were nothing more than white trash, and that putting on airs would only get them in trouble.

■   ■   ■

The rumble of deep-throated aircraft engines shook Harold from the memory. A Braniff DC-7 was climbing out of Dallas Love Field. He leaned against the Buick and sighed, feeling the passing shadow of depression. The marriage was deteriorating. It was time to admit it, though there was nothing to be done about it with two little girls dependent on them both. Whatever they had felt for each other was slipping away rapidly, and he hadn't a clue how to get it back or change her feelings.

The night air felt suddenly chilly, and Harold shivered as he climbed back into the car, holding the heavy door open a few moments to take another deep breath of country air redolent with the aromas of freshly turned fields.

He headed the car home to Oak Cliff, letting his mind close off the hurtful thoughts of Penny's estrangement and shift instead to a brief hallway conversation several days before with Jack Rich. He'd almost forgotten the exchange, but now it came swimming back to prominence. Jack had mentioned that someone at Republic had a small bank for sale.

Why didn't I remember that? Harold chided himself. *I'll call him in the morning.*

He would refrain from mentioning the subject at home, of course. The reaction would be all too predictable.

■   ■   ■

"You may not know the place, Harold," Jack told him the next day. "It's a little hole in the wall north of Austin called Jarrell."

"I know Jarrell. The Jarrell State Bank?"

"Probably. Give him a call if you're interested."

The news that 51 percent of the Jarrell Bank was held by a friend of a fellow employee at Republic triggered a flood of ideas and excitement in Harold. The owner had been unable to use the Central Texas bank for his intended purpose of placing loans from the small Dallas finance company he also owned. Yes, he told Harold, he was indeed interested in dumping his shares. And as soon as possible.

Harold began to search immediately for ways to finance the buyout. With most of the money from the Lavernia deal already gone to buy and furnish his new house, his only hope was to finance the entire purchase price without a down payment, and for that he should find someone closer to Jarrell than the big banks of Dallas.

There was, he recalled, a man he'd met who ran a small bank across Guadalupe Street from the main campus of the University of Texas in Austin. It took a trip back to the capital to convince him, but the bank president finally okayed the deal.

"Okay, Harold," Tom Joseph said, "... provided *you* agree to compensating balances. You know the routine. You keep enough of the Jarrell bank's deposit money in my bank to equal or preferably exceed the amount I lend you to buy it, and we're golden."

Harold had accepted the deal on the spot, and walked with metered steps from the bank as he tried to control the temptation to let a large smile take over his face. This was the beginning! A few years of clever investing of the bank's money, a few years of making it a far more efficient and profitable institution, and he could sell his bank for a substantial profit and buy something with even more potential.

My bank! I like the ring of that, Harold thought.

With nothing left but the paperwork and final signatures, Harold settled behind his desk again in the Republic credit department with his mind already prowling the little bank in Jarrell, looking for ways to bring it up to date.

He couldn't help smiling as he thought again about the $7,000 Lavernia Bank option he'd sold so effectively. It wasn't that buying and selling banks and bank options was easy; it was the fact that he'd figured it out without any capital. There was a truth there. Harold realized it was the challenge of the acquisition that felt so good—the challenge of buying the right thing at the right time for the right price. That was the game, and the game was exciting.

CHAPTER 8

JARRELL, TEXAS: 1957

"*M*r. Simmons?"

The voice of the president pulled him back to the dimly lit interior of his bank. He could hear the wall clock ticking steadily, and almost taste the cigar smoke from one of the board members as it hung thick in the air.

"Yes?" Harold said.

The woman looked around at the other board members, betraying her nervousness with a slightly wide-eyed look. In the background, the door to the bank creaked open to admit a customer. Harold could hear the lone teller speak a familiar greeting.

"You had mentioned the bonds, Mr. Simmons. The corporation bonds you had us buy?"

"Sorry. I was thinking about something else," Harold said, meeting the woman's gaze. "You mentioned the bonds the other day on the phone. You said you were concerned about them."

Harold watched the woman swallow hard and try to find the right words to oppose the new owner, who was young enough to be her son. The bonds Harold had directed her to buy as an investment for the bank were worrying her to death. Neither she nor the three grim-faced men sitting in various chairs around her desk for the board meeting knew anything about the buying or selling of corporate bonds. He had tried to explain that the bank could make double the interest buying high-grade corporate bonds instead of government bonds. He'd even told her about Charlie Walker, the Republic's economist, who had said flatly several months back that interest rates were going to go down and the bond market was going to appreciate. But in the end, he'd had to almost order her to buy the bonds.

It took less than a month to prove Walker right. The bonds in the bank's portfolio had already appreciated some $7,000, but their presence was scaring the bank president. "I called the bank examiners, Mr. Simmons," she began.

"You called the *examiners?* Why?"

"Because I'm very concerned about the bonds being improper."

"So what did the examiners say?" Harold asked, already knowing how he would have responded.

"They didn't really give me an answer, but I don't want us doing anything wrong, and I just know we shouldn't be putting deposit money there."

Harold looked away and sighed. Getting the bank president to add a small service charge to all the checking accounts had been hard enough. "But those are our customers and our neighbors!" she'd protested. "We can't charge them anything. Those accounts have always been free."

Change was very difficult for such folks, Harold realized. Maybe the bonds weren't worth the battle. He certainly didn't want his bank president quitting in panic, and she was clearly panicked.

"Okay, look," he began, "if y'all are worried about them, why don't I just personally buy the bonds back from the bank for exactly what they cost us?"

The woman almost leapt out of her chair, her eyes wide with relief. "Oh, *would* you Mr. Simmons? That would be wonderful! I'd really appreciate that!"

The other board members, all locals, were nodding almost in unison, and Harold had to suppress a laugh at their relief, and their folly. The bank would get back the money, but he would get the profits.

"Okay. Done. I'll take care of it when I get back to Dallas."

When the bonds were sold and the money had been sent to Jarrell reimbursing the original cost, $7,000 remained in the account, all of it the property of Harold Simmons. A $7,000 profit, and he still owned the bank!

Once again it was hard to suppress a smile during the day. The cash would give him money for a down payment to buy something else. It wasn't, he thought, that the money was easy, but the profits for using his head were reliable. Insert know-how and a little luck here and get profit out over there. That was the way he described it to Glenn, who was even more impressed than before with his follow-up monetary coup, a reaction Harold deeply appreciated, since there would be no approval at home.

He thought about his next move, which would have to be plotted carefully. Jarrell needed to be more profitable, but he could only shove them so far. Maybe he ought to buy a second bank or think about owning a chain of them. Running a small empire of Texas rural banks while enjoying a slow but satisfying progression up the ladder at Republic would be a reasonable goal, he figured. After all, heavy-hitting Dallas bankers like Jimmy Aston and Don White and Jim Keay had all made the same steady climb, although he didn't know whether they owned banks and businesses on the side. If not, he would pioneer the art of doing both.

Keay was a problem. He was head of the credit department, and therefore Harold's boss, but he was more than a little wary of the young man from Golden. Harold had befriended him in a subordinate sort of way, but Keay wore the cautious demeanor of an old lion watching a new male circling at a respectful distance and sizing him up. There were too many suggestions from Simmons, too many ideas, too much desire to change. To Jim Keay, reining in Harold Simmons was part of his responsibility.

Keay was quite a contrast, Harold thought, to someone like Don White. White was not a native banker, but a former finance officer for the Graybar Electric company, having worked for them to retirement. For some reason he had come out of retirement to join Republic, serving as a senior vice president and a financial wizard. White understood financial statements like no one else, and Harold felt he was slowly mastering what White was teaching him about how to analyze what a financial statement *really* meant, and he valued the association. At Republic, Don White was rapidly revolutionizing the bank's ability to make loans with far more safety and intelligence than the competition could muster. He was slightly gruff, aging, and often disagreeable, but he was a genius and a pioneer. In his head, Harold thought, were answers for which most of his contemporaries hadn't even formed the questions.

And, Harold realized, if he could learn to read and interpret the financial statements a company presented to a bank to secure a loan, he could learn to decipher their annual report as well. In that arcane art, he was sure, would lie the key to making smart investments.

The sight of Don White approaching Harold Simmons' desk in the credit department was somewhat of a rarity in itself, since Harold usually went to him. But on an otherwise unremarkable morning in mid-December of 1958, Harold looked up to find his respected friend and mentor doing just that.

"Mr. White?"

"Harold, you have a few minutes?"

"Sure."

"Why don't you follow me." It was a command, not a question, and Harold got up immediately. Don White led him back to his office and closed the door. The space was nowhere near as opulent as the upstairs corner office of the president, Jimmy Aston, or that of bank founder and CEO Fred Florence, but White's office was filled with mementos and a couple of comfortable chairs on the other side of his desk. White settled into one of them while motioning Harold into the other.

"Harold, when in heck did you buy a bank?"

"Last spring. It's down in Jarrell. Just a little country bank. I bought controlling interest last spring."

"Well, apparently our correspondent banker was down there at Jarrell last month urging them to keep more deposits with Republic, and the manager tells him, 'Hey, don't ask me. One of *your* men in Dallas owns this bank. Go talk to him.'"

Harold nodded, ignoring a small ripple of apprehension. "That's what I heard, and he was laughing about it. He dropped by my desk up here with the same request, and I said I'd do what we could, but I've already got a certain amount I have to keep in Austin. Is that a problem?"

Don White sat back and studied his young friend for a second. "Jim Keay got wind of this, Harold. He's not happy."

"Jim wants me to keep more money up here?"

"No, he wants to fire you. He went running up to Jimmy Aston this morning and recommended we throw you out right now. Immediately. He's all concerned that this is a terrible conflict of interest."

"But it's not a conflict! I mean, I don't even run it, and I'm doing my job here."

White shook his head. "I told them you were doing a real good job, Harold. I told them you're a smart, diligent, hard-working young banker, and we don't even have a set policy on this. But Keay is all lathered up to get rid of you, and I don't know what Aston's going to decide."

"I . . . Mr. White, I can't support my family on profits from that little bitty bank. I need this job, and I really like the Republic. That thing's just an investment!"

"I understand, Harold. But you're going to have to get rid of it. If they let you stay, that is. I told them upstairs, 'Let him stay and have him sell the damn bank.'"

"And Jim Keay?"

"He doesn't care. He wants you out of here. He put on a big show of righteous indignation." White got to his feet and gestured toward the door. "You go on, now. I'll let you know what they decide. I did the best I could to convince Jimmy."

"Should I talk to anyone?"

White shook his head sadly. "I'm sorry, Harold. I'll let you know as soon as I hear."

Harold sailed back to his desk on a rising tide of alarm, his face slightly flushed from embarrassment, as if the other employees around him could read what had just happened. How on earth, he wondered, could ownership of a tiny, nothing little country bank threaten the mighty Republic?

He already knew the answer. There was no threat to Republic. But his purchase of Jarrell State Bank had given Jim Keay, whom Harold believed felt threatened, the perfect opportunity to get rid of him.

The grip of apprehension constricting his stomach was increasing. Now he'd have to wait. Try to do substantive work at his desk and wait for the axe to fall, or not. And he couldn't even argue his own case. Don White had done that for him.

Harold left his office early on the pretense of lunch and walked around downtown Dallas, oblivious to the cold air. What, precisely, would he do if they fired him, which they were almost sure to do if Keay had his way? After all, Keay was over White, and the president, Jimmy

Aston, hardly knew Harold Simmons existed. Aston was bound to listen to Keay.

He stopped at a street corner, ignoring a Salvation Army worker ringing her bell amidst a throng of holiday shoppers. He stared up at the gleaming metal of the Republic tower, trying to reason away a growing feeling of loss. Controlling his emotions was seldom a problem, but the internal turmoil over what to do if he lost the job, how to handle Penny, and how he had gotten into this position, were already eating at him.

Christmas was little more than two weeks away. There was money in the bank, but that was for future deals and expansion, not to live on. Where could he get another great bank job in Dallas, since he was already at the best bank in town? To get fired would also be a permanent blight on his personal record.

In a twisted way, Penny would love it, he thought. It would be the final validation of her visceral opposition to his "uppity," "grandiose," "hair-brained" schemes. He was acting just like her stupid father, she had said. It would all come to grief. He had no right to try to move up. His ambitions were "nothing but B.S."

There was a hollow feeling inside him surrounded by a shell of self-doubt, but he would have to work it out himself. There was, quite simply, no one to talk to, not that he wasn't used to making decisions and facing crises alone. But even if he had wanted to talk to someone, there was no one to call. Penny wasn't an option. And Glenn? Well, Glenn was his brother. He hated the idea of Glenn losing faith in him.

Harold squared his shoulders and took a deep breath. The act of walking back into the building would feel roughly like climbing a gallows, but he had no choice. Whatever was going to happen would happen.

The rest of the day crawled by, each unusual sound a form of torture. He looked up countless times, expecting to see the malevolent grin of Jim Keay approaching with the coup de grâce.

But Keay didn't come, and Don White was nowhere to be seen.

The drive home was an agony. It was twilight when he left, and an overcast sky accurately reflected his feelings as he crossed the Trinity River bridge en route to Oak Cliff, just to the south of downtown Dallas.

He resolved to say absolutely nothing to Penny about the volatile situation, a resolve he knew he could keep. Penny seldom asked him about work anyway. She had long since stopped caring whether he'd had a good day or bad.

The night passed slowly and without sleep, leaving him tired and troubled the next morning as he sat behind his desk and tried to ignore the sick feeling in his stomach. Another agonizing eight hours passed, but the other shoe had yet to drop.

The third day was equally numbing, until Don White appeared at long last, his expression unreadable at first.

Harold didn't spot him until the older gentleman was practically at his side. White supported himself on the edge of the desk and looked down at his young student.

"Well, Harold . . ."

"Hello, Mr. White. What . . . did they decide?"

White smiled suddenly, a rarity for him. "Jimmy decided to keep you."

Harold let out a small sigh, but maintained iron control over his expression. "I'm very glad to hear that."

"But you've got to sell that bank as quickly as you can."

"Okay. I'll get it on the market immediately."

"That's the deal: 'Tell Simmons he can keep his job if he sells that bank right now.'"

"I'll do it."

"Good." Don White slid off the desk and started to leave, then turned and offered his hand, which Harold took gratefully.

"Glad it worked out this way, Harold. Hate to lose you."

Harold watched him walk away and then sat back in his chair, part of his mind latching onto the job of planning a bank sale, and part of it reeling at the close call. The other part of the reaction took a few hours to set in: What would he do for investment now that building a small rural banking empire was not a feasible sideline for a Republic Bank employee? If not banks, then what? Time was passing, and there was money to be made. Surely there was something profitable he could buy out there that wouldn't get him in trouble.

CHAPTER 9

SOUTH OAK CLIFF, DALLAS, TEXAS: 1959

*T*he sudden emptiness of 1430 Summertime Lane was an alien feeling to Harold. Scheryle and Lisa were in their beds and already asleep.

Harold walked in a trance back to the living room and sat down around 9:00 P.M., his mind still reeling. Since they'd moved in, he couldn't recall a night Penny hadn't been there. Most of her evenings were spent in the bedroom with the ritual Dr Pepper and a mountain of magazines, of course, but physically she was always there.

Until tonight.

He shook his head and closed his eyes at the ludicrous nature of it, the memories flashing past: her packed bags in the hall when he'd returned from work; her declaration she was leaving him, but needed him to drive her downtown to the YWCA where she planned to get a room; her refusal to answer when he'd asked, "And what about the girls?"

"I need time alone to think," she had said.

It wasn't as if the marriage hadn't been sinking for some time. But why now, when his steady job at Republic couldn't be going better? Why now, when he'd mentioned virtually nothing for months about buying banks or companies?

And what about her own daughters?

What do I do now? Harold wondered.

He'd long since hired a black woman who took care of them during the day. She was basically a housekeeper, yet he knew he could rely on her to help if he needed her.

But the void was still there, like a vortex of blackness. Suddenly, he wasn't just responsible for his daughters' overall welfare, he was responsible for their tactical care, too. Day by day. Hour by hour. Night after lonely night. He would have to be both mother and father to them while making a living and trying to get ahead in the business world.

Maybe it was time, though. Somewhere deep inside, a small glimmer of hope began to burn that the lonely nights lying by Penny's side were over.

■　　■　　■

It was January before Penny Simmons finally relayed her request for an immediate divorce. Harold could have the girls and everything else. He should file and pay for everything. She would contest nothing.

Harold reluctantly acceded to all of it.

Now he threw himself into work at the bank with even greater zeal, trying to substitute concentration on business for the constant raw feelings. There was a deep pain there, but he successfully shielded it from everyone except Glenn, who could sense the terrible toll Penny's rejection had inflicted on his brother's emotions. The wounds were deep and visceral, Glenn felt, and bound to influence all his brother's future relationships with the fairer sex. Harold would weather it, of course, but life was teaching him a harsh lesson about love and trust and women.

For years after the divorce Harold would catch himself remembering Penny from time to time as he'd known her back in Austin at the university, wondering how he could have missed the signs. The diverse personality traits that had doomed them as a couple seemed so obvious in the perfect light of hindsight, but he had been so young and so very naive. Never again. He needed a woman who could embrace life and all its possibilities, a girl and a wife to help him forge a grand future, taking real pride in his accomplishments. After all, he was a risk-taker.

■　　■　　■

Harold had already noticed an attractive brunette working as one of the pages at Republic Bank. He'd watched her bright smile and flashing eyes from a distance or while walking past her. She was a college girl fresh from the Ozarks named Sandra Kathereen Saliba, Harold discovered, when he finally introduced himself in May of 1960.

"I've seen you around, Harold. You're on the loan floor, right?"

"That's right. And they tell me you're a student at the University of Arkansas?"

"I was. In my freshman year. I ... uh ... sort of got kicked out," she said. "Which is why I'm down here living with an uncle until I can get transferred somewhere else."

"Grades get you?"

She laughed easily, he noted. "No, a few too many drinks in the dorm got me," she said. "They get kind of upset about that sort of thing."

Very little time elapsed before Harold asked her out. There was no specific plan of courtship, merely the enjoyment of time with an exuberant young woman who seemed in awe of the world around her, as well as in awe of the young banker who was happily paying attention to her.

He knew he was on the rebound and vulnerable to latching on to the first girl who treated him well, but Sandra was fun to be with after a long void of feminine companionship, and they spent more and more time together over the ensuing months, getting to know each other.

Without dwelling on it, Harold was well aware his inner compass was pointing toward a replacement for Penny, and to a certain extent, Sandra was auditioning for the role with every date and every hour they spent together. If he'd thought about it at all, he would have said the personality he was looking for had to be markedly different from Penny's.

Harold appointed himself the guardian of Sandra's education and talked her into re-enrolling at the University of Arkansas the following fall to finish the semester she'd left behind. He would help with the paperwork, the phone calls to the university registrar, and even buy her a new wardrobe before purchasing a bus ticket to take her back to Fayetteville.

"When you get it all finished up there and come back to me, we'll get you enrolled right here in Southern Methodist. You can get your degree from SMU."

"How am I ever going to afford SMU, Harold?" she laughed. "They don't let poor girls go there."

"Well, you might just have to marry me so I'll have to pay for that, too."

Sandra's departure left a new void in the house on Summertime Lane. They had become lovers, and Sandra seemed taken with his daughters, though the feeling wasn't necessarily mutual. While Scheryle at age eight was diffident and cold, five-year-old Lisa had begun to respond to Sandra's overtures, and Harold let himself dream about having a household with a bright, loving wife who would truly care about both him and his accomplishments at the end of each day.

Many evenings, late into the night, he'd talk to her about what he was planning to do with careful investments and diligent work. She appeared to hang on his words, asking intelligent questions and smiling in all the right places. Getting rich was a perfectly good quest in Sandra's opinion. She'd had too little of everything growing up in Arkansas. Her mother had died early, and she'd been raised by a grandmother in a poor household. Getting into the University of Arkansas had been a major accomplishment, and her suspension a corresponding disgrace.

With Sandra in Fayetteville, Harold settled back into the routine he'd established in the months following Penny's departure: coming home as early as possible and spending many a late afternoon playing with his girls. Nighttime would find him reading to Lisa and Scheryle, cutting their fingernails, combing their hair, rubbing their backs, holding them in his arms and frequently singing them to sleep. The day belonged to Republic Bank, but the rest of his time after 4:00 P.M. he devoted to his daughters, even if his mind was sometimes elsewhere working out the possibilities of a new investment idea, such as the idea of finding an undervalued company somewhere that others with substantial money might be persuaded to buy.

The heat of the North Texas summer of 1960 had not yet begun fading when the first truly exciting target crossed Harold's sights—a mid-sized corporation back east, clearly undervalued, which could grow substantially if properly managed. He'd come across their annual report, and with the knowledge he'd gained in understanding financial reports in the years working at Republic Bank beside Don White, the prospects seemed to leap off the page. The fact that the targeted company wasn't a bank made it even more attractive. How could Republic object?

The amount of money needed to purchase such a company was way beyond what Harold Simmons had, or could borrow directly. The "deal," if he could structure one, would have to be brokered by him to someone with money and vision and business acumen, and in 1960, that meant someone in New York City. The more he studied the idea, the better it sounded. It became an article of faith that any sophisticated investor good enough to prosper in New York could be sold on the same vision, and the rewards could mean instant riches for Harold Simmons. It was logical. Perhaps not as easy as winning the jackpot at Dessau Hall back in Austin, but doable.

An up and coming young banker making $500 a month didn't just up and blow three-quarters of his monthly pay on a round-trip coach ticket to New York, but there was no time to drive. Instead, Harold borrowed the money for the airline ticket from two friends, Bill Petree and Jerry Jacobs, who were interested in whatever deal he could broker in the big city.

■   ■   ■

There was an element of manifest destiny to his thinking as he settled into a window seat in the coach section of an American Airlines Electra and watched Dallas slip away beneath them. The logistics of planning a business trip to a bustling metropolis like New York were completely new to him, and he'd hardly considered doing anything more than bringing along his business plan and the names of the businessmen he wanted to talk to. He alighted that afternoon at La Guardia Airport with no hotel reservation and no real idea of just how big and overwhelming New York City really was. Neither was he prepared for the princely sums the major downtown hotels were demanding for a room the size of a phone booth. The rest of the afternoon and early evening was consumed looking for a place he could afford, a search which ended in a somewhat seedy off-Broadway hotel that had seen better days but charged an affordable rate.

The following morning Harold, slightly off-balance but undeterred, began calling the men he wanted to see. With one turndown after another, the process became more frustrating and disturbing with each hour. But finally he booked one appointment in the financial district and made contact with another man who, surprisingly, invited him to lunch at his yacht club.

Working the phone from the confines of a small room with a dull roar beyond the window was one thing, but emerging in the midst of the jarring and confusing contrasts of New York in midday was another.

The living circus of sights and sounds so markedly different from Dallas washed around his consciousness as Harold left the rundown hotel around 11:00 and headed for the appointed yacht club, having no clear idea what the place would look like, let alone how his proposal would be received. His confidence in the efficacy of his ideas and plans was solid and unshaken, but as he merged into the cacophony of the streets he sensed a startling momentum, a monstrous energy and depth to the amazing city around him that automatically belittled and intimidated.

This was the city that John D. Rockefeller had conquered. It had been the financial playground of Jay Gould, and Andrew Carnegie, the Astors and the Mellons. This was the home of the New York Stock Exchange and Wall Street, the global epicenter of finance he essentially intended to conquer, but he hadn't known or even thought about how incredibly large and important and *established* the place was! The deep rumble of the city seemed to mock his self-assurance.

Here at the gates of the castle of American finance stood a solitary son of Golden, Texas, essentially demanding its surrender while armed with little more than an idea propelled by superior intellect. He fought to suppress a gut-level, unspoken fear that he was badly mismatched, and his naivete about the hotel situation did nothing to allay such worries.

■　　■　　■

Not even in the executive dining room of Republic Bank back in Dallas had Harold experienced the degree of opulence which now surrounded him in the New York yacht club. After explaining his idea to his host, a prominent financier, Harold sat back and waited hopefully for the reply.

The man took his time answering, signaling to the uniformed waiter for another drink and raising an eyebrow in question toward the young Texan before beginning the process of dismembering Harold's proposal.

But it wasn't the idea that was bad, Harold realized. It was him. The young man bringing the idea to New York had no track record, no significant connections, no credibility.

Harold glanced around again to memorize the richness of the club's interior, fighting a strange mix of embarrassment and loss.

Embarrassment at not having whatever the financier expected, and loss borne of seeing a world he couldn't possess.

At least not yet.

The club was New York City itself, beckoning him to keep trying at the same moment one of its sons was blackballing his "application" to join the dealmakers.

The second appointment in the financial district proved even more cursory and frustrating. The man he'd come to see was in a hurry to leave and bypassed a handshake to check his watch. "You've got five minutes," he said, standing near the door, as Harold attempted to squeeze the essentials of his idea into an acceptably short briefing.

When he'd finished, the businessman instantly shook his head "no" and departed, leaving an increasingly disillusioned young Texan in his wake.

Harold made his way back to the depressing little hotel, winding his way through the filth of the subway system without really seeing it, his mind focused intently on the problem at hand and the need to line up more appointments. What was it going to take to get their attention?

Credibility, he decided. *And I have none.*

Who was he, anyway? Just a bright young man from somewhere else with an idea of how to use other people's money to make even more money. The fact that he was right was immaterial. The city was full of bright young men who believed in their own good ideas, but it was only those with a track record, or the right connections, who could marshal the credibility to inspire the level of financial participation he needed.

Harold's first night in New York had been vibrant with hope, even in the surroundings of the third-rate hotel room.

The second night was darker, and the second morning sealed the fate of his mission: there were no more appointments to be had, and no point in trying further.

Harold took a cab back to La Guardia and boarded the next flight for Dallas, feeling depressed and naive.

■   ■   ■

Back at his desk at Republic Bank in the following weeks, Harold's mind churned away at the problem of gaining the experience and respectability he needed. If it was too soon for him to broker deals, then he needed to start smaller and work up, and there was another possibility.

In 1959 Congress had passed a law called the Small Business Investment Company Act, a program which provided new capital for small businessmen trying to get started. Harold was well aware of the new law, and had spent considerable time trying to figure out how to utilize it. Sometimes in the evenings, rocking with the girls on the front porch glider or just sitting with his arms around them on the small living room couch, his mind would return to the problem of forming such a company. The charter from the Small Business Administration required about $50,000 of seed capital, but once that was accomplished, the government would loan twice as much as the seed money at low interest rates. Fifty thousand dollars, in other words, could instantly become $150,000 of investment-ready capital. In 1960, when $4,000 would buy a substantial car and $40,000 would buy a 4,000-square-foot home, $150,000 was a significant sum.

Over the years Harold had come to know a slightly older entrepreneur named Herbert Oaks who banked with Republic. Smart and likeable, Oaks was several years ahead of Harold in making smart investments and trying to build wealth. Harold approached Oaks and a friend named Jerry Jacobs about forming a qualifying SBIC company under the new act. "We'll call it OSJ Capital Corporation," Harold suggested, "for Oaks, Simmons, and Jacobs." The men reached quick agreement, and within the space of four months, OSJ Capital came into being with the expected government funding, and the principals began the process of looking for investment targets.

Once again the senior officers at Republic Bank got wind of Harold's involvement in an outside venture.

"There he goes again," Jim Keay complained.

"It's not a bank!" Harold protested, completely puzzled at their response.

And once more the edict was handed down from the third floor: Sell your interest in that company, or resign.

While Harold wasn't expecting the reaction, in many ways it wasn't a surprise. When Republic had forced him to sell the Jarrell State Bank (leaving him with a profit of $7,000 from the resold bonds), the episode had left seeds of discontent. By imperiously dangling Harold over the edge for a few days, Republic had tarnished its own image in the young banker's mind and triggered a slow but steady rethinking of his career plans and the desirability of being a career banker in the first place.

He thought back to how Penny's departure had removed the pressure to remain in a steady job with a predictable paycheck. Harold began to realize just how slow and glacial any progression to the top at Republic was likely to be. Worse, many of those above him had already made a career out of doing nothing fast, yet they were trusted blindly, even when they ignored good ideas and discounted profitable changes. Harold wanted to be an engineer of profitability, a banker whose intellect could help guide Republic to greater heights over the coming decades.

But he knew now that his career in banking would consist of years of discounted initiatives frustrated by threatened managers. They might run a steady ship forever, but this was not the place where a bright young businessman should be spending his career.

No, Harold decided, it was obvious that his talents weren't appreciated at Republic. The bank had been a great training ground, but now was the time to move forward. Besides, hadn't he just formed an investment company to give him the needed credibility of being an up and coming young businessman with a respectable track record?

I can make it without them, he told himself as he submitted his response to their ultimatum in the form of a resignation.

At long last Harold Simmons would be on his own and ready to prove that he was, in fact, as smart as he thought. It was as frightening a moment as it was exhilarating, but once the decision had been made, he was determined not to look back.

Republic's leaders accepted the resignation graciously. But for twenty-nine-year-old Harold Simmons, the future was getting brighter. In mid-December, nineteen-year-old Sandra Saliba honorably finished her freshman courses in Fayetteville and left Arkansas with a clean transcript and the ability to transfer to SMU. Suddenly, the vibrant young brunette was back in Harold's life on a daily—and nightly—basis. And as Christmas of 1960 came and went, they decided to marry, setting the date for mid-January.

BOOK THREE

The Ground Floor

CHAPTER 10

FORT SMITH, ARKANSAS: 1961

*G*oing to Fort Smith, Arkansas, to marry Sandra Saliba had seemed a good idea in a mild December, but winter blew in with the January wedding date, bringing freezing cold temperatures, an ice storm, and snow blowing across western Arkansas in the hours before the ceremony. Heavy coats and shivering dashes between cars and buildings were the order of the day, making the arrangements for the modest ceremony more difficult.

Several of Sandra's girlfriends from the University of Arkansas had planned to drive down to be in the wedding, but the roads were becoming treacherous and they canceled at the last minute. Sandra's folks had already made it in from the tiny community of Alma, and Harold's mother had arrived the day before from Austin. Harold recalled his mother's warm smile as she hugged her two granddaughters, Lisa and Scheryle. She saw them often, but never often enough.

And Glenn, his brother, had come as well, standing for the second time as his best man.

The ceremony was held in a small Baptist church, followed by a modest reception Glenn had arranged, complete with a wedding cake that had barely been cut before Harold and Sandra climbed into their new Buick Century and plowed through the snow and ice on the westbound highway out of town, headed for a honeymoon on the rim of the Grand Canyon in Arizona.

Harold eased his car into a parking space and set the brake as he studied the front of the business. He had seen the drugstore before.

University Pharmacy. The sign is okay, but plain, he thought.

The store occupied the north end of a single-story building across Hillcrest Road from the stately Georgian campus of SMU. The location should mean the store would pull in regular business from thousands of Southern Methodist students as well as the surrounding town of University Park, a well-heeled incorporated community enfolded by the much larger city of Dallas.

"It's a really good location," he'd told Sandra, "right there across from your classes."

"You going to buy it, then?" she'd asked with a smile.

"Don't know yet. I'm looking at a lot of businesses. But this one's interesting."

The idea was growing in his mind. He knew nothing of the drugstore business, but he could certainly learn. And there was no doubt he could improve its profits. Of course, the store's books would tell the tale, since he knew how to read the financials of a small business.

Harold sat a minute in thought, squinting through the bright sunlight bathing an otherwise cool and crisp winter day.

The ad had been in the *Wall Street Journal* off and on for weeks when he answered it. He'd been answering a lot of business-prospect ads lately, and getting closer to admitting that OSJ investment corporation, which he'd spearheaded and left Republic Bank to run, wasn't going to be enough.

Harold got out of the beige Buick and closed the door, his eyes traveling the length of the storefront, taking in the Varsity Shop adjacent to it and the number of parking spaces out front.

OSJ corporation was barely three months old, but he was already tiring of a basic reality: although he was the managing partner, his percentage of the business was small. What had seemed a great idea had already begun to pale with the constant need to consult Herbert Oaks on every significant decision. Even if they made a killing on some deal, only a minor amount of the profit would be his, and that bothered him a lot more than he'd expected.

Not that Oaks and Jacobs were being difficult. Jacobs was essentially a silent partner and Oaks was very accommodating. But the dream of building a business of his own played like a siren song in his mind, a business that only he would own. He could make a success of any such business, he was sure, if he had enough time to concentrate and learn it.

But not if he had partners to satisfy.

The *Wall Street Journal* ad had been placed by the store's accountant, who called as soon as he received Harold's inquiry.

"Why don't you go over and take a look at it, Mr. Simmons?" the man suggested.

"I may do that."

"I could meet you there . . ."

"That's not necessary. If it looks interesting, I'll get back with you. What's the inventory book value?"

There had been a hesitation on the other end since the asking price of $100,000 had already been stated.

"Well, remember it's a great location."

"And the book value?"

"About sixty thousand, Mr. Simmons, but the store clears about thirty thousand per year on revenues of around three hundred thousand."

"I'll take a look."

■　■　■

Harold crossed the parking area and entered the store, taking in the counters and shelves of a typical full-service drugstore, the pharmacy in the back, a small soda fountain to one side. The owner, a Mr. Bright, was the father of prominent Dallas businessman Bum Bright, one of the future owners of the Dallas Cowboys football franchise. Bright senior was a retired salesman from the Johnson and Johnson Company. He'd been running the store for ten years and now, at his son's urging, wanted to fully retire—but not without realizing a substantial profit from the store he'd built.

Small retail stores had traditionally been priced according to their book value, but Bright was holding firm at an asking price of $100,000, and University Pharmacy had languished on the market for some time as a result.

But there was substantially more value in the store than a $60,000 inventory, and Harold understood that point better than most. Successful businesses generated cash flow, and cash flow—in terms of how much was profit and how much was expense—was a far better measure of the worth of a business than the value of the inventory. If the business generated enough after-expenses cash every month, a young owner could pay himself a decent salary and still have enough left over to pay the monthly principal and interest on a large enough loan to buy the store with almost nothing down. The business, in other words, could be purchased with its own funds over time, and essentially pay for itself from the beginning if one was careful and clever.

Of course, Harold cautioned himself, the success of a traditional drugstore was considered highly dependent on the pharmacist and the worth of the staff.

Harold smiled at a clerk as he headed back toward the street. "Howdy."

"Can I help you, sir?" she asked. An older woman, he noticed, who had probably been working there for years. Good. A loyal staff of well-trained people would help.

"No, thanks. Just lookin'," Harold replied, pushing back through the doors, pleased with what he'd seen.

It was time to call the accountant back and see the books, he decided, suppressing a small sparkle of anticipation as the idea grew. He would need to plot out the plan in his head to turn his small equity stake in OSJ into enough financial leverage to buy Mr. Bright's drugstore, but the idea was making sense.

It would all depend on Herbert Oaks, Harold realized. The books of the store looked solid, and his figures made sense. The owner had agreed to finance part of the purchase, and now what he needed was to raise the rest of the purchase price from Oaks and the very investment company he'd helped create, since a bank was out of the question. Most bankers would laugh him out of the building at the idea of paying so much more than book value.

"You want to do what, Harold?" Herbert asked when Harold presented the business plan and his proposal to sell Oaks his share and leave OSJ.

"I want to sell you my interest in the company, Herbert," Harold had told him.

"For how much?"

"Well, I have five thousand in it, and that would be the price. Five thousand. But I need a loan in return. You and Jerry would have to have OSJ make me a fifty-thousand-dollar loan."

"To buy the drugstore?" Oaks asked.

"That's right."

"For fifty thousand? Didn't you say the book value is fifty?"

"No, the book value is sixty thousand, but the sale price is a hundred thousand. The rest of the money comes from the owner taking a note back."

"That's a pretty high price, Harold. You want to pay a hundred thousand dollars for a sixty-thousand-dollar store?"

"It'll be worth it, Herbert. Once I build it up, it'll be a gold mine. But this is a good deal for you, too. If I'm out of OSJ, you'll have only one minority partner left."

"I know that, Harold. And I'll make you the loan, but you're taking quite a risk. You've never run a drugstore before, have you?"

"No."

"Drugstores can be dangerous investments. They're labor intensive, slow inventory turnover, dependent on the pharmacist ..."

"I know."

There was a long hesitation as the older man thought about it. "You *sure* you want to do this?"

"I'm sure."

"Okay, then. We'll do it."

With Herbert Oaks' agreement in his pocket, Harold accepted the asking price for University Pharmacy and returned home that evening to 1430 Summertime Lane in high spirits, explaining the deal to Sandra, who put aside her homework to listen intently.

"So, Mr. Bright's going to take back a forty-five-thousand-dollar note with no interest for several years, just regular payments, which will be secured by the fixtures in the store," Harold told her.

"Fixtures?"

"You know, the counters, the shelves ... the displays."

"Okay," Sandra replied.

"They're not worth a lot, but he'll take a lien on them, and with the fifty thousand from OSJ and the five thousand dollars Herbert Oaks is paying me for my share of OSJ, we can do it."

"So we'll both be driving all the way to North Dallas from here every morning?" she asked.

"Not at first," Harold replied. "I'm going to get used to the store for a while. Mr. Bright will keep running it."

"Then maybe we should move to North Dallas," Sandra said, planting an idea Harold hadn't really thought about. "We'd be a lot closer."

Harold nodded silently, his mind already back on the business of making a modest drugstore an immodest success.

■   ■   ■

Within two weeks Harold was shaking the hand of Bright's attorney as he sat down in the man's office for the closing.

"Is your lawyer coming?" Bright had asked him in the hallway.

"Don't have one," Harold replied, smiling, and deciding not to add what he really thought: that lawyers are an impediment to doing deals.

The papers seemed in order, and in his judgment, Mr. Bright was a good man, so there was no need to be suspicious of anything. Harold knew he was buying only the name of University Pharmacy, the ongoing business, and the inventory. That was it. The building was owned by someone else. It never occurred to him to ask to see the lease under which University Pharmacy held its lucrative location.

Instead of driving home from the closing, Harold motored to University Pharmacy, his new business, with Mr. Bright following. He fully expected Bright to continue managing the store for at least a month while he learned the ropes.

But within two weeks the old gentleman was gone, and Harold Simmons was on his own.

Life began to accelerate ever so slowly. The days began long before the store opened at 7:00 A.M., since the drive from Oak Cliff took a half hour. Coordinating the schedule with Sandra's classes made things even more complicated, but the two of them made it work as Harold immersed himself in the esoterica of the retail drug business and began to make some startling discoveries.

"Hey!" he said one afternoon to the pharmacist as he inventoried the shelves of prescription medicine. "Half these bottles are out of date!"

"They are?" the pharmacist replied.

"They were all part of the inventory, but they're mostly out of date. There are hundreds of them back here!"

The pharmacist nodded, looking sheepish. "We know."

"We do?"

He nodded again.

"I paid good money for all this stuff, and it's probably too late to send most of it back."

Harold shook his head at the emerging picture. What was supposed to be $60,000 of saleable inventory might, if he was lucky, be worth $50,000. There was a chance of getting credit on some of the items, but there was no doubt he'd been outfoxed by the previous owner.

However, where many would have turned immediately to litigation and stopped paying on the note Mr. Bright had taken back for selling the store, Harold Simmons considered it *his* problem. He'd simply been bested by a tough trader, and he should have caught it himself. Getting angry was a waste of time.

Then there were the products that kept growing legs and leaving on their own. It was a sad commentary on SMU's normally well-heeled student population across the street, but their propensity for theft was apparently staggering, and according to his salesladies, anything not nailed down or too heavy to carry would find a way to disappear if the staff wasn't watching closely enough. Even with the checkout counter at the front door, it was hard to police, and the very nature of a drugstore meant thousands of small items on open racks and shelves. He would have to find some way to reduce loss from pilferage.

CHAPTER 11

DALLAS, TEXAS: 1962

"*W*hat do you think, Sandra?" Harold asked his young wife as they stood outside a new two-story home on a crisp, clear winter day, ignoring the real estate agent who was trying to busy herself in the distance. Sandra had whirled around the interior like a child in a candy store, looking wide-eyed at rooms that were huge by her childhood standards, modern bathrooms, inside garages, and a dream kitchen. The thought that such a house could be hers was more than exciting.

"I love it! I mean, Hockaday is right across the street, Harold, and we're just a few miles from the campus and the store ..."

"It's expensive. Thirty thousand, if they accept the offer."

"But it's perfect. It really is. Buy it."

He nodded, grinning. "It is pretty great, isn't it? Four bedrooms. Pure luxury. The girls can have their own rooms."

■   ■   ■

Moving from Oak Cliff to North Dallas was more than a step up in house size for Sandra Simmons. It was also her first tangible proof of social existence in her new town. Coming as she had from a relatively impoverished family in small-town Arkansas and having not grown up in the shadow of Dallas' rarified social atmosphere, Sandra nevertheless rapidly latched on to a 1960s fact of life on the North Texas prairies: Anyone who's anyone in Big D lives *north* of downtown.

That included the so-called Park Cities of University Park and Highland Park. And it included a growing area of new homes and estates ranging from tract houses to monstrous mansions stretching from a small tributary known as Turtle Creek (lined with old-money manor houses) to Forest Lane in what was then far North Dallas.

And it certainly included any nice home rubbing elbows with the preeminent Dallas private girls' school, Hockaday, which had abandoned its inner-city origins for a sweeping new campus only a few years before.

At the ripe age of twenty, Sandra was not only a junior at SMU, she was also the wife of a businessman and the owner of a beautiful new North Dallas home, and she intended to enjoy all of it—when she could.

Time was always a problem. Sandra was attentive to her stepdaughters Scheryle and Lisa, but the demands of being an undergraduate at SMU kept her occupied as well. It was turning out to be harder than she'd figured to set priorities.

And Harold was becoming a perennial fixture at the store, putting in extremely long hours as he dealt with the daily problems and made plans to expand, improve, or accelerate what the store—and he— could accomplish. Careful plotting was required to find the time to spend together. Still, Sandra could drop in on her husband at any time by just crossing the street between classes.

Weekends were family days, but they were also the heaviest business days for University Pharmacy. SMU students migrated over in waves to cash checks and buy everything from aspirin to ice cream, crowding the store aisles and leaving the sales staff and pharmacist hard-pressed to keep up. Increasingly, the absence of an employee would pull Harold into the store on a weekend. It was a fact of retail life he took without complaint, but it was draining.

The soda fountain was especially demanding. Most of the staff were young black women from South Dallas working under the sergeant-major control of a heavyset black matron in her fifties named Minnie, who treated the girls like a stern mother. But, even with Minnie's help, it wasn't always possible to get all of the soda fountain crew to show up every day, and the sight of the young store owner working side-by-side with his people behind the soda fountain became anything but unusual.

"I'm going to build a coffee shop in there," Harold announced one day to Sandra as they stood at the back of the store and looked at the soda fountain. "We'll install some big curved windows along the street there so it'll look inviting, and we'll put in booths, and have a really good little menu."

"Why? I like the soda fountain."

"Well, SMU's going to keep growing, and look at all these kids coming across the street, escaping from the dorm food."

Sandra laughed. "That's the truth."

"So we'll get 'em to buy lunch from us."

"Harold, Scheryle and Lisa are waiting in the car. Let's go. It's Sunday, remember? We're going water-skiing."

"I'm coming," he said, his eyes still calculating where the booths would go and what had to be changed as he laid aside a hand towel and waved to one of his employees.

Harold stopped at the front door and turned around, mentally etching the dimensions of his store into his mind.

His store! He'd succeeded in setting it up just right, and they were making money. But this was just the first step, and he was anxious to get on with the process of proving to himself how well he could transform a steady business into a spectacular success by figuring out what others had missed.

The business of running a retail store was perplexing enough, but the drug business—the pharmacy—added an entirely different set of problems and challenges, including the irritating state regulation that not even the owner could enter the area where the pharmacist worked.

I've got to get these fixtures changed! Harold thought, his eyes running along the store's faded interior. The ragged set of counters and cash registers he'd inherited were more a liability than benefit.

He recalled a brief conversation with one of the store's suppliers during the previous week. "Why don't you call Southwestern Drug Company, Harold?" the man had suggested. "They'll help you design a new interior, sell you new fixtures and finance them, because then you can sell a lot more of their merchandise."

"Harold? *HAROLD?* Are you coming or not?" Sandra had left the car again and was standing on the sidewalk, her hands on her hips.

He turned and smiled at her as he let the front door of University Pharmacy close. "All right, darlin'. I was just thinking."

"You're always thinking."

■   ■   ■

The paperwork for a $25,000 loan to completely re-outfit the interior of University Pharmacy was completed within a month, with Southwestern Drug Company doing the installation and setup.

The old shelves and counters were worth less than $5,000, but they were part of the security for Mr. Bright's $45,000 loan that had enabled Harold to buy the store, so he secured them in a vacant store a few feet away until he had time to talk to Mr. Bright. It was a small matter, and he gave it little thought. After all, a healthier, more robust University Pharmacy would be even better security for paying the senior Bright's note off. The thought that Bright would be pleased with Harold's progress crossed his mind.

But Mr. Bright was anything but pleased.

Harold was across town the afternoon the previous owner decided to drop by his former store. Within minutes he was storming around the drugstore, from soda fountain to front counter, his face several shades of red, ranting at his former employees about the new fixtures and counters and shelves and snarling that Harold Simmons had no right to change anything.

"I'm gonna sue that young bastard!" he bellowed as he pushed his way out the door.

Within a few hours he was back, trailed by a local photographer retained to "document" the changes. The staff, frightened and visibly upset, kept trying in vain to reach the boss, but the story couldn't be relayed until Harold returned in late afternoon and was greeted by the details of Bright's onslaught.

There might have been a chance of calming the older man, but his disruptive foray into Harold Simmons' store seemed to demand an immediate response that an older, wiser Harold Simmons might have handled differently.

"What's the matter with you, Mr. Bright?" Harold said to the former owner by telephone. "I didn't sell your fixtures! They're almost worthless anyway, but they're stored. They're okay."

"You're gonna put them back in place, Simmons! You understand me?"

"No, sir, I'm certainly not going to do anything like that. I'm making the store better. You should be pleased."

"Our agreement specifically prohibits you from removing those fixtures, and I'm gonna sue you for the entire note."

The arrival of a summons several weeks later confirmed the former owner's fury as Bright filed his threatened lawsuit to foreclose on the $45,000 note for breach of the contract's provisions.

And for the first time in a business matter, Harold had to hire a lawyer—one who rapidly discovered that the note Harold had signed with Bright *did* prevent him from removing the old fixtures from the store without written permission.

To Harold Simmons, the whole brouhaha was little more than a tempest in a teapot. Bright knew that if he succeeded in accelerating the note, he could conceivably force the store into bankruptcy; however, that could backfire. He could be forced to come out of retirement and run the store once more if Simmons failed. Obviously, Harold reasoned, Bright didn't want that. He was just an old man set in his ways who didn't like things happening without his permission. Either that, Harold thought, or Bright was using the small contract violation as an excuse to get the loan paid off faster.

"Don't worry," he told Sandra. "It's a ridiculous little thing. We'll get it settled."

There were far more important things competing for Harold's attention in the late spring of 1962, including the chance to buy something new and make even more money. Despite the lawsuit, University Pharmacy was doing well and extra cash was building up in the coffers. Not enough to go wild with, but enough to look for another drugstore to buy. After all, Harold reasoned, he was getting the hang of running University Pharmacy. If he could run one, why couldn't he run two or more? Same challenges, same methods, same lessons. It was all in figuring out the patterns.

And he had already spotted two possible targets.

Each drugstore was operating out of leased space on the end of a small strip mall, one on the north side of Walnut Hill Lane just east of Marsh Lane, and the other on the south side of Walnut Hill, facing the competing store. Each seemed to be pounding the profits out of the other, and both businesses were for sale.

What if, Harold thought, *I buy both of them and shut one of them down, and move all the customers and accounts to just one store, which will then have the volume of two stores and the expenses of one? I'll bet that'll work! And I could sub-lease the floor space of the one I shut down to a different kind of business.*

He began researching the area, verifying the fact that the housing developments to the north were booming with new families and a growing base of business.

Harold met each of the two owners in turn, careful not to tip his hand to what he was considering. The store on the north side of Walnut Hill was doing almost $400,000 gross a year, the one on the south side about $225,000, and both war-weary owners indicated they might be willing to finance their own sale with just a little down.

If I could work an almost-nothing-down deal with University Pharmacy, Harold decided, *there's no reason I can't do it here.*

Before he could take on any more debt, however, the matter of *Bright v. Simmons* had to be settled.

Harold took his new attorney and met with Mr. Bright and his lawyer one afternoon to hammer out a simple agreement: Harold would start paying 6% interest on the previously interest-free $45,000 note, and Bright would drop the lawsuit. It was a significant win for Bright, who began collecting an extra $200 per month from Harold Simmons, but it seemed worth it. Suddenly, Harold was freed up to do the new deal, and he wasted no time.

Moving rapidly, quietly, and alone, he made an offer for the first store at Marsh and Walnut Hill, pulling enough cash from University Pharmacy's accounts for a down payment of $20,000. When the deal had closed and Harold Simmons was the sole owner of his second store and its accounts, he withdrew almost the same amount from the newly acquired store's cash reserves to make the down payment on the third store, later taking the cash from the third store's accounts to replace what he'd borrowed from University Pharmacy.

"The upshot of it," he later told Glenn, "is that I essentially bought both stores with their own money and zero equity, and all I had to do was slow down some of the payables and increase the cash flow of both new stores to make up the difference. And the beauty of it is, everyone gets paid, everyone makes a profit, and the stores will be better managed when I get through straightening them out."

Within weeks Harold initiated a quiet campaign to run down the south store and eventually close it, shortening the store hours, diminishing the merchandise, and telling the customers that they were gradually merging the store with the other location—all the while unaware that the operation would seriously antagonize the landlord of the shopping center.

Even with the heavy workload, he was discovering a rhythm to his own management of time. Taking the girls to school each morning was never a chore—he loved seeing them on their way and giving them a goodbye kiss and appropriate encouragement. It buoyed his drive down Hillcrest to University Pharmacy. Attending field days at their school and PTA meetings took more planning, but after all, he was the boss, and as long as he could cover the various minimum positions required to run the store, his kids' need for their dad's presence was more important. It was early, he knew, in the business career he was planning, but one facet would be constant: he would make every game, every PTA meeting, every play or performance, and be there for his girls almost every night, just as he had since Penny left.

■　　■　　■

With his management duties now tripled overnight and no real office to work in, Harold decided it was time to add on to University Pharmacy. In one project, he decided, he could build both his coffee shop and a much-needed little office loft for himself. The project took another loan of $35,000, but this one was relatively easy to finance. After all, the applicant was now the owner of not one but *three* stores, and anyone smart enough to do that was undoubtedly good for a paltry store improvement loan. The more receptive banking attitude didn't make the paperwork any simpler, but the presumption was beginning that Harold Simmons was a comer, a bright young businessman who was going places.

And as he knew so well from being a banker, such assumptions opened doors.

CHAPTER 12

DALLAS, TEXAS: 1963

*T*here were apparently no limits to what the new corporate stars of Dallas could accomplish, and watching them was almost awe-inspiring. In the wake of the spectacular success of Texas Instruments, which had exploded from the status of a sleepy company in the fifties to a major, growing national electronics force in the sixties, Dallas corporations seemed to be positioned to compete with the best and the richest America had to offer.

And already one of the most successful new ventures was a company called LTV. Cobbled together by a brilliant financier named Jim Ling, LTV was an uneasy amalgam of his tiny Ling Electric Company, an aerospace firm called Temco, and aircraft builder Chance-Vought Corporation. Ling-Temco-Vought was becoming one of the nation's fastest growing and most spectacular conglomerates—a corporate collection of dissimilar companies acquired through complicated stock swaps and financial maneuvers. The forging of conglomerates in general, and LTV in particular, involved far more complexity than corporate America was used to. Suddenly, a sparkling new steel and smoked-glass office tower was rising in downtown Dallas to house LTV's corporate offices, and the entire business community was busily paying homage to its creator. With new bank buildings rising on the North Texas prairie and fast-moving, go-go bankers transforming First National and Republic (and even the more stodgy Mercantile) banks into responsive risk-takers fueling a new Texas business boom, not even the sky was the limit, as NASA's selection of Houston for its head-quarters seemed to prove.

Ling, for his part, thought in grandiose terms. He was the new breed of non-oil Texas wildcatter, using brains and chutzpah where the Clint Murchisons and H.L. Hunts had used instinct and a gambling spirit thirty years before to make millions by drilling for oil. Ling was light-years ahead of his staff and his legal team in conceiving deals and financial maneuvers that were often literally without precedent. In less than six years he had rocketed from obscurity to ownership of one of the most palatial homes in North Dallas and a position of power almost unequaled in Dallas history. Quite simply, in Big "D," other than Troy Post, the chairman of Greatamerica Corporation, Jimmy Ling was the man to know. He was the dealmaker.

Harold Simmons had watched Jimmy Ling's rise with great respect and interest. Harold didn't want to *be* Jim Ling, but he wanted to know how Ling was managing to acquire major corporations with their own money so successfully. While Harold's purchases of University Pharmacy and the two ill-fated drugstores on Walnut Hill Lane in-volved hundreds of thousands of dollars, largely financed with little to nothing down and utilizing some of the acquired companies' money to stabilize the deals, Ling was wheeling and dealing with *hundreds of mil-lions* of dollars in highly complex acquisitions that often left LTV own-ing companies outright for effectively no expenditure of LTV cash. In some respects, Ling was living Harold's dream, not to own fancy houses or capture the public spotlight, but to develop an unparalleled prowess with complex corporate transactions. Just like Harold, Jimmy Ling had *figured it out* before anyone else, and was living proof that a smart guy who refused to give up could span the distance from financial obscurity to financial dominance inside a decade. In the late fifties, Ling had owned only a tiny company called Ling Electric. By 1963 he was well on his way to becoming the most powerful businessman in Dallas, with a growing personal fortune already based on LTV's success and stock.

If anyone could understand the opportunity Harold suddenly thought he saw in a particular New York-based corporation, it would be Ling.

Harold had learned at the knee of Don White how to read not just financial statements but also the required filings of public corporations, and he'd developed a habit of picking out interesting companies and sending for their annual reports. If the company looked like it might be undervalued, an interested person could look for the Security and Exchange Commission filings known as the "10K" and "10Q" reports and begin to get a feel for what the corporation really owned and how much it was really worth.

The company that had tweaked Harold's interest seemed terribly undervalued. Bath Iron Works in Maine had been around for a long time, steadily building ships and earning a profit. It was a company of little debt, substantial cash, and even more substantial capital, owning most of its own real estate, and having already paid for the vast majority of its buildings.

But Bath was far from a glamour stock, and despite its steadiness, the price per share was far less than what Harold thought it should be. Someone with enough cash, he thought, could probably gain control of it with a relatively small percentage of shares, and, once in control, could cash in some of the hidden value and even reimburse most of the cash needed to acquire it in the first place, while improving the business considerably with a revamped management.

It was just too enticing an opportunity to leave alone, Harold decided, but it was many orders of magnitude beyond his financial capability.

Harold wrote a letter to Jim Ling from his office in University Pharmacy, asking for an appointment. It was worth a shot. He knew Ling would have no idea who Harold Simmons was, even though his brother, Glenn Simmons, was approximately three tiers below Ling as an up-and-coming LTV executive. "You've managed to do what no one else has ever accomplished," Harold wrote. "You've convinced the world that common equity is no longer a necessary ingredient in corporate finance."

It was a moderate thrill when Ling's secretary called a week later to confirm a date and time for a meeting.

■   ■   ■

Within the month, the owner of University Pharmacy walked out of the elevators on the thirty-first floor of the sparkling new LTV Tower in downtown Dallas and instantly recognized the decor. It was Corporate Success, the same motif he'd seen in New York on his ill-fated trip. From the thick carpet to the art objects and huge windows, everything about Jimmy Ling's company and his spacious corner office bespoke incredible accomplishment.

Ling was friendly and gracious as Harold entered. He directed his secretary to close the double doors and leave them alone, and sat listening attentively as Harold pitched his idea: the investment opportunity the undervalued firm presented, what could be done with the assets, and how it could be financed.

When Harold paused, Jimmy Ling adjusted his thick Clark Kent glasses and smiled. "Well, Harold, you've certainly done your homework. So happens, we took a good look at Bath a few months ago, and you've got it right in every particular. I don't think it fits LTV right now, but it could be a hell of a deal."

Harold rode the elevator down to the lobby with a soaring feeling in his gut. It would have been better if Ling had decided to act on his ideas, but to have someone with the facile mind of a Jimmy Ling basically give him an A+ on his analysis confirmed that he was on the right track, and that was worth its weight in gold for the moment.

When Harold looked at himself in the mirror during the months that followed, increasingly he saw the face of an exceptionally smart fellow who knew he could accomplish precisely the same spectacular degree of success Jimmy Ling had achieved, provided the timing was right.

■　　■　　■

With a small war going between his pharmacist and the unyielding woman he'd hired as his front store manager, the number of weekly trips Harold had to make to his north Walnut Hill and Marsh Lane store was becoming a major aggravation.

And now this. The pharmacist was threatening to quit in the middle of the day, and the manager was complaining bitterly yet again about the pharmacist. The lack of cooperation between the two was hurting the bottom line, and although he hadn't seen them snarl at each other in front of the customers, he was sure their attitudes were driving people away.

Harold sighed and slipped out the side door of University Pharmacy to find his car.

Less than a year had passed since he'd closed the deals on the new stores, and the money was draining out faster than he'd planned. Not enough to spark a panic, but enough to get him thinking about a recent conversation with his new lawyer, Dudley Andrews, about trusts.

"A trust can protect you, Harold, as you build your businesses."

"Protect against what?" Sandra had asked one evening when he'd tried to explain.

"In case we get sued again and someone wants to take our house and everything we own," Harold replied, "instead of giving me time to pay them back."

"So, if everything's in a trust and somebody wins a big suit against you, you don't have to pay?"

"No, I'd have to pay. They just wouldn't be able to touch our major assets, whatever those might be. That's the way Dudley Andrews explains it. And that means I can keep on building my business and pay the creditors off on *my* schedule. The main reason for the trust is to allow me to control when and how my creditors would be paid off if I got in trouble."

"And it's still our money?"

"Well, I mean it's all the same thing, but it's a legal deal. Technically the trust owns everything, but since I control it, it's pretty much the same thing."

Dudley Andrews had sent an early draft of a trust for Harold to study, but he'd been too busy and it was still sitting on his desk. Besides, he had no intention of "getting into trouble" financially anytime soon, so there was no urgency.

■   ■   ■

The trip to Marsh and Walnut Hill took less than fifteen minutes. It was a gray day with a chill north wind slightly uncharacteristic of early March, and the overcast weather matched his discomfited mood.

Harold pulled his car into one of the parking places in front of the store and got out as something caught his attention to the west. A collection of orange warning signs had cropped up along the crowned blacktop road that was Marsh Lane as it ran alongside the store. Why?

What the heck is this? Harold thought, pulling his topcoat more tightly around him against the wind as he walked toward the point where Marsh intersected Walnut Hill.

They've blocked it off! He noted the number of men and pieces of heavy road equipment that had sprouted up and down the closed roadway. They hadn't been there the day before. Small wooden stakes with fluttering orange flags were everywhere, and in the distance he could see half of a surveying crew busily setting additional markers.

A worker in a hardhat was leaning on an idling bulldozer, looking at what appeared to be a set of blueprints. A cloud of diesel fumes encircled the man, but he seemed oblivious as he studied the plans and chomped on a cigar, absently blowing a smoke plume back at the huge machine.

Harold stepped over a ditch and caught his eye.

"Hi."

The man looked up and smiled the smile of a busy individual suddenly required to be nice. He pulled the stump of a cigar from his mouth, his voice gravelly and weathered. "Hi."

"What are you fellows fixing to do here?" Harold asked.

"What are we doing to Marsh Lane?" the man asked.

Harold nodded, glancing over his shoulder back toward the north, unsure where they'd cut off southbound traffic. He looked back. "Yeah."

"Expanding it. Paving it. This is the big expansion project you've been reading about."

"I didn't read anything about it," Harold said.

"Well, neither did I, but I was told it was in all the papers."

"But you're ... closing the road down?"

The worker shook his head. "Not completely after today. It'll usually be one lane at a time. Why?"

"Because I own a drugstore over here and we're really dependent on the traffic that comes down Marsh," Harold said, wondering if he sounded a bit plaintive.

"Traffic will be slow for a while, all right," the man gestured broadly with his cigar. "In fact, it will probably be a nightmare. But this'll be a real nice four-lane road when we finish."

"When's that?" Harold asked, already calculating the loss if his customers decided not to brave the construction project and went somewhere else.

"I don't know. Maybe by December. Maybe next year."

Harold's heart sank as he left the man and walked into the store to arbitrate between his two feuding employees.

■   ■   ■

His plan to close the south store was already going badly.

Harold could sense it before he could see it in the bottom line. Once again he was having trouble with what was supposed to be an easy move: the decision to close the south store. The landlord of the shopping center was furious, claiming that he'd broken the store's lease by shutting it down. While Harold's master plan included sub-leasing the space the south store had occupied to a non-drugstore operation, the landlord was determined to find *another* drugstore operator to come in and take over the location.

Once more, Harold had to pay for a lawyer to tell him he hadn't checked everything out as well as he should have. The landlord had pulled up in a truck after closing one night and emptied out what re-mained of the stock and fixtures in the south store, effectively finish-ing the job Harold had begun. The man then had the locks changed, leaving Harold a formal notice declaring that the leasing contract for the space was now null and void.

"He can't do that," Harold said when he reached his lawyer's of-fice.

"No, he can't," the lawyer quickly agreed.

"It's my store. I own the thing," Harold said, pointing to the loca-tion of the south drugstore on a map on the lawyer's desk. "I can close that store anytime I want to. And I can sub-lease that space."

"Well ... not necessarily, Harold," the lawyer replied. "He wants that store left open and healthy, and if he can't have that, he wants to take back the lease and sub-lease it to someone else to start a rival drugstore."

"That's crazy. If I keep that store open, both stores will go belly up, which would be terrible for the value of his little shopping center. You know—don't put a store in there, you'll go bankrupt? But if I consoli-date the stores and sub-lease his space to another type of retail opera-tor, not a drugstore, he still gets his rent."

Harold knew that that part of the problem was relatively small compared to his central headache: the Marsh Lane street-widening project and what it was doing to the customer base of his north Marsh Lane and Walnut Hill store.

He had expected the loyal customers of the south store to come across the street to the north store, and he'd even merged their charge accounts to make it easy. But not all of them were coming. Some were scared off by the growing disruption of Marsh Lane, which was one of the major routes to the store, and some were put off and run off by the confusion of not understanding what the new owner was doing in shrinking and closing the south store. Too many customers were simply deserting the area for other drugstores.

And then there was the basic problem of getting existing customers to brave the construction on Marsh when there were easier stores to reach farther to the north. Not only was his customer base shrinking, but there was little new business, and the master plan required keeping the existing customers and adding new customers at a healthy rate.

This isn't working, Harold had to admit to himself. *If something doesn't change here, I'm going to be in a survival posture. Forget the profits.*

Managing three stores meant even longer hours now for Harold, and the struggle to spend enough time with Sandra and the girls became more acute. While University Pharmacy was making money as usual, it was in a massive state of flux, especially with the start of the coffee shop construction project, and he needed to stay close by. Before opening the small restaurant, he would have to hire a good manager, train a new wait staff, secure health department inspections and licenses, and take care of a thousand other details—including making up a menu. He hoped it would all be completed by the beginning of Sandra's senior year at SMU.

CHAPTER 13

DALLAS, TEXAS: 1964

*A*s Dallas began working through the shock of John Kennedy's assassination, workers across from SMU were finishing the new interior of Simmons' University Pharmacy, and Harold began planning a grand opening.

The new coffee shop occupied the north half of the store and was separated from the main retail side by a half-wall which let the customers survey items they might want while they munched their hamburgers and fries. The interior sported wide, freshly built and upholstered booths flanked by several tables, all of them visible and inviting through the sweeping new plate-glass windows separating the interior from the sidewalk. As Harold had planned it, the coffee shop customers would not be able to enter the coffee shop directly; instead, they would enter through the main door of University Pharmacy and traverse the heart of the retail side to get to the tables or booths. It was a clever design that enhanced impulse sales of items carefully placed near high-traffic aisles.

And at last Harold had what could pass as an office atop a tiny circular metal "stairway," in what amounted to a tiny loft. The little office became the diminutive nerve center for both University Pharmacy and the Marsh Lane operation. Harold's hours on the job increased steadily. If not in the tiny loft office or on the retail floor, he could be found many days working in the kitchen, flipping burgers, washing dishes, or anything else that needed to be done.

"Who *is* that guy?" was a typical question from coffee shop customers startled to have a man taking their orders instead of the usual waitresses.

"I think he owns the place," was the typical response. "I've seen him around."

It was a spring day in 1964 when one of the customers who had wondered the same thing walked brazenly past the staff and into the kitchen area at the back of the coffee shop to confront the owner.

"I'm looking for the boss," the man announced.

"You've found him."

"You're Harold ... *Simmons?*" The question seemed strained, as if the man asking it was incredulous that someone washing dishes in the back of a drugstore coffee shop could be the boss, let alone the owner.

Harold looked up from the stack of dirty dishes and wondered for a minute if this was some sort of joke. Standing before him was a short, fat little man who looked for all the world like a clown slightly out of costume. He was wearing a yellow shirt under a pink suit coat with a huge carnation, and had a cigar sticking out of his mouth. The only thing missing, Harold thought, was Bozo's bulbous nose and carrot-colored hair.

"Believe it or not, I'm Harold Simmons," Harold replied, controlling his reaction.

The little man turned with a startling suddenness to survey the front end of the coffee shop, then turned just as abruptly back, looking Harold in the eye. He pulled the cigar from his mouth long enough to whistle. "I'll be damned! There used to be a soda fountain here."

"That's right."

"And you've put in a coffee shop."

"Apparently."

"So, you're the *Simmons* of Simmons' University Pharmacy, as the sign now says out front?"

"Yes. Who are you?"

The man ignored the question, his eyes falling to the dishes Harold was pushing into the dishwashing shroud. "What are you doing back here?"

"Well," Harold replied, feeling a bit irritated but holding his temper in check. "I'm washing dishes. We do that in coffee shops these days, especially when my dishwasher steps out for a while."

"But you're the owner."

Harold pulled a towel across the stainless steel counter and began drying his hands, his curiosity piqued.

"May I ask who you are?" Harold asked again.

This time the man's face virtually erupted in a sudden 50-megawatt grin as broad and flashy as the toothy smile of a sideshow barker. He stuck out a pudgy hand. "Why, I'm George Sirbach, regional sales manager of S&H Green Stamps. I imagine you've heard of me."

Harold met his hand and shook it in guarded fashion.

"No."

"Yeah, well, you probably just forgot. This is my territory. Harold, is it?"

"Yes."

"You can call me George. I'm really impressed, Harold! A store owner up to his elbows in dirty dishes is a regular guy, and I like regular guys."

"What can I do for you, Mr. Sirbach . . . George?"

"Well, you can buy me a cup of coffee and tell me all about your plans for this place! You never know. Maybe S&H can help."

"I think we already give Green Stamps."

"Of course you do. That's why I'm here."

Harold studied the strange little man and hesitated before nodding.

Maybe it was a waste of time, but something instinctual was warning him that anyone as bizarre and self-assured as George Sirbach might just be a person worth cultivating. And in any event, being discourteous was not a Harold Simmons trait.

Harold smiled and put the towel back on the rack. "Okay, Mr. Sirbach. I guess I can afford to take a break."

CHAPTER 14

DALLAS, TEXAS: 1964

The realization that the purchase of the Walnut Hill stores had
been a mistake was slow in coming. There were specific reasons
why his plan hadn't worked, but the plan itself had been sound. Of
course, Harold admitted to himself, he'd grossly underestimated the
amount of managerial hand-holding he'd have to do to keep the north
drugstore going, and he'd equally underestimated the interference of
the landlord of the south store, who was still upset and still trying to
cancel the lease.

But the worst problem was simply the cash flow which hadn't developed. Unless Marsh Lane was finished very soon and traffic into the
north store picked up significantly, there wasn't going to be enough
cash coming in to pay the two loans without deeply raiding University
Pharmacy profits.

Several weeks before, his lawyer, Dudley Andrews, had sent a re-
fined draft of the family trust idea. "Harold," he'd said on the phone,
"now's the time to do this, not when you're having a financial problem."

"What do I put in the trust? And tell me again who really owns it?"
Harold had asked.

"Technically, your kids will own it when you die, but in the meantime, they just have a remainder interest and the trust owns itself.
You'll be trustee and can manage it without interference."

"So, I can't lose control of my money?"

"Nope."

"And . . . I can pay myself a salary and decide how to invest or use the trust money at my discretion?"

"Absolutely. It's called self-dealing, and we'll waive the normal prohibition against that. We'll draw it so you have complete power to self-deal without having to account to the trust for what you do. I mean, the whole focus of the trust is managing the assets so they'll grow, but I know that's what you have in mind anyway. The law allows you to create such a thing because you're trying to build up a lot of money to pass on to your kids."

It seemed like a reasonable move, especially with the growing uneasiness that maybe he'd taken on too much debt to get the two Walnut Hill stores, only one of which could now be sold in an emergency.

The trust was prepared and signed almost as an afterthought. It was just another small detail in the process of doing business, and a type of estate planning. Even the documents that transferred all his shares of University Pharmacy to the trust were signed in the course of a normal business day, although with the stroke of their pens, Harold Simmons and Sandra Simmons ceased to own the SMU store.

Instead, Harold became the trustee, able to do anything with the shares he wanted *as* trustee, even though he no longer had the legal ability to say he owned them. Full control and full benefits with none of the dangers, his lawyer had said, and that amounted to a good solution to the problem of protecting the wealth he fully intended to compile.

While the shares of University Pharmacy went to the new trust, the shares of the other two stores did not. Harold knew he might yet have to deal with the former owners of the Walnut Hill and Marsh Lane stores if he had trouble paying the loans he'd taken out to buy them, and he didn't want the trust involved if it got ugly.

■　　■　　■

By late summer it was clear to Harold that he was out of options. The one remaining Walnut Hill store had to go, even though the sale price was unlikely to be anywhere near enough to pay off the two loans he'd originally taken out to buy the north and south stores at Walnut Hill. The payments on the University Pharmacy loan (which now included interest, thanks to the settlement with Mr. Bright) plus the heavy payments on the other two loans were becoming a dangerous burden, and the amount of money being leached monthly from the profits of University Pharmacy was threatening his ability to pay for the improvements to the store. Reluctantly, Harold placed an ad to sell the north store at Walnut Hill, well aware that any sale would require the approval of the men who held the two notes, each of which was secured by the respective stores, one of which was now defunct. The south store was unsaleable and gone. But by his best estimates, the north store might bring $50,000 for the inventory and fixtures.

He owed $100,000.

In a year in which a luxury car cost around $6,000 and a brick home with 3,500 square feet of floor space in a good North Dallas neighborhood brought around $35,000, a debt of $100,000 was incredible. Even if he could find a buyer, Harold realized he would be left owing $50,000 on the Walnut Hill deal, and about $25,000 on University Pharmacy plus the fixture loan for $25,000 borrowed to build the coffee shop. Debt servicing $100,000 would cost over $1,500 a month, which was about one-half of University Pharmacy's profits. Despite the continuous improvement in the SMU store, it was going to take years to dig out of the hole the Marsh Lane expansion project— and his own premature exuberance—had created.

But he would dig out. It was just a matter of time and a calm reliance on his own abilities. There would always be setbacks, and there would always be solutions.

And he was protected from sudden foreclosure by the family trust.

CHAPTER 15

DALLAS, TEXAS: 1965

*H*arold glanced at his watch as he slipped behind the wheel of his car in front of University Pharmacy. His immediate mission was clear. Work out a new payback deal with one of his biggest creditors, the man from whom he'd purchased the now-closed south store at Walnut Hill and Marsh.

The sale of the north store had brought in little more than half the money he needed to pay off the notes from both stores, and he was left still owing nearly $50,000 for two properties that were now history. Even worse, the holders of the notes had no security left, with one store closed and the other sold. In order to avoid trouble, he had to convince both men to trust him to pay the loans off in full from the profits University Pharmacy generated.

The owner of the north store had already agreed and given permission for Harold to sell the store. The other owner would have no practical choice but to agree as well; however, approaching him as a supplicant made Harold uncomfortable.

"What are you proposing, Harold?" the older man asked when Harold had made his case.

"The summers are my slow time. If you could let me skip the payments for the three summer months when SMU is closed down, and then let me resume paying in September, I can concentrate and work hard on improving University Pharmacy and pay you off in a few years."

"What security will I have?" the man asked.

Harold looked him in the eye. "My word. I'll pay back every penny. I just need breathing room."

The decision was several minutes in coming, but as Harold had expected, the approval was given. He drove back toward SMU thinking about the next step he had to take. It would be painful for Sandra, but he had no choice. Their beautiful new house across from Hockaday would have to go. It would take a few years of restricting the family spending to allow time for recovery, and he knew that would be difficult for Sandra.

■　　■　　■

Sandra was at home and the housekeeper was just leaving when Harold pulled into the driveway. Since her graduation, Sandra had made an effort to be a good mother to her two stepdaughters.

With college courses no longer a daily battle, there would be more time for children, and the early 1965 news that she and Harold had conceived had left a frequent smile on Sandra's face—a smile he knew wouldn't remain with the news of his decision to move.

Harold waved to the housekeeper as he closed the car door and walked toward the house, stopping to look at it, his mind deep in thought.

There would be other houses in the future, he knew, just as there had already been a succession of them in his past. In fact, the decision to sell wasn't really bothering him. It was the fact that he had failed to learn all he needed to know before jumping into the Walnut Hill deal that bothered him. He knew he could do better than that. The Marsh Lane expansion project would have been easy to discover had he thought to ask the city. No, he'd been too sure of himself. He hadn't done all his homework.

And he wouldn't allow that to happen again.

■　　■　　■

As he expected, Sandra was very upset. She loved her house. She was pregnant. The news that they had to put it on the market was more than troubling. Why did they have to sell it if University Pharmacy was still theirs? They had money, but they didn't have money? None of it made any sense to her.

"We'll rent a house near here somewhere for a few years, and when I get everything paid off, we'll buy an even better one."

She stared at him for the longest time before turning and fleeing to the bedroom.

Harold sighed as he sank into one of their new wing chairs, his mind already proceeding to the necessary steps of finding a real estate agent and beginning the process. Sandra would get over it. She was still very young and very emotional. She'd get over it, and they'd be fine.

■　　■　　■

A week would pass before Harold could open his personal relief valve and take to the highway in his car. Driving was still a soothing balm, an anesthetic to whatever was bothering him, a dynamic world of kaleidoscopic sights and insulating sounds he could control without the interference of telephones, employees, ledgers, or even his wife and daughters. His car was a space capsule, adrift on an endless sea of concrete, his life-support system the cheap gasoline in the Buick's tank.

He'd pointed the car southward, then navigated off on an endless series of small farm and county roads, rolling the window down every now and then to breathe pure Texas aromas of hay and sorghum, the pungent signature of an occasional feedlot and the smell of freshly turned black dirt, underscored by the perfume of wildly mixed meadow fragrances borne on the shoulders of summer humidity. It was the bouquet of his boyhood, the enjoyment of which confirmed him as a true son of Texas, not just a concrete-pounding denizen of a flashy city like Dallas.

As he often did, Harold would stop occasionally and get out, standing by the car or someone's barbed wire fence to drink in the landscape and listen to the cicadas and the occasional buzz of an unseen insect flashing past his ear.

Here I am, Harold caught himself thinking, *owner of a good business, married to a woman I love, father of two, soon to be three, and doing well.*

He hadn't thought about the loans or the Walnut Hill stores or even the impending move to a rented house for the past week. Past was past. Now he had to figure out the future, and when to expand again.

Even if it took a year or two to amass the cash, it didn't matter. The time would give him a chance to learn much more about the business of running a drugstore, and when opportunity presented itself again, he would be ready, this time with all the right questions.

Harold's mind drifted back to University Pharmacy, causing him to chuckle. He had a staff of good people working for him.

Harold leaned against a fencepost and watched a buzzard practicing aerobatics in the distance. He thought about the constant, wonderful getaways with Sandra and the kids: waterskiing at Grapevine with the little boat they'd purchased; meeting with the Dallas Ski Club in Aspen last winter and learning to go downhill without killing himself. Dallas was a whirl of socialization and parties, but he was more an observer than a willing participant, except where the girls were involved. He loved doing anything with them.

He thought of Golden, and Austin, and his mother.

He thought of his father, the Fessor, and how far he'd come since his dad had passed on. It wouldn't take an appointment to the Supreme Court, Harold knew, to please his father. If Leon Simmons was still alive, he'd already be proud of what his boy had achieved.

And it was just the beginning.

BOOK FOUR

One Giant Leap

CHAPTER 16

DALLAS, TEXAS: AUGUST 1966

*A*t least he hadn't been up to his armpits in dishwater when Blanche found him in the back storeroom and handed him a business card.

"This fellow wants to talk to you if he can."

"He's a drug distributor, Blanche. We already have a drug distributor."

"He told me to tell you he's not selling anything today."

"Behrens Drug," Harold said, reading the card.

The Behrens salesman quickly accepted a cup of coffee and sat in one of the booths in the coffee shop as Harold sat across from him.

"So, what can I do for you?" Harold asked.

"Well, you know we sales types get around a lot."

"I'm sure of it."

"And we hear things, and I heard you were buying the Simpson chain in Tyler."

Harold nodded. "I was interested, but I'm not buying it right now."

Best not to tell him, Harold decided, that Sam Passman, his lawyer, had scared Mr. Simpson out of the deal a month before by asking for too much information on the Simpson drugstores. That was an important lesson, Harold figured: Always keep the lawyers out of a deal until there's a handshake.

The salesman was tapping a fountain pen on the Formica tabletop and watching Harold carefully. "The reason I dropped by, Mr. Simmons

... I happen to know of a small drugstore chain that's available. If you're interested."

"Really? Where?"

"In Waco. Seven stores. The Williams Drug chain."

Harold sat forward slightly, his interest immediately piqued. "I don't know them."

"Traditional stores, all with soda fountains and the normal markups. Delivery service, charge accounts, the whole thing. But very solid, and no debts. You interested? Because Behrens would like to get *all* their business, and we only have a small bit of it now. So, we were hoping someone new ..."

"Might come along and buy them and use your services." Harold finished the thought.

"Something like that," the man said, relaxing slightly. "So you *are* interested?"

Harold had smiled at that. He'd been interested in expanding even as he sold the Walnut Hill store and rearranged the loans he couldn't pay off. He had a third daughter now, named Andrea, his first child by Sandra, now barely a year old. Time was passing. And now he knew the formula.

He was ready.

"You bet," Harold replied. "I'm always interested."

A trip to Waco came the following week. Harold dropped by several of the Williams stores before his planned appointment with the owner of Behrens Drugs, Lacey Clifton, and was pleased by what he saw: a traditional chain waiting to be transformed into a much more profitable enterprise.

It was an economy of scale, he figured. Using the very same lessons he'd learned making a success of University Pharmacy and incorporating some of the methods of the successful Ward's Cut-Rate Drug chain in Dallas, he could probably double the Williams chain's profits in a few years.

■   ■   ■

Harold settled into a chair in Lacey Clifton's Waco office several weeks later with a tentative smile. The deal was coming together, but one more, completely critical piece remained.

"Well, Williams and I have a deal, Lacey," he told the older man.

"Great, Harold!"

"But now I need to raise the money."

"I figured."

The purchase price for Williams' Drug Company and its seven stores was $650,000, which was close to book value. The company was solid with no major debts and a backlog of good stock, locations, and buildings, including a Waco warehouse with a small office Harold figured he could use.

"What'd you think of Berry Williams, Harold?" Lacey asked. "Aside from the fact that he's agreed to sell to you."

"I like him a lot," Harold replied. "Nice fellow. I offered him three hundred twenty-five thousand in cash and he agreed to take back a three hundred twenty-five thousand note on the company for five years at six percent, and take the inventory as collateral."

"Okay."

"Now, Lacey, why I'm here ... I can do this deal, buy these stores, and give you the business if you can help me by guaranteeing a note for three hundred twenty-five thousand. I've got to find a bank for that money, and I know they'll want a guarantor, and I know that if I factor Williams' charge accounts receivables as soon as I have the sale complete, I can pay most of that loan back immediately."

"How much are their receivables, Harold?"

"Two hundred thousand. With a reasonable discount I can raise one hundred seventy thousand by selling those accounts."

"You sure can," Lacey grinned, "and you can consider that problem solved, because we'll buy those accounts."

"I was hoping you'd say that," Harold replied.

"We've got a new computer-based billing system here, and we can factor the accounts and then have a new spate of customers, since Berry would never give us that business."

"Well, that leaves the bank."

"Don't worry about that, either, Harold. I can get my bank to do that."

■　　■　　■

The news that the Harold Simmons who had transformed University Pharmacy into *Simmons'* University Pharmacy was leaving

Dallas to actively manage his new stores left his employees stunned and apprehensive.

For those who understood what he was doing, there was some quiet cheerleading from the sidelines, but for several of the longer-term employees who had struggled with all the previous changes and learned to trust Harold implicitly, this one was seismic.

"Mr. Simmons, who's going to run things here?" Blanche asked.

"I'm working on that," he told her, "... but we'll get someone good. You interested?"

"Heavens no! I'm not management material."

The store bore only a remote resemblance to the sleepy little pharmacy it had been. Paintings by local artists hung throughout the coffee shop, each of them for sale. The array of available merchandise made the store a first stop for almost anything the student population needed, yet the inventory turned over steadily and efficiently. "The World's Most Unique Drugstore!" Harold had labeled University Pharmacy in a series of ads. An SMU student newspaper sniffed sometime later that "the phrase 'most unique' is entirely redundant!"

But grammatically repetitious or not, the store *was* unique, and more so than any other drugstore in the entire state of Texas at the start of 1967. More important, it was very profitable.

There was no last day on the job for Harold. It was more of a gradual fadeout as the Williams deal closed, a house was found in Waco, and a new manager named Jack Smith, a pharmacist and former drugstore manager from Kansas City, was hired to manage University Pharmacy.

By October of 1967, Harold was gone—instantly reachable by phone in a small warehouse office a hundred miles to the south, but physically removed from the store that bore his name and imprint. University Pharmacy was now doing more than $500,000 of business annually, an improvement of more than a third in six years, all of it made possible by innovations Harold was getting ready to apply to his newly acquired chain.

CHAPTER 17

WACO, TEXAS: 1967

*H*arold had just arrived home and closed the front door when Sandra's car screeched into the driveway of their leased Waco house. He walked to the window and peered out as she leapt from the driver's seat and raced toward the front door of the house with a huge smile on her face.

I guess that tells the tale, Harold thought as he waited for her to burst in. After months of pilot training at Waco Regional Airport, it was time for her FAA checkride for her private pilot license. When he'd left for the office many hours earlier, she was still studying and more apprehensive than he'd ever seen her.

But now she was back, bursting through the front door with a war whoop.

"I DID it, Harold!"

He feigned puzzlement. "Did what?"

She hit him gently. "As if you didn't know! I'm all officially blessed by the FAA now as a private pilot."

"Good! But now I suppose you're going to want me to come fly with you," he said, smiling.

"Yep. This weekend. We'll go cross-country to Dallas or something. I've already reserved one of the Cessnas."

Harold nodded and watched her rush off toward the kitchen to call some of her girlfriends.

He'd had mixed emotions about the flight training. On one hand, Sandra had been so unhappy about the move to Waco that the announcement months before that she wanted to learn to fly was almost a relief. At least it would be something to take her mind off her apparent discontent.

On the other hand, the quest worried him. What if something happened to her? Flying was fairly safe, but crashes happened, and she was responsible for raising three girls. Even if safety wasn't a problem, the image of a wife and mother out wheeling a little airplane around the sky seemed somehow incongruous. Although he didn't feel that a woman's horizons should be limited to home, motherhood, and family, flying just wasn't one of those skills he expected his wife to possess. Harold felt vaguely threatened by it. If anyone in the family should be learning to fly, shouldn't it be the breadwinner who might be able to use the skill in his business?

Harold masked any reservations he had, because it was clearly making her happy.

The following Saturday he worked hard to seem enthusiastic as they drove to the airport. Sandra preflighted the single-engine Cessna 172, poking and prodding her way around the small four-seater before assigning her husband to the right side and climbing in herself. Start, taxi, and takeoff were uneventful, and Harold found himself enjoying the view and the feeling of being aloft as they gained altitude and Sandra struggled with her flight plan and maps to keep them on course.

"So how're we going to find Dallas? Shouldn't we climb up higher than three thousand five hundred feet? You can see Dallas from Waco, I'm told, if you're high enough."

She shook her head, speaking loudly over the roar of the engine. "Dead reckoning."

"Dead what?" Harold asked.

"Dead reckoning. I fly a particular compass heading for a precise amount of time, based on my correction for the wind coming out of the west, and it puts us just about where I want to be."

"Oh. Awful phrase," Harold chuckled. "Sounds like if you reckon wrong, you're dead."

"Charles Lindbergh found Paris the same way."

"But we're only going to Dallas, right?"

She rolled her eyes and nodded. "That's right, Harold. I don't have enough fuel for Paris."

"And I don't have enough time for Paris. Besides, I've already been there."

She looked at him wide-eyed. *"Paris, France?"*

"No. Paris, Texas. It's not that far from Golden."

The two of them fell silent as Harold resumed scanning the horizon beneath fluffy cumulus clouds. Sandra was checking her watch more and more frequently, her eyes darting from the map to the ground and back to the map until Harold leaned over to her.

"Something wrong?"

"Well ... nothing's where it should be," she said. "We've been underway for twenty-five minutes and we should be ... *here* ..." she pointed to a spot on the aviation chart, "and Dallas should be right in front of us."

"I don't see Dallas," Harold said.

"Neither do I. That's the problem."

"It's hard to miss, Sandra. It's kind of big."

"Don't tease me, Harold."

"I'm not. It really is big. Remember? We lived there."

She shook her head in disgust as she resumed the search between map and reality.

"There's a small town just ahead," Harold added. "And it has a water tower."

"I'm really happy for them. But what town is it?"

"It's written on the water tower. Most towns do that, remember?"

"Oh. Yeah."

"Maybe we could descend and read the water tower."

"I get the point," she said, pulling the power back and beginning a gentle descent to about five hundred feet above the ground, aiming just to the right of the town and circling left as they passed the water tower.

"Fairfield," she said. "Where the heck is Fairfield?" She shot a warning glance at her husband. "And don't you *dare* say Texas."

She increased power and pulled the little aircraft into a gentle climb as she looked at the map, trying to find Fairfield.

"What're these things, Sandra?" Harold asked, pointing to a bank of radio control heads on the forward panel.

"One's the communication radio we used to talk to the tower in Waco, the other one's called a VOR."

"For navigating?"

"Yes."

"Suppose we might turn it on?"

"I wasn't going to use it. I ... they really haven't taught me much about it. They did teach me how to use dead reckoning, though."

"Couldn't we turn it on and try it?"

"Yeah, you're right." She checked the map for the appropriate frequency and dialed it in, working a small knob left and right and trying to read the course to the Waco VOR.

"I think this means Waco is ... *west* of here, bearing two-six-five!" Sandra said, stabilizing the Cessna in a small bank to the left and tracing the direction backwards on the map. "And here we are, at Fairfield. How did that happen?"

"Look here," Harold said, pointing to the compass on the panel in front of her. "You were flying zero-four-zero degrees from Waco, right?"

Sandra nodded.

"But your flight plan says zero-zero-four."

"Good grief!"

"I think I need to pay for more flight instruction," Harold said, smiling, as his unamused wife banked westward toward Dallas.

Even before they touched down back at Waco, the idea of learning to fly himself was taking hold in Harold's mind.

"You want to do *what?*" Sandra replied when he mentioned the idea sometime later.

"Well, flying with you convinced me that I need to know how to fly, too."

"Why?" she asked, suspicion tinging her voice.

"How about self-defense?" he replied.

"Not funny, Harold."

"No, seriously, I think it'd be a smart idea so we can keep each other safe when we're tooling around the sky with the girls in the back. Maybe we can buy a small airplane and I can use it in the business. You know, as we expand."

"We're expanding?"

"Sandra, I like Waco, but I'm not planning for us to be here very long. It's a stepping stone."

She hugged him suddenly. "I'm *very* glad to hear that."

CHAPTER 18

WACO, TEXAS: MAY 1967

*B*y 1960, Waco, Texas, had changed little from the sleepy, rural Southwestern town that had hosted an Army Air Corps training base during World War II. Larger than dusty Texas burgs like Jarrell, Waco was still a tiny place compared to Dallas or Houston. To most urban Texans, it was little more than a dinner stop at the Elite Café along U.S. 81, arguably the town's most famous eatery in the fifties. Even though Waco was beginning to come alive with new industries by the mid-sixties, it was destined to remain deep in the shadow of Dallas a hundred miles to the north.

Dallas had recovered from the stigma of the Kennedy assassination and was booming with a fervor and intensity that would have made most businessmen on their ascendancy hesitant to leave, especially for the likes of Waco. But Harold's faith that Waco was merely a stop along the way remained rock-solid. He was making substantial progress. *After all,* Harold told himself as the days of 1967 moved toward summer, *last year all I had was one drugstore and a lot of debt. Now I own eight stores. And I know I can analyze these things correctly.*

The promise and the prospects were unlimited, and he had snagged the same dazzling optimism that hung in the heady air of the Dallas business community and forced it to follow him south to surround the small brick warehouse and office complex in downtown Waco where Harold had been captaining the conversion of Williams Drugs.

The Williams conversion, however, was not going as planned.

In the final analysis, Harold concluded, the Waco community was not going to grow fast enough to get him where he wanted to be. Over time, conversion to the cut-rate form of high-volume drugstore business with no soda fountains and no delivery and no in-house charge accounts would turn a nice profit, but nothing would increase exponentially unless the University Pharmacy Corporation (which now owned Williams Drug in Waco) expanded further.

And fast.

Into that atmosphere on a day in May 1967 walked the powerful little man Harold had once mistaken for a clown back at University Pharmacy: George Sirbach of S&H Green Stamps.

The Sperry and Hutchinson Company (aka S&H Green Stamps) was a public corporation of immense wealth because of the way it did business. Retailers all over the nation bought the trading stamps by the tens of millions from S&H, paying in cash, and distributing the stamps over time to their retail customers as a premium incentive for each purchase. The stamps had become so popular by the sixties that for many retail businesses, *not* giving trading stamps was a significant handicap, since many customers would consciously flock to competitors that did. While gas stations were in the forefront of the S&H Green Stamp distribution network, so were drugstores. But customers needed to amass quite a few completed books of stamps before redeeming them for merchandise, and therefore months and years would typically elapse between the time the money flowed into S&H's accounts for any given stamp and the time S&H had to use the cash to pay for the merchandise the customers were entitled to receive when they redeemed that stamp. S&H had an immense cash float, and in the southwestern United States, flamboyant George Sirbach had the responsibility of not only maintaining S&H's preeminent market share but also constantly watching for profitable places to put some of S&H's vast pool of cash.

"Harold Simmons! How are you doing?" Sirbach boomed one afternoon as he came around the corner to the small office Harold used in Waco.

"Just fine, George. How've you been?"

"Never better! So, you're the big drugstore chain owner now, huh?"

"Well, eight stores is hardly big."

"Nonsense! By the way, I want to thank you for making sure the Williams Drug customers continue to get their Green Stamps."

"You're welcome, George. We like Green Stamps. It's hard to keep customers without them. You know that."

"I do. I do. And I work hard to make sure everyone continues to feel that way." He plopped in a chair opposite Harold's desk, his huge smile once again bisecting his face, the ever-present cigar wagging from the right corner of his mouth.

"So tell me what you're planning to do here, Harold. Gonna make Waco your permanent home?"

The conversation flowed easily between the two men, Harold feeling comfortable enough to sit back at one point and sigh, deciding there was no reason *not* to share a small frustration.

"You know, George, I figure I've got to buy more stores if I'm going to make my overall plan work. Waco just isn't booming."

"I understand that."

"I've been scouting around, and I found an oilman down in Houston who has a block of stock in a chain of stores you may know, Mading Drugs. About thirty stores."

Sirbach nodded. "I know 'em, all right. They *don't* give Green Stamps."

"Really? I didn't realize that."

"You wanna buy Mading?"

"Well, I figure if I could get that fellow's stock, which is about twenty-five percent of the outstanding shares, I could get control of the company, and ..." Harold smiled and sat forward, "... then, George, I could get Mading started using S&H Green Stamps."

"How much do you need?" Sirbach asked.

"Sorry?"

"To buy the man's stock. How much?"

"Oh. I figure he'll sell for five hundred thousand dollars. I just need to find a way to borrow that money, and I'm already—"

"Okay, you got it," George Sirbach said, smiling broadly again.

Harold fell silent for a few seconds trying to make sense of the non sequitur.

"I ... excuse me, George. I've got what?"

"The five hundred thousand. S&H will loan it to you. You've got the loan. Go do it."

"I've . . . *got the loan?*" Harold said in abject disbelief.

Sirbach was nodding.

"Just like that? You must be kidding!"

George Sirbach's smile faded as he leaned forward and poked a pudgy finger at Harold Simmons. "Hey, man, when I say you've got something, you've got it. Count on it! Now, we've got some pencil pushers in New York you'll have to talk to, and they'll have to push their little pencils around, but there's no question about it. You've got the loan because I say you've got it. Now, go make your offer. Get that company."

The remainder of the afternoon brought a bizarre mix of emotions. Harold knew Sirbach was a powerful man in his own way, but could he really trust his word on something that big? Then again, what would it hurt to make an offer to the Houston oilman? If something happened and Sirbach couldn't come through with the loan after all, the deal would simply fall through.

But . . . *just like that?* It seemed far too easy.

The negotiation required to get a sale agreement on 25 percent of the stock of Mading Drugs was minimal, and within weeks Harold found himself sitting in a Braniff 727 flying back from New York with copies of the completed loan for a half million dollars in his briefcase, just as George Sirbach had promised.

"He was right," Harold told one of his friends in Dallas by phone. "They pushed their pencils around and asked me a bunch of questions and made me fill out enough paperwork to choke a horse, but the loan sailed through."

"So when do you take over, Harold?"

"Well, it's not that easy. I'll go to the next board meeting and have them put me on the board and then we'll see."

"You think they'll cooperate? I mean, you don't have a majority of the stock."

"Sure they'll cooperate. Why wouldn't they? I own twenty-five percent of the stock, and there are no other big stockholders."

CHAPTER 19

HOUSTON, TEXAS: JUNE 1967

*H*arold checked his watch as he wheeled into the entryway of the plush Rice Hotel. His timing had been perfect. Fifteen minutes remained before the board meeting was scheduled to begin. He turned the car over to the doorman and walked into the lobby, wondering whether to go directly to the hotel conference room reserved for the Mading Drug board meeting, or wait a few minutes and walk in precisely on time.

I'll wait, he decided. He moved to one side of the lobby and found a chair out of sight of the entryway to spend a few minutes reviewing what he was going to say.

Even with 25 percent of the company stock under his control, the leadership of Mading Drugs had seemed less than overjoyed to have Harold Simmons in their midst.

Lewis Lynch was the chairman. A man without formal management training, Lynch was the embodiment of the traditional Mading way of running a drugstore, having worked his way up to chairman from manager of a soda fountain. Harold had introduced himself as soon as possible after closing the deal for the stock. Surely, Harold thought, Lynch and the other five board members would positively consider the cogent recommendations he was going to make about what Mading needed to do to transform itself into a more profitable chain.

Harold asked to be voted onto the board, and the board quickly complied at the first meeting. They even pretended to listen with interest when he spoke. But it became painfully obvious by the second meeting that neither Lewis Lynch nor his intensely loyal board members had any interest in letting Harold Simmons influence their company, let alone run it or transform it. A 25 percent stockholder was a minority stockholder, and that's the role they expected him to play.

Patience, Harold counseled himself. *These old boys are kind of set in their ways.*

There were six directors, one of them a prominent, well-known Houston lawyer named George Rice, who was senior partner in one of the more powerful firms in town. Regardless of their own business reputations, all of the men appeared determined to defer to Lynch in most matters.

But Lynch is killing Mading Drugs, Harold concluded after the second meeting. *He's scared to innovate, not knowledgeable enough of what's happening to the drugstore business to realize they're dying, and determined to hang on personally,* he thought. *If I can't get them to change, this investment is in real trouble.*

It was supposed to have been simple, but that wasn't happening. The new stockholder was being politely ignored in the apparent hope that he'd eventually go away.

■   ■   ■

Harold glanced at his watch. *It's time,* he thought, getting to his feet to attend his third board meeting.

Two hours later he headed for the lobby on a rising tide of conflicting emotions. Nothing had changed, and he realized that nothing would happen as long as he was pursuing his goals with this company by himself.

He returned to Waco determined to carry out an idea he'd voiced to them about bringing a friend to the next meeting, a financier who might make a good addition to the board. Harold was hardly in the door back in Waco before calling Russell Kibbe in Dallas to see if he was interested.

Buttonholing Kibbe to join the Mading board seemed a good idea. Harold desperately needed an ally, and Kibbe—who, until the previous year, had been the financial vice president of Texas Industries and had become a good friend—could fill the bill. With Kibbe's business experience and résumé, the rest of the Mading board might be persuaded that Harold's reform ideas weren't just the loony ravings of some entrepreneur but a true blueprint of what needed to be done to make Mading prosperous. Harold had met Russell Kibbe years before when they lived near each other in Dallas and Kibbe's daughter began babysitting for the Simmons girls. Russell loved to talk about big deals, and the prospect of getting involved in an exciting salvage operation immediately interested him.

The next board meeting, held in the same hotel meeting room in downtown Houston, seemed cordial enough at first. The directors knew Russell Kibbe would be coming, and none of the members had voiced objections.

Harold introduced Russell and then asked him to wait outside as they opened the meeting and reached the point Harold had waited for.

"Gentlemen, you've met Mr. Kibbe and heard his extensive financial background, and I've told you I firmly feel that as the owner of a quarter of the company I should be entitled to two seats on this board, so now I'd like to enter a motion that we elect Mr. Kibbe to the board."

"So noted, Harold," Lewis Lynch said evenly from the other end of the meeting table. "Do I hear a second to the nomination?"

Silence.

What on earth? Harold thought, looking around the table. No one was meeting his eyes.

"Okay," Harold said at last, off balance at the lack of reaction. "We need someone to second Mr. Kibbe's nomination."

The deep silence that descended on the little room was immediately deafening. George Rice cleared his throat and studied some papers in front of him while the director on his left rubbed his ear and glanced at Lewis Lynch, who seemed unruffled.

No one spoke, and Harold felt his face flushing with anger.

These guys discussed this ahead of time! Harold realized. *I told them I was bringing Russell down here, and they set me up!* He cautioned himself to remain civil, but he could feel the reins on his temper slipping. Did they really think a man who'd paid a half million dollars for his quarter share could be frozen out?

"Okay," he said, glaring at the various men around the table one by one as he got to his feet slowly. "All right, so be it. None of you want to second my nomination. But if you think I'm going to sit here and let you gentlemen run this company without my participation, you'd better think again! You understand me? I'll just go out and buy enough stock to take over this outfit and maybe I'll fire all of you. You can just count on it. You haven't heard the last of this."

"Ah, Harold ..." Lewis Lynch began, looking thoroughly alarmed, but a furious Harold Simmons had already turned and left the room, slamming through the door and briefing Russell Kibbe as they both headed toward the elevator.

No one gave chase.

■　　■　　■

"Listen, Russell, I've got to get another twenty-six percent of Mading," Harold told him as they left Houston.

"Only twenty-six percent?"

"That's all I need to unseat these guys. Otherwise, I've got stock in a dying company."

Within the daily pressures of keeping the reforms on track at Williams Drugs' seven stores in Waco, Harold began shoving the throttle up on the acquisition machine he was determined to build to take over Mading Drugs' thirty-one stores in Houston. He had to make his heavy investment perform, and in the hands of Lewis Lynch, the Mading chain was slipping toward further stagnation. If that happened, he could be left paying off a $500,000 loan left over from purchasing a worthless company, and, by contrast, the $50,000 he'd been left to pay after the Walnut Hill debacle would seem like peanuts.

Borrowing a half million dollars for the first 25 percent of Mading had been frightening, but now he had to do it again. Harold wouldn't let himself consider the emotional implications of adding that much indebtedness. Three-quarters of a million dollars was too much to count, but he'd need every penny and more to buy the extra stock in Mading necessary to take control.

In the final analysis, though, the numbers weren't important. Seizing control was.

"Russell, I think I've got her figured out," he told Kibbe by phone one morning a week later.

"Okay, tell me."

"I just need a little favor."

"Sure, Harold. What?"

"Russell, I need you to help me raise at least a half million dollars."

"Oh. Is that all?"

"Yeah. Nothing too great. I think I can borrow the rest from the bank."

"Let me check the petty cash drawer here, Harold."

"No, seriously Russell. If you can help me find enough investors to raise that amount of seed money, I think I can get a bank to loan the rest, because the book value of Mading is good enough to sustain it."

"Harold, do you ever sleep?"

"Of course. But not when there's a deal that needs doing."

"I suspected as much. Let me think a while and I'll call you back."

The small whirlwind of an idea accelerated into a tornado of activity as Kibbe assembled a group of five wealthy Dallas businessmen headed by Larry Hart and Preston Reynolds, Jr.

"I've changed the name of University Pharmacy Corporation to Williams Drug Company," Harold told the men during their first meeting in Dallas, "and I want to sell you half the company for five hundred thousand dollars. I'll take that cash to a bank, and get the loan for the remaining funds I need to buy the controlling interest in Mading. Then we'll merge those stores together, make them all cut-rate marketers, significantly raise the value of the investment, and we'll all make money on the deal."

After a flurry of refinements, they all signed on, and Harold rapidly found himself in the office of Harold Blacksheer of the Bank of Texas, who agreed (after significant back and forth negotiation and paperwork) to finance the tender offer.

"But what *is* a tender offer?" Sandra asked one evening when everything was coming together and Harold couldn't quite contain his enthusiasm. "Some sort of nice and gentle offer?"

"No, it doesn't mean a kind and gentle offer. It means if they'll *tender* their shares to us, we'll pay so much money per share to buy them."

"Oh. Tender."

"Yeah. As in 'to offer.' We're offering to buy them out."

"Who owns the stock you need to buy?"

"A lot of folks. We're going to have to chase them down, I guess, one by one. I need twenty-six percent more. It's kind of complicated."

In fact, the legal and financial complexity of the deal he'd hatched had suddenly thrust Harold Simmons into an entirely different arena, one that required the services of investment bankers and corporate lawyers to handle aspects he'd never dealt with before.

Dean Gurerin, a fellow member of the Dallas Ski Club, who ran an independent investment banking company, Epler, Gurerin and Turner, signed on as the financial expert, while a Dallas firm known as Jenkens, Anson, Spradley, and Gilchrist supplied a lawyer in the person of senior partner, Walter Spradley. Spradley, a tall, gregarious man with a great sense of humor and a keen legal mind, had been one of the lead corporate lawyers for oilman Clint Murchison. With the two professionals working hard to guide Harold through the regulatory and legal minefield, the tender offer was announced ten days later to the sound of thundering silence. Despite the dismal prospects of Mading, the stockholders were not flocking to sell.

Mading Drugs had been slipping for some time, and everyone with money in the stock knew it. To some extent, the investors had already written it off and moved on, not that they were ready to give their shares away. But a tender offer for a moribund stock attracts little immediate interest when the stockholder refuses to realize that the stock value is never going to go *back* up. At fifteen dollars per share, the tender offer was somewhere between appropriate and generous. Nevertheless, those stockholders willing to sell to Harold Simmons were only trickling in.

Harold began dashing in all directions trying to talk to individual stockbrokers, but the effort was wearing thin. Weeks were passing, and still his percentage of ownership remained below 51 percent.

"Let's reduce the price some more," someone on the team suggested. "We've offered fifteen, now let's scare them and offer thirteen fifty per share. If they don't sell now, the implication is it'll go even lower."

The new offer was launched, and the ploy—which would in later years be rendered an illegal takeover method by the Williams Act—worked. The final small blocks of stock came in, the final payments were issued, and Harold Simmons' University Pharmacy Company (now changed to the Williams Drug Corporation) became the 51 percent owner of Mading Drug Company, Incorporated.

The Mading board and Lewis Lynch caved almost immediately, but Harold decided not to fire any of them as he'd threatened. In fact, the only one of the original board to leave was Lewis Lynch himself. Suddenly gracious and cooperative after being informed of the change in ownership, Lynch decided to retire, remaining only long enough to help Harold transition the company to a new management team headed up by Harold Simmons himself.

■   ■   ■

"So when are we moving?" Sandra asked when the news had been announced at home in Waco.

"As soon as possible," Harold replied. "You upset?"

"Are you kidding?" she asked, smiling. "Houston qualifies as a real town."

CHAPTER 20

HOUSTON, TEXAS: 1967

*T*he task ahead of Harold in Houston was daunting, but he wasn't thinking about it in those terms. Where the workload and challenge of taking on three drugstores had been a shock three years before (when he'd made the ill-fated Walnut Hill purchases), the sudden senior management challenges of running a thirty-nine-store chain was going to be many times greater. But that reality never triggered serious self-doubt. After all, he'd purchased a senior management team along with Mading's stock, and they could handle the day-to-day challenges while his mind and focus remained on the horizon. He could guide them in changing to more cut-rate and efficient operations precisely the same way they were changing Williams. They could do it in time. There was no long-range concern about servicing the huge debt he'd now amassed.

"There are a hundred ways to get into financial trouble, and a thousand ways to get out of it," someone had once told Harold, and he held it as almost a mantra of justification when the potential realities of what he had taken on threatened to contaminate his resolve. After all, hadn't he weathered the Walnut Hill problems and come back within two years?

"There's a huge opportunity out there," Harold had explained to Russell Kibbe and the other investors who now owned a sizable chunk of his company. "Texas is still full of these archaic drugstores which are full of book value and can be put together under a common name and vastly improved. We can build a huge business doing that, if we move fast enough. Speed is the key, because others are going to figure this out sooner or later, and those stores that are left after everyone else gets in the game may be too far gone under the weight of cut-rate competition to be worth buying."

■   ■   ■

Life continued to accelerate, the days blending into a blur of happily productive activity punctuated by time with his family. The move to Houston was relatively painless, and he and Sandra were able to lease a house as big and as plush as the one they had been forced to sell in Dallas two years before.

The west side of Houston in 1967 was still full of wide-open spaces, many of them heavily timbered and reasonably close to the heart of the city, and within a month Harold had located a property that excited him.

"You've got to see this," he told Sandra. "It's got three acres, more than a hundred fifty trees by my count, a five-bedroom house, and our own swimming pool."

"Three acres?"

"Big place. The yard's huge, too. I'll have to get a riding lawn mower to cut the grass."

"Bigger than our house in Dallas?"

"Bigger and better, Sandra."

With the purchase complete several weeks later, the Simmons family moved into their new house with great enthusiasm. It seemed like a grand estate, and it was theirs, a perfect place to raise the girls. It promised a new tranquility, Harold thought, especially since he'd made the decision to send his increasingly rebellious fifteen-year-old daughter Scheryle to a private school.

Harold was busier than ever, but he took great pride in being home almost every night, the exceptions being out-of-town trips. His record of attending his daughters' plays and games was still perfect, his praise of their accomplishments constant, and he was there every night being a supportive father. He took them waterskiing, horseback riding, driving, flying, and hiking. He bought a riding lawn mower and gave them endless rides around their new property, something that Andrea loved the most. Whatever they wanted, Harold tried to give them—in material goods as well as his own love and attention.

Full-blown vacations were more sporadic, but they traveled often as a family and even began flying as a family after Harold soloed and passed *his* private pilot flight check (which he had completed before leaving Waco).

"I really do think we should buy an airplane," he told Sandra one afternoon in Houston, delighted at the huge smile he got in return.

"Oh, Harold! That's great! What type?"

"How about a little Cessna? Maybe a 182?"

"Wonderful."

"I can fly it on business trips to Waco and Dallas."

"And if we get it fully instrumented, I can get my instrument rating and my commercial license."

Harold had paused as he studied her eyes. "I ... can understand why we both ought to have an instrument rating, but why a commercial license?"

"I don't know, Harold," she said, tossing her long hair and giving him a teasing look. "Maybe I'll get a job as an airline pilot someday."

■　■　■

At work, Harold moved into Lewis Lynch's old office, a sizable affair in a suite of offices in the two stories built above the Mading warehouse. With thirty-one stores in the chain—not to mention his seven stores in Waco and one in Dallas—there was now a constant river of correspondence to deal with and people to talk to. He needed a gatekeeper—a secretary. This was a real milestone, though he didn't view it that way.

Harold had never thought much about having a secretary. It wasn't a rite of passage or a badge of achievement, but merely a fact of business. Until this point he had always typed his own letters and stamped his own mail and answered his own phone.

■　■　■

If Harold Simmons was getting to know Houston in the fall of

1967, it was without any particular anticipation of being noticed. But Houston *was* noticing him, and even though his arrival as a new resident was hardly the top news of the season, the fact was that an exceedingly young man from Dallas had come to town and snagged the largest retail drugstore chain. Anyone who could do that was someone to cultivate.

Houston in the year before Richard Nixon's election was not the same type of boomtown metropolis as Dallas. Less posh and much less preoccupied with social standing, Houston was an oil town that still thought nothing of letting eighteen-wheeled mobile drilling rigs roll routinely through the heart of downtown. Refineries and major oil company headquarters ruled, and where Dallas' optimism centered around the bankrolling and controlling and building of industries, Houston *was* those industries—with a wildcatter's blue-collar heart and bawdiness to boot.

Decades before the rust-belt cities of the Northeast began losing large portions of their populations to Houston, the town had become the largest city in Texas, characterized as much by its voracious hunger for annexation of adjacent towns and lack of municipal zoning as Dallas was for the opposite attitude of controlled growth and careful city government.

Houston, in other words, was a great place for empire builders, whatever the scale of their empires. And as Harold knew well from personal experience, for bankers intending to build their own banking empire, ferreting out the young lions of industry was a good beginning.

Harold was such a man, and Ben Love was such a banker.

Newly recruited to Texas Commerce Bank in Houston and quietly assigned the task of acquiring Harold Simmons as a new Texas Commerce customer, Love set about meeting the new controlling shareholder of Mading Drugs to see if he, perchance, needed any banking help in the Bayou City.

"Well, I already have a banker, Mr. Love," Harold remembered telling him. After all, Harold Blacksheer's bank had backed the pivotal acquisition of Mading Drugs, the acquisition that had attracted Texas Commerce's attention in the first place. Harold's loyalty was to Blacksheer.

But Ben Love was not about to give up. As Harold began angling for the purchase of another Houston drug chain called Dugan Drug

Stores, Ben Love began introducing Harold to the movers and shakers of the city, inviting Harold and Sandra to fancy balls, showing him the sights, and becoming a good friend. While socializing was anything but a comfort or a goal for Harold, it became a tolerable means to an end. Besides, he knew instinctively that the better known he was among important members of the Houston business and financial community, the easier it would be to borrow more money and buy more businesses in the future.

The chance to attend gala society balls and other glitzy parties suited Sandra just fine, and as she had in Dallas, she kept her wardrobe at the forward edge of the envelope.

But Sandra was beginning to see other horizons, both from the cockpit of their new Cessna and from the innate sense of competition that seemed to leave her uncomfortable with Harold's increasing public notoriety. After all, she was *Sandra* Simmons, not just *Mrs.* Simmons. She was a pilot, and had become a pilot first. She was a college graduate and a capable person and far more than just a cute thing in a micro-miniskirt. Harold was concerned that she saw herself increasingly in her husband's shadow, and that shadow, in her perception, was stunting her growth.

Sandra began work on her advanced pilot ratings with a vengeance, driven by an unfocused, unspoken sense that she was competing with her husband every inch of the way.

CHAPTER 21

HOUSTON, TEXAS: 1968

*H*arold zipped up his jacket against the chill wind blowing across South Texas and knelt down behind the tail of his single-engine Cessna 182, his eyes following the linkage on the trim tab as he moved the elevator up and down to complete another vital part of his preflight.

It was warmer in Aspen! he thought, shivering slightly and flashing back to the ski trip Sandra and he had just taken to Colorado. He was getting better at skiing, although the extreme slopes were still intimidating. But it was being in the mountains that mattered. He loved the magnificent scenery and the crisp nights and always looked forward to the next visit, though returning to the world of his expanding drugstore chain was somehow even more exciting than speeding down the steepest ski slope.

Harold's thoughts turned to Scheryle's latest induced agonies and her impossible behavior at school. Her rebellious nature knew no bounds, and no amount of counseling was having any apparent effect. At home, her relationship with Sandra was deteriorating monthly into a constant fight.

He stood up and forced himself to put the worries aside as he turned to finish the walk-around. He checked his watch, calculating the flying time to Tyler, Texas, where he was headed, his mind turning automatically to the recently completed, successful conclusion of the Dugan deal in Houston.

Another thirteen stores! And each of them was a top quality facility, much larger than the thirty-one stores of the Mading chain.

Harold seldom let himself indulge in a burst of pride, but he couldn't help being proud of taking on the small company, as well as proud of how it had happened. McKesson and Robbins was one of the largest distributors of pharmaceuticals in the Southwest, and they hated losing any of their customers. But they knew the small Dugan Drug chain of Houston was foundering, with Mr. Dugan, the owner, financially overextended and sinking fast. It was a measure of how his reputation was growing, Harold thought, that McKesson and Robbins had come to him to see if he might be interested in yet another drug chain acquisition. They were well aware of the dynamic changes being made at Williams Drugs in Waco, and they also knew that the Dugan chain had to be converted like Williams to a low-price, high-volume format in order to survive.

Harold smiled to himself as he ran his hand along the Cessna's propeller looking for dents. The meeting with the McKesson and Robbins officials had been brief, and his response just as rapid.

"Sure," Harold had said when he heard the asking price of $750,000. "I can do that."

In fact, it turned out to be relatively easy to arrange the loan in payment for his stores. The older man was happy to be rid of the financial pressures and accepted quickly, adding thirteen stores to the Harold Simmons mini-empire.

It was at once a gutsy deal and a great deal. The chain was seriously undervalued, especially in view of the greater market penetration and the efficiencies of volume, when added to Mading. Harold instantly knew he'd been handed a tremendous bargain.

He was far less aware, however, of how startlingly crafty and clever the acquisition would look to the local business community. A young man in his thirties wheeling and dealing around Texas, buying up companies and stores, was not your run-of-the-mill entrepreneur. He was exceptional. He was someone to watch.

He was someone to *know.*

Once again, Harold Simmons' name went up in lights in Houston.

A sudden chilly gust of wind ruffled Harold's hair and fluttered the collar of his jacket, causing him to look around to the northwest. A few small, puffy clouds could be seen in the distance, aligned in a ragged row, a meteorological afterthought in the teeth of a stiff upper-level wind raking across a deep blue sky. They looked almost comical, tropospheric puff balls marching past with urgent determination, as if an alarmed procession of white, fluffy, overweight chicks were chasing an unseen mother across the horizon.

Probably be bumpy up there, Harold cautioned himself, recalling the fact that they were known formally as alto-cumulus cloud forms.

With more than three hundred flying hours under his belt, taxi and takeoff were almost second nature now, and within minutes he had the small Cessna cruising nicely at 4,500 feet as he set a course for Tyler, Texas, and glanced at his watch.

Plenty of time. Should touch down at Tyler by 2:00 P.M., get a rental car, and be there by 3:00.

The prospect of the meeting he was flying to made him smile. He'd failed the first time around to buy the small chain of drugstores based out of Tyler, but this time Mr. Simpson, the founder, wanted to retire, and Harold had thought up a new way of cashing the man out with little if any impact on his bottom line.

"First stock," he'd explained to Russell Kibbe, now one of his stockholders in Williams Drug. "I'm going to offer him preferred stock in our company, in return for his company. I know Simpson needs a steady income, so I've built in dividends that'll give him a regular check until we cash out the stock."

"So, no cash outlay?"

"No cash. We get his company, some of the debt, and all the assets, and he's well paid by the preferred stock."

Better not get excited, Harold cautioned himself. There were a few thorny problems to solve first, but Simpson—the same owner who'd bolted from negotiations when Harold's lawyer had asked for too much information several years before—had called *him* this time around.

This little plane sure makes it easy, Harold thought as he scanned the instrument panel and rechecked his altitude, momentarily upset with himself for drifting off altitude. He'd been thinking more and more lately about moving up to a faster, heavier, twin-engine aircraft such as a Cessna 310. He already had an instrument rating and good experience flying himself all over the state, but there were times that a single-engine aircraft just wasn't enough. He needed that extra engine and that extra speed that a 310 could provide. He needed to be able to zip across Texas at close to 200 knots, some 80 knots faster than a 182. A 310 could shrink the boundaries of his growing drugstore empire, especially if he decided to start opening drugstores in almost every Texas city.

And that was part of the plan he'd been hatching: the "Wal Mart" approach to rural retailing, an idea that had grown on Harold as eminently logical long before Sam Walton began changing the U.S. with the very same idea up in Bentonville, Arkansas.

Everyone needed a drugstore, and Harold knew that the vast majority of Texas' small-town drugstores were just as inefficient and high-priced as the ones he was busy buying and converting. The memories were very fresh of driving to Mineola from Golden to get a prescription from the only pharmacy in town, paying whatever price they asked. No one really thought much about it, but what if the residents of Golden and every other tiny Texas community could drive to the same closest town and find a choice? Would they insist on spending their hard-earned funds on the regular prices in a full-service store if a new cut-rate operation had opened down the block selling the same goods at a substantial discount?

Of course not. Retail loyalty only went so far.

That's what we need to do, Harold thought. *As soon as it's financially feasible, I should be opening new stores in small towns.*

The prospect of being *the* retail drug merchant to most of Texas had both a commercial and personal appeal. It could develop into a type of mission, he thought, and to carry out the management duties that that would entail, he'd need to be almost everywhere at once.

I do need a bigger plane, he told himself, making a mental note to write Cessna in Wichita, Kansas, for the latest specifications on the 310.

■　■　■

"Harold, are you going to change my stores much?" Mr. Simpson asked as they shook hands several hours later and Harold got to his feet to go.

"Well, I'm going to make the same changes I did in Waco."

"You're going to make it like a Ward's Cut-Rate store, then?"

"Not exactly. More volume, lower prices, no delivery, no soda fountains, no in-house charge accounts, yes. But the stores should still look good inside and feel comfortable."

"We've been doing charge accounts for a long time, Harold. My . . . *your* customers may get angry at you if you cut them off."

"I won't cut them off. I'll just phase them out, or change them over to some central charge operation."

■   ■   ■

The flight back to Houston in late afternoon was too routine to remember. With the skies still clear, he'd elected to fly by visual rules instead of instrument rules, which meant that he didn't have to talk to anyone on the radio until asking permission to land back in Houston. It was just he and the steady drumbeat of the engine, and Harold had already discovered that flying brought the same joy of detachment as driving, only perhaps more so. He could fly along in deep thought in far greater safety. There were no oncoming cars to dodge at 6,000 feet. Flying was becoming instinctive, and even though he took it very seriously, all he had to do was keep the heading and altitude constant while his mind was looking for new ways to build his business.

Not that the acquisition of Simpson's nine stores wasn't a milestone.

"Well, Glenn, guess what?" Harold told his brother a few nights later by phone. "You're related to the guy who owns the biggest drugstore chain in Texas now."

"I wondered if maybe you'd become the biggest," Glenn replied. "Someone sent me a clipping from the *Houston Chronicle* with your face spread out all over the front page, and I figured I'd better call and find out what on earth you think you're doing."

"Building a business, Glenn."

"Yeah, I got that impression. Let's see. Your poor little company owns only *sixty* stores now?"

"Yep. Want to come join me down here? I'll give you a job."

"I've got a job, remember? I've been with Chance-Vought and LTV going on twenty years now."

"Well, maybe I can give you a better job. I could sure use some help down here."

"I don't know, Harold. I mean, I'm mighty impressed at what you're doing, but . . . what would I be doing?"

"I need management help I can trust, Glenn, and we're just getting warmed up. I've got a lot of people reporting to me, and you've always been good at keeping people organized."

"You'd want me to move to Houston?"

"Yes."

"I'll have to think about this, Harold. I'm going to have to see how Binky feels."

"I know."

"I'll have to get back to you."

CHAPTER 22

HOUSTON, TEXAS: SUMMER 1968

*D*uring the scorching summer of 1968, Harold began to turn his attention to the fact that several other major financiers—including Warren Buffet up in Omaha—were buying casualty insurance companies as a way to raise investment money at low cost. The idea made sense, Harold decided, and when a man named Harry Stuth approached him to urge the purchase of a small casualty insurance company in Dallas called Dealers National, Harold was ready to explore the opportunity. Stuth, who firmly believed he had enough experience to manage such a company with conservatism and a very good underwriting program, finally convinced Harold, and the purchase of Dealers National Insurance Company became a reality.

Around the same time, the accounting firm that Mading-Dugan had been using in Houston urged Harold to look at a company called Texas Consumer Finance Corporation, which happened to be the largest consumer finance company in the state, headquartered in Fort Worth.

"You might want to meet with them, Mr. Simmons," one of the accountants told him. "I know they're looking for some sort of deal to increase their equity base." A meeting in Houston with Wallace Jay, the president of Texas Consumer, was promptly arranged.

Texas Consumer Finance Corporation had a blue-ribbon board of independent directors, was a publicly traded corporation with stable profits, and had bank lines from several major banks, but the stock price had never gone anywhere. It, too, looked like an opportunity, and making the possibilities even better was the fact that TCFC's management seemed eager to make a reasonable transaction. After negotiations with Jay and Gene Engleman, the chairman and CEO, a plan was devised: Mading-Dugan and Dealers National Insurance Company would invest $3 million in new TCFC stock for a controlling interest, then create a new holding company to merge with TCFC, thereby taking TCFC private, with the new holding company becoming the public vehicle for further acquisition. The new holding company, named Contran, would have more than $5 million net worth and zero debt. Contran could then acquire the drugstores from Mading in exchange for stock in the holding company, which would create a larger diversified company with growing profits.

Harold had been careful to pick up the auditor's report and examine it closely. Price-Waterhouse was the major accounting firm involved, and he checked to make certain their man had properly signed off on all aspects of the annual audit. That was a key requirement. He'd learned *that* at Republic Bank. Fully audited financial reports signed by someone from a major, reputable accounting firm could be trusted.

"You going to buy it?" Glenn asked.

"Yeah. We're going to do that deal," Harold replied. "We're incorporating a holding company called Contran."

"Okay, but which company owns what?"

"Well, remember when I changed the name of Simmons' University Pharmacy Corporation to Williams Drug Company, and then bought Mading Drugs, and I ended up with Williams owning Madigan Corporation, which is the holding company that owns the stock of Mading-Dugan?"

"I think so."

"Okay, when Harry Stuth brought me the Dealers National Insurance deal, I had Mading-Dugan invest five hundred thousand to buy it, then we had Dealers National turn around and buy five hundred thousand dollars worth of bonds from Williams, which cashed out the original investment. In the end we used our existing equity more efficiently, but with no net cash outlay."

"Right. Of course."

"So, the trust still owns all of Williams, which in turn owns Madigan Corporation, which will own the new company, Contran.

Once we create Contran, it will merge with Texas Consumer Finance Corporation and become our main public holding company."

"Harold, what about your co-investors in the Williams Drug Company?"

"I'm buying them out, Glenn. They're scared of the insurance business, so I'm cashing them out, and they're doubling their money, so they're feeling pretty good, and so am I."

■   ■   ■

By the end of the year, 1968, the TCFC deal had been completed, and Harold turned his attention to the dual questions of how to expand his insurance and finance company holdings while expanding his drugstore chains, using one to fuel the other. Two more insurance companies had been added to the Contran list, one called Fidelity General Insurance Company based in Chicago, and another based in Fort Worth.

From his experience at Republic Bank, Harold was very familiar with the financing structure of consumer loan companies. Texas Consumer Finance had about $75 million in revolving lines of credit from numerous large banks. Periodically, the company would pay off the balance of one of the loans by borrowing the payoff money from their revolving loan account at another bank, and a few months later they would pay off *that* loan with other borrowed funds. As long as the overall balance of the money it borrowed didn't continue to increase, TCFC could continue making enough money from the high-interest-rate small loans it issued to service the debt it incurred from the banks that provided those funds, and to add profits to its equity base. As long as none of the big institutions called in *their* loans, the system could continue indefinitely. There were some noncurrent loans, of course, but the default rate seemed low, very steady, and very predictable. As long as the customer made payments on a regular basis, their loans were considered "current," and the amount the customer still owed counted as part of the value of TCFC. And most of TCFC's loans were current, at least on the books of the company.

The TCFC purchase, Harold concluded, was going to turn out to be one of his best moves.

CHAPTER 23

HOUSTON, TEXAS: 1969

*J*n some ways, it seemed to Harold like an eternity since he'd sat in a booth at University Pharmacy's coffee shop and learned that a small Waco drug chain was for sale.

In other ways, it seemed like yesterday afternoon.

Life had been accelerating continuously, and although he'd never worked harder in his life and he felt his mind all but smoking after most days of decision-making and trying to keep up, he was also having an enormously good time.

So this is what "wheeling and dealing" is all about, he said to himself in mid-January, when, in the space of one afternoon, he'd seen the consummation of the Texas Consumer Finance Corporation purchase, the activation of Contran Corporation as his main company, and the discovery of a menswear chain that might make another profitable acquisition.

He'd observed that each new company purchase would trigger new articles in the local newspapers, and those articles would, in turn, create new interest in the financial community which would bring more opportunities to his attention.

Clyde Campbell's Men's Shops was such an example. It was a small but lucrative chain of well-run men's stores in the Dallas area, and its owner wanted out. It wasn't the drug business or the insurance business, but the stores generated good profits. And Harold had watched Cully Culwell make money with the Varsity Shop next door to University

Pharmacy over the years. Even if vicariously, he knew something about the business, and Clyde Campbell's had a good executive team.

"This is really interesting, Glenn," he told his brother during late November as they continued to discuss Glenn coming aboard. "No matter how leveraged I am, I buy stuff and immediately I've got even more people wanting to lend me money to buy *more* stuff!"

"You complaining?"

"Heck no. It's just funny. As long as all these companies can generate enough cash to pay for the loans I'm taking out to buy these companies, why stop?"

Glenn had smiled, his head cocked to one side in a gesture Harold had always thought of as exclusively Glenn's. "Well, Harold, when you went barging in to see Jimmy Ling about that ship company a few years back, I remember saying to myself, *God almighty, Harold's going to be another Jimmy Ling.*"

Glenn watched Harold's smile broaden, then fade as he struggled to control his response. The effort was failing, and for good reason, Glenn thought. He knew his brother deserved to be proud of himself.

"Well," Harold said, "things have worked out so far."

■   ■   ■

Deckerd Jackson, CEO of the Dallas-based investment firm of First Southwest Corporation, had become somewhat of a legend in Dallas financial circles by 1969. He was the type of financier others watched carefully, and he was counting on that reputation—and a steady stock market—to launch his latest venture: the first public offering of stock in Ward's Cut-Rate Drugs Corporation.

Founded by three brothers—Milton, Erwin, and A.J. Weinberger—Ward's was built on a combination of conservative management and first-in-the-market use of low-margin, high-volume drugstore merchandising. By 1969, Ward's had become the drug chain success story to emulate in North Texas, and the Weinberger brothers—having worked since the forties to achieve that success—were ready to cash out when Deckerd Jackson made an offer for the company.

While the Weinbergers sold Jackson their stock, the brothers stayed on to manage the chain under contract. Jackson, meanwhile, monitored and encouraged their growth from the sidelines as he waited for the perfect moment to take Ward's public in an IPO—an initial public offering.

Early 1969 had been the target date, but by mid-January, it was obvious that the market was declining rapidly, not an environment for an IPO. There were indications that it might be several *years* before the time would be right again. Perhaps, he concluded, it was time to find a private buyer and forget the public offering.

Deckerd Jackson had met Harold Simmons some years before. He'd followed the young Texan's progress from the purchase of the Williams chain in Waco in 1967 to his newly minted position as the dominant drugstore owner in Texas, with sixty operating stores.

And he'd researched where Harold Simmons was trying to go in financial terms, and whether Ward's chain could fit into those plans.

Jackson had many decades of experience dealing with men who wanted to make more money and do more deals. He knew the lean and hungry look from that of the casually interested, and he could instantly cull the sort of unprincipled daredevil who was likely to let his bravado bankrupt a company, from one who was an uneasy walking amalgam of careful investor and calculated risk-taker.

Harold Simmons was clearly the latter, and even though Simmons' company was heavily burdened with debt from buying all the components of his new chain, Deckerd Jackson knew the Ward's deal would be all but irresistible to him. As long as it was dangled in the right way at the right moment, the Ward's deal would be akin to tossing meat to a hungry tiger.

It was time, he figured, to call Simmons.

"Sure, I'm interested," Harold had replied by phone. "When would you like to meet and talk about it?"

■　　■　　■

"How much, Harold?" Glenn had asked when his brother returned to Houston and told him by phone that Ward's Cut-Rate Drug Stores, Incorporated, was for sale.

"Eighteen and a quarter million dollars," Harold replied.

Glenn tried to suppress a gulp. "What'd you tell him?"

"I said, 'Sure, I can handle that.'"

"Can you?"

Harold grinned. "Sure, I can handle that."

"Harold, *eighteen and a quarter million dollars?* That's far and away the biggest deal you've ever gotten close to!"

"I know it. Well, there was the idea for buying Republic Insurance Company that would have been bigger, but I can make this work."

Harold left the office for home that evening without ever seeing the highway, his mind running at flank speed over the possibilities. Ward's was a solid investment, with a strong and stable profit picture and strong management. Borrowing money against Ward's as a company shouldn't be too difficult, especially for the new Contran Corporation, with its strong balance sheet and public ownership.

"Here's how we're going to do it," Harold announced a few weeks later. "This is a staged deal, and we're buying Deckerd Jackson out in three lumps. First, Contran is going to raise about eighteen million in cash." He pushed a piece of paper across the table to two of his executives. "That shows you where and how we're raising that cash. Contran buys thirty-five percent of Ward's stock. Then, with a ten million dollar loan from First National secured by shares of Ward's, plus these other sources I'm listing here," he pushed across another sheet, "we'll have Mading-Dugan buy sixty-five percent of Ward's. Then, I'll have Contran do a stock swap with Madigan for all of Mading-Dugan's shares, making Contran the one hundred percent owner of Mading-Dugan Corporation. Since we'll then own it in full, we'll merely transfer the sixty-one percent Ward's stock to Contran to mix with the thirty-five percent we already will own. We'll then sell about thirty percent of Ward's in a public offering and repay the First National loan."

"And that ends up ..." one of the men asked.

"Well, my family trust owns all of Williams Drug Corporation, which in turn owns all of Madigan Corporation, which owns the majority of Contran Corporation, which ends up owning one hundred percent of Ward's along with all of Mading-Dugan Corporation. Contran also owns Clyde Campbell's Men's Shops, and ninety-eight percent of Texas Consumer Finance. Dealers National Insurance is still owned by Madigan. As soon as all that's done, we'll start converting our other stores in Waco and Houston to the Ward's name and system, and do a public offering of some of the Ward's stock, which will raise enough to pay back the First National loan and give us more cash for expansion."

"Whew," one of them said, sitting back with a smile. "Harold, have you run the numbers on the Ward's stores?"

Harold looked irritated. "What do you think I've just been talking about?"

"No, I don't mean the financing. Obviously you've done enough of that to make me queasy. No, I mean the number of stores you'll end up with. I count forty Ward's stores, plus thirty Mading stores, plus thirteen Dugan stores, plus seven Williams stores, plus nine Simpson stores, and little old University Pharmacy for an even one hundred."

"I don't get your point."

"My point is, that in October 1966 you had one store. Here it is February 1969, and you own an even one hundred drugstores. And Harold, that's really big!"

"Well, at least it's a good place to start."

■   ■   ■

When the Ward's deal had been consummated, Glenn Simmons finally agreed to come aboard.

"I'm going to give it a try, Harold," Glenn told his younger brother. "At least a year."

"Well, that industrial psychologist we went to says we passed all his tests. We can work together without getting on each other's nerves."

"He said, Harold, that it will work as long as we don't try to do the other's job. That's part of it, but the other part is LTV. I went to the president, and he said to go give it a try for a year, and if it doesn't work out, I can come back."

"Okay, that's good."

Harold found himself counting the days until Glenn arrived. He needed Glenn's organizational help desperately. Managing people was Glenn's long suit, but it was a struggle for Harold to deal with the daily relationships in the office environment, when all he really wanted to do was concentrate on the strategic. The mundane minutiae of managing a company tended to get in the way of strategic planning. Besides, the office payroll was already growing, as were the ranks of people who worked for his companies on the front lines. In late fall Harold had hired an executive vice president-finance named Dale Wood and a corporate general counsel by the name of John Brunson. But he always seemed to need more people to handle the tidal wave of details that he, himself, kept creating with each new corporate maneuver.

CHAPTER 24

WEISNER FIELD, MINEOLA, TEXAS: 1970

Johnny Dowell walked around the right tip tank of the shiny new Cessna 310 and patted the metal skin of the twin-engine aircraft with a big smile.

"That's quite an airplane, Harold."

Harold Simmons smiled at his high school buddy as he stepped down from the right wing of the aircraft, carefully placing his foot on the small metal step.

"Yeah, I sure like it."

"You want to go take a look around town?" Johnny asked, his right hand still resting on the tip tank.

Harold nodded and pulled on a windbreaker as they headed for Johnny's car, a large, late-model sedan, which he promptly aimed toward State Highway 37, his arm resting on the open window sill as the fresh aromas of East Texas in spring filled the car.

"We're all pretty excited for you out here, Harold, buying a hundred stores and being so successful," Johnny said. "I hear you bought Haddon Simpson's stores in Tyler, too?"

"That's right."

"And . . . I hear tell you just had another daughter."

Harold nodded again with a broad smile. "We named her Serena. She was born in January. Andrea's five now, Lisa's fifteen, and Scheryle's eighteen."

"You get to see them much, being so busy?"

"Johnny, I'm home every night."

"Well," Johnny continued, "Thomasene's been keeping up with you, and she's working on a clipping book of your newspaper articles. You running the business yourself?"

Harold shook his head. "No, I've got a lot of folks helping me, including Glenn."

Johnny nodded. "I know. I talked to Glenn Reuben last month. He said y'all are really doing well. Said you owned insurance companies now, and clothing stores, and a finance company, and said you'd probably own Jimmy Ling's company in a week or two."

"Glenn exaggerates. I'll need at least a month." Harold grinned.

"Well, how's it feel to be rich and famous?"

"Come on, Johnny, I'm not rich and famous. I'm just me."

"Oh, sure, you're not rich. You own a hundred stores and your own airplane an' you're not rich? Harold, do I *look* like I just fell off the watermelon truck?"

"I actually saw you do that once."

"I was pushed, but you're avoiding the question."

"I'm mortgaged to the eyeballs, Johnny. I owe a bundle from buying all those stores. I only look rich."

"Well, it's working. Seriously, Harold. How's it feel to be so successful in just three years?"

"I never think about it."

"Sure you do."

"I'm too busy, Johnny."

"Okay, so tell me about it."

They fell into easy conversation as Johnny turned onto old Highway 69 to head north toward Golden. Harold found himself relating some of the tumultuous events of the past year, the acquisition of Ward's, the insurance companies, the building of his management team in Houston, and his sudden popularity among the wealthy in Houston.

"They seem to be real taken with how utterly brilliant I am as a conversationalist, Johnny. That's why I get invited to all the big parties in Houston."

Johnny turned to him with a surprised look. "Really?" Belatedly he noticed the twinkle in Harold's eye. "Oh . . . Okay, you're pulling my leg."

"Well, I mean I've got people trying to lend me money, and Sandra and I get invited to stuff, but it's all business. How're *you* doing?"

Harold listened as Johnny talked him through the last few years of his life, and his return to the Mineola and Golden area.

Johnny pulled the car to a halt a few yards from Golden's old country store and the two men got out and walked in silence for a few minutes, enjoying the view and the crispness of the early spring air as a gentle breeze rustled the newly grown maple leaves overhead.

"Really pretty this time of year, isn't it?" Johnny said, noting that his friend was nodding silently. He turned to Harold. "You ever miss it out here?"

Harold pushed his hands deeper into his pockets and took a deep breath as he studied the horizon.

"In some ways, I always miss it," he replied. "But I'm having a lot of fun, Johnny, just seeing how far I can push things, ya know?"

"I guess."

"I mean, I see so much opportunity out there in these different businesses. I've been really naive about a bunch of stuff, but I'm learning, and everything's going great. I'm expanding Ward's, getting ready to open more stores around the state, especially in smaller towns. I've got a bunch of good people in addition to Glenn helping me run things. And it all seems balanced . . . It's like everything is preordained to work."

BOOK FIVE

Into the Valley

CHAPTER 25

AUSTIN, TEXAS: 1971

The flight to Austin's Mueller Airport had been routine, the 180 miles from Dallas covered in just about an hour, but the overcast weather had forced Harold to fly an Instrument Landing System approach from which they broke out into visual conditions just 400 feet above the ground.

Glenn and Harold had made the trip several times before. It was something Harold had looked forward to in the previous days: parking his new, cabin-class Cessna 421 on the western, private ramp of the airfield, jumping the fence with his brother, and walking the short hundred yards or so to their mother's brick home on Airport Drive.

The afternoon had been pleasant and relaxing, with Mrs. Simmons insisting on fixing lunch for her boys. The plan was to take her out to a fancy restaurant for dinner, but the afternoon had been an enjoyable respite of sitting around the house and talking.

Now Glenn was on the phone in the other room, dealing with some problem back at the office in Dallas as Harold sat at the kitchen table with his mother.

"You look worried, Harold," she said after a few moments of silence.

"Well, mostly things are good. I told you about the little brick office building we built alongside the Ward's warehouse in Dallas on Harry Hines Boulevard, didn't I?"

"Yes."

"It's near Love Field, and it's a pretty neat little office, Mom. I had a good one in Houston, but this one is better. Glenn's office is in there, too."

"Are the drugstores a problem, Harold?"

"No. No, Ward's is great. I mean, the reason I moved the office, and Sandra and the girls from Houston back to Dallas, was because the original owners who were staying on to manage it, the Weinberger brothers, decided to retire. I had to replace their management team. But we're doing great! In fact, we're getting ready to open a bunch of Ward's stores down here in Austin next year."

"So, then, what is worrying you?" Harold's mother probed again.

Harold sighed as he wondered how he had ever managed to trust someone like Harry Stuth and his glib assurances of how to run insurance companies. His trust in Stuth had been unfounded, and Contran was far from through with the worrisome problems the insurance companies had created.

"Mom, you remember those insurance companies I bought?"

She nodded.

"And that finance company, TCFC?"

She nodded again.

"They've all collapsed."

It hadn't taken long, he told her, for Harry Stuth to reveal himself as totally incompetent, in Harold's judgment, at the task of evaluating the three casualty insurance companies before purchase, but also in managing them thereafter. Unbeknownst to Harold, Stuth had been incredibly naive, writing dangerously bad policies in markets no one else wanted, insuring (among other bad risks) merchants along the Gulf Coast against a hurricane that had promptly come roaring ashore in the form of Hurricane Camille, wiping out $100 million of insured value from Gulfport, Mississippi, through New Orleans.

"I had no idea, Mom," Harold added, "that they'd been writing bad business and failing to properly estimate their reserves. They hadn't set aside enough money to cover the claims, and since my main company, Contran, owned *them,* it made Contran look like a loser."

"I see," she said, watching her son's eyes intently.

"Well, then, because we'd used Contran stock to beef up the capital base of the insurance companies, when Contran's shares went down in value, the insurance companies suddenly weren't showing enough of a capital base to operate safely, and the Texas insurance commissioner down here leaned on us to do something. So what I did, and it seemed like a good idea, we put one of our best assets in the insurance companies, one that wouldn't go up and down in value in the stock market."

"What asset, Harold?"

"TCFC. Our finance company."

"And that didn't work?"

He shook his head. "No. Mom, you remember reading in the papers how the stock market crashed back in May?"

She nodded, but he wondered if she really had been following it.

"Okay, well, the money markets all but collapsed, too. The banks suddenly didn't have any cash to loan because the Federal Reserve was tightening the money supply to slow down the inflation rate, and all of a sudden it's the worst financial panic I've ever seen."

"Like nineteen twenty-nine? Like the depression?" She looked alarmed.

"No, no, Mom. Not that bad. But it hurts business, and our finance company relied on having all these credit lines they could borrow from. You know, they borrow ..."

"... from the banks, and lend the money to regular people at higher rates," Mrs. Simmons added. "I know. You explained that."

"Well, when the panic started, by midsummer several of TCFC's lead banks reduced their credit lines, and by August they'd filed for Chapter Eleven. You know, a petition to hold off the creditors while they reorganize."

"I understand what a Chapter Eleven is, Harold."

"Okay. Well, when that happened, it ruined the capital base of my insurance companies, and *they* all filed for Chapter Eleven."

■　　■　　■

There was visceral anger leaking through from Chicago, and Harold was determined to ignore it. The worst rumblings were coming from the executive who'd headed Fidelity General Insurance Company of Chicago, a man Harry Stuth had insisted was trustworthy, but who had apparently been deeply involved in a long-term effort to keep the company alive no matter how risky its practices.

"Apparently it works like this," Glenn had explained after spending months trying to sort out what had happened and why. "It looks to me like they not only purposefully understated how much they needed to set aside in reserves against possible future claims, but even when they *knew* they were going to get clobbered in court for claims they'd refused to pay, I think they grossly understated what they thought the settlement costs would be, hoping they'd have enough in the way of new premiums coming in the door to pay for those judgments when the various lawsuits became final, or when they reached a final settlement. As long as they could play the float, they could *stay* afloat. But now that they're in reorganization, it's all coming out."

"And it's our company," Harold added, "so the assumption is that we, too, knew what was going on?"

"Exactly. We did nothing wrong, though," Glenn said, turning to three lawyers in the room. "Isn't that right?"

All three heads were nodding. "Absolutely right, Harold," one of them replied. "Neither you, nor Glenn, nor Contran, nor any of us down here did anything wrong. Problem is, the guy you fired up there in Chicago is running around calling you fellows crooks and claiming you raided Fidelity's accounts, and by doing so, forced them into bankruptcy. He's trying to blame it all on you, and we can expect litigation."

■　　■　　■

"We're down to sixty stores now," Harold told Sandra one evening in mid-1971.

"So the sale went through?"

He nodded, sitting heavily in an easy chair. "Yeah. Jack Eckerd, the guy who started the big drugstore chain in Florida, is paying us five million for them because he wants to move into Houston. I'm going to use that to pay down what I owe First National, since we didn't get enough money on the public stock offering for Contran to pay back the loan like I'd planned."

"But you're sinking to sixty stores?"

"The Houston stores weren't making enough money, Sandra. I was having real trouble servicing all the debt that I took out to buy them. So now that that's paid off, the extra money makes us more healthy. Besides, we'll be opening more stores and be back up to a hundred or more real soon."

She sat uneasily at the dining room table, bouncing their eighteen-month-old daughter Serena on her knee. "Which one are you opening next?"

"Fort Worth. South Fort Worth. They've got the usual opening hoopla planned. You know, searchlights, live music, free food."

"Who's playing?"

"I think they've got some country star named Porter Wagoner and some girl."

■   ■   ■

The possibility of foul weather messing up the opening party for a new Ward's store was always a worry, but the skies were clear and the starfield above the shopping center was starkly visible even with all the nearby light pollution. Harold usually left the formative details of such openings to his staff, and if they prevailed on him to say anything as head of the company, he always kept it to a few words and a quick snip of the oversized ribbon-cutting scissors.

His duty done, Harold would usually walk to the back of the crowd and observe, as he'd done tonight.

It was time for the entertainment, and he watched as country music star Porter Wagoner climbed onto the flatbed truck which served as a makeshift stage. Several rented searchlights were frantically raking the night sky overhead.

Radio ads had been blaring the existence of the opening party all day, and the crowd was gratifyingly large and enthusiastic—obviously the result of good promotion. Their response to Wagoner's arrival on the flatbed stage was loud and sustained applause, much of it aimed appreciatively at his performing companion, a startlingly buxom young woman with a guitar and an infectious smile. As they launched into their opening numbers, the woman's distinctive warble and electric enthusiasm caught Harold's attention.

Dolly ... what was it? Oh, yeah. Dolly Parton. Interesting.

Not exactly the type of hard-core Texas country he'd grown up with, but good, basic music.

His mind flashed back over the voices he'd listened to through so many Golden evenings: Bob Wills and His Texas Playboys, the former singing governor of Texas, Pappy "Pass-the-Biscuits" O'Daniel, Hank

Williams, and the Lightcrust Dough Boys sponsored by Fort Worth's Burris Mills, all unforgettable. But country music wasn't as important to him as knowing the show tunes and happy songs he loved to belt out by himself in the car—and occasionally when the girls were with him. "Over the Rainbow," "The Sunny Side of the Street," and others had melted away many a mile and shepherded him to work with a positive attitude.

He turned and headed back to his car, his mind on the flight school at Love Field he was buying.

"It's not much of anything," he'd explained to Glenn when the subject came up, "but I think we might make some money on it, and it'll keep her happy. She wants to have an aviation business, and our accountant tells me we can buy one of those new Cessna Citation jets, use it in that school for training and for chartering, use it myself when I want to, and make some money on the deal."

"A jet, Harold?"

He'd pulled out the four-color sales brochure from Wichita and opened it up on his desk.

"Really kind of neat, Glenn. It's a pure jet with straight wings, real forgiving, just like our piston-powered Cessna 421, but the Citation flies at over three hundred knots and can land almost anywhere, including at our place in Arkansas." Harold thought about the small landing strip they planned to build on the acreage he'd just bought near Fort Smith. If he paved the runway, a Citation could use it.

"So, Sandra will learn to fly it?" Glenn asked.

He nodded. "We both will. *I'll* fly it on business. But she says she wants to make a career out of aviation, so she can fly copilot for me on trips, and I'll just buy this guy's little flying service and let Sandra run it."

"Can she handle it, Harold? She doesn't have any experience in business."

Harold shrugged. "I don't know. It's not much to risk."

CHAPTER 26

DALLAS, TEXAS: 1972

*B*y the last half of 1972, the tiny, one-room, one-person outfit called Flight Proficiency at Dallas Love Field was growing. Contran had purchased the sleepy little outfit for $30,000, but Sandra's attempts to run the company had proved less than stellar and Harold had decided to listen to advice from his Contran advisors and take matters into his own hands. The first step—locating and hiring a professional manager with flight school experience—took only a few months. As soon as the new manager was aboard and Sandra had agreed to step aside and take a lesser position, the man approached Harold with a proposition.

"Mr. Simmons, if you're not using your Citation daily, the company could lease it from you and use it as the basis for GI training to train students for their airline transport pilot rating and instrument ratings."

"GI training?"

"Anyone who served in the military can get all their expenses and tuition paid if they enter training to qualify for a new profession. Aviation is included, and that means anyone who wants to be a professional pilot. There are literally tens of thousands of veterans in flight training right now on the GI Bill, and the schools who qualify are making a mint. Braniff Airways, for example, right across the field here, has built a school they call BESI, Braniff Educations Systems Incorporated. Every would-be airline pilot knows that to have a chance to be hired as a Braniff pilot, you first have to come pay them around five thousand dollars to get trained as a Boeing 727 flight engineer. Most of them do it on the GI Bill, and BESI is raking in ten million a year."

"You're not suggesting we get a Boeing 727?" Harold asked.

"No, no! We wouldn't do flight engineer training. But with nothing more than your Citation, we can get some of that government money and provide a good product. Good training."

Harold authorized the move, and with Sandra participating as chief instructor, Flight Proficiency expanded their office space and added training facilities and instructors, qualifying easily as a veteran-approved flight school. Within six months the revenue stream had jumped substantially, and Harold's Citation began flying constantly and earning a profit.

■　　■　　■

As September of 1973 rolled in and Lisa Simmons, now eighteen, departed for Duke University, Sandra decided that being a flight instructor for her own flight school wasn't enough.

"I'm going to put in a pilot application to Braniff, Harold," she told him one evening.

"A what?"

"I'm going to apply to be a Braniff International pilot. It's something I've been thinking about for a long time."

"Since when do they hire women, Sandra?"

"They'd better start with me. From what I hear, federal law won't let them shut out females anymore."

"Sandra," Harold responded, "how can you be an airline pilot and a mother at the same time? Serena is barely three, Andrea is just entering third grade, I'm busier than ever . . ."

"Still always about you, isn't it? This isn't negotiable, Harold. I'm going to do it. We've got a housekeeper and she takes care of the girls when I'm not here, as you well know. The question is, are *you* going to support me or not?"

Harold sighed. "I always have, haven't I? Okay, if you've got to do it, then go ahead."

She began the preparations almost immediately, acutely aware that

Braniff required a certain number of flight hours, certain ratings, and certain licenses.

The first step was going to the same Braniff Educations Systems course Harold had been told about earlier in the year. Two weeks of intense study and nearly $5,000 secured Sandra her Flight Engineer-Turbojet FAA rating, and her pilot log book was now sporting enough flight hours in jets to qualify, but there was still the basic hurdle: the fact that would-be Braniff flight officer Sandra Simmons was a girl.

Braniff didn't hire "girls" as pilots. Although a few females had been admitted tentatively to the ranks of professional airline pilotage in other airlines such as United and Frontier, Braniff was largely populated by the traditional masculine cockpit culture which exuded the attitude that "girls couldn't handle big airplanes." Lost in that jingoistic and discriminatory attitude was the reality that most big jets had hydraulically powered flight controls and were as easy to fly physically as a Cadillac was to drive. Even though the constitutional prohibition against discrimination had already been extended to include sexual discrimination, the day of the guaranteed sexual discrimination lawsuit had not yet arrived—and Braniff's lawyers had not yet convinced the personnel department that maintaining the old point of view could be hazardous to the company's financial health.

But all that was about to change.

Sandra's application was met at first by thundering silence, and then by the somewhat surprised tones of a secretary who pointed out that since Sandra "was a girl," and Braniff didn't hire such delicate creatures, except as flight attendants, she need not darken their doorstep further.

The reaction was swift and effective. With Harold's help, Sandra retained a lawyer who scheduled a meeting with Braniff's leaders, a confrontation that was anything but an appeal.

"You have a choice," Braniff was told. "Either hire Mrs. Simmons right now as a full-fledged pilot with no tricks and no intent to sabotage her training, or we're going to sue you to hell and back and make a national example out of you. You have no defense. You will lose, and you'll gather terrible publicity in the process."

Braniff was an innovative airline spending untold millions annually on its image, and on trying to convince the upscale customer that flying on Braniff was the most exciting, most chic and innovative way to travel. Braniff's marketers were well aware that in tens of thousands of cases, the person who made the critical decision on what airline to book was someone's secretary—almost always a female. The thought of having Braniff's traditional anti-feminine cockpit attitude paraded all over the newspapers by determined lawyers for the SMU graduate wife of a prominent Dallas businessman was far too risky.

"Ah, congratulations, we'd like to hire you as a Braniff pilot," was the rapid response, and with a single stroke the gender barrier at Braniff's cockpit door shattered. (Within two years Braniff would hire several more women, a trend which accelerated slowly until the airline's 1982 demise into bankruptcy.)

As Sandra launched formal training for her new career and began flying the line as a second officer/flight engineer, Harold found himself working hard to pick up the slack and spend more time with Serena and Andrea. The additional focus on his girls was no burden. He had always been a constant presence in their lives, with them each and every night.

Harold had felt Sandra slipping away for a long time. Now she had engineered lengthy absences as a professional pursuit, and while he struggled to applaud her accomplishment, there was a growing void. The smart young man from Golden, Texas, was still human, with human feelings and human needs, and the bulwark of spousal support he'd taken for granted when he'd married Sandra was no longer there.

He could be an iron man, of course, steady and unbendable, but now it was even more important for him to maintain his remarkable capability, noted and commented on by his staff, to stay unfazed and steady in any storm.

And the heavy storms were just beginning. There *were* darker concerns lurking just beyond the fire circle of his small empire. The legal ruminations and recriminations, the financial claims, and the outrageous charges stemming from the collapse of Texas Consumer Finance and the three insurance companies were escalating, all the more because the bankruptices had inevitably placed the glaring spotlight of hindsight on the $5 million of equity Texas Consumer Finance had shown on its books—its sturdy capital.

"Don't worry about TCFC," Harold had reassured his staff numerous times, Glenn among them. "It's a sound company with real equity."

"All those little loans, right?"

"Absolutely," Harold would say. "Not a problem."

But the audits had suddenly revealed something entirely different. To the utter disbelief and shock of Harold and Glenn Simmons, the equity of TCFC was evaporating before their eyes because of improper practices it suddenly appeared almost everyone at TCFC should have known about.

The longtime chairman of TCFC, who had already left the company, had apparently approved a questionable practice and made certain that all the company's office managers maintained it year after year. Annually, just before the end of the fiscal year—and using dollars and even quarters from petty cash—the branch managers would credit small payments against loans which had otherwise seen no activity and no payments for many months. *Any* payment activity within the previous three months, by their accounting rules, meant that the loan could be classified as "current," even though the loan had essentially become uncollectible. "Current" loans counted as equity, while *noncurrent* loans had to be removed from the capitalization side of TCFC's annual financial report.

"Oh, my Lord," Harold said when first briefed on the practice the auditors had uncovered. "How many were done this way?"

"Just about all the noncurrent loans in each office. The managers knew to do it this way. It was an annual duty."

"You're not telling me the entire list of loans is bad?"

"Not all, Harold, but a disturbing number."

"But those reports were audited! I checked the reports myself! They were from one of the national accounting firm branches."

There were more solemn nods in the room.

Harold was stunned by the news. One of the rock-hard foundations of finance had become quicksand beneath his feet. If you couldn't trust a certified CPA audit of a company, what could you trust?

"And what does that do to our capitalization for TCFC?" Harold asked.

There was a long hesitation in his office as the men who had assembled to deliver the bad news glanced at each other before launching the coup de grâce.

"It . . . just about wipes it out, Harold. You remove all those sham noncurrent, uncollectible loans, TCFC has just about zip."

"It's the *appearance* of impropriety, not the fact, that's hurting you," one of Contran's lawyers, Walter Spradley, explained. "Here these guys are in Illinois trying to discredit you and claim you stole their company, which we know was already on its tail, and you buttress your position with a company that essentially has been lying about its net worth from the get-go. Naturally, they're going to claim that you knew about it all along."

"And you know damn well we didn't have a clue," Harold added.

"Of course I know that. You'd never have bought the puppy if there had been anything wrong with it. But this may lead to some bigger troubles, Harold."

"How big?"

Spradley shook his large head and sighed. "I don't know, but I do know we're facing a bunch in Illinois who are frantically looking to divert attention from the fact that they were running a bad insurance company."

CHAPTER 27

DALLAS, TEXAS: 1973

*T*he small group of serious men arrayed around Harold's office in the Ward's Cut-Rate Drug Company complex had been waiting for several minutes as he read through the legal papers that had arrived an hour before from Illinois. Harold carefully picked through the numerous paragraphs outlining a major lawsuit filed in federal district court in Chicago, a suit seeking tens of millions of dollars from Harold personally and from his companies and alleging nothing less than an evil scheme to loot and bankrupt Fidelity General Insurance Company.

"This is nonsense, of course," Harold said at last, closing the last page and dumping the offensive instrument on his desk.

There were nods around the room, but the faces remained serious and worried.

"Okay," Harold said, leaning forward in his chair. "Let's get this to Walter Spradley and see if he'll represent us."

Two days later, senior attorney Walter Spradley himself was settling into one of the same chairs in Harold's office and gesturing to the lawsuit filing.

"This *is* serious, Harold," he said.

"I figured it was, but it's all wrong."

Spradley nodded. "You know that and I know that, but a federal court has to be convinced of that."

"You can take this, can't you?" Harold asked, startled when Spradley began to shake his head in the negative.

"Harold, this is complex stuff, and very serious, and what you need is not so much a corporate lawyer as a master litigator. Someone really top-notch in the courtroom."

"You have someone in mind?"

Spradley was nodding. "Yes, I believe I do. A fellow named Fred Bartlit of Chicago. Best courtroom lawyer *in* Chicago, and very well at-tuned to corporate matters."

"Can we get him?"

Spradley hesitated. "I don't know, Harold. He's in heavy demand, but I'm going to call him."

■ ■ ■

While Harold's desire to acquire insurance companies completely evaporated with the shock of the insurance company bankruptcies and the Chicago lawsuit, there was a growing recognition in Harold's mind that he should be looking for new corporate bargains in other indus-tries. There were people better suited to running the retail drug busi-ness on a national scale, and one of them was a person with whom Harold had already become acquainted, Jack Eckerd.

Eckerd's purchase of the Mading-Dugan collection of forty stores in Houston had catapulted the Eckerd chain into the Texas market, and Jack Eckerd was hungry for more. Originally the owner of a three-store chain in the Washington, D.C. area, Eckerd, while vacationing in Florida, had seen a need for a low-cost chain in the Florida market and filled it. He opened store after store during the sixties and had ex-panded into adjacent states with no end in sight. Like the Weinberger brothers in Dallas when they built Ward's, Eckerd had figured out tech-niques for maximizing the production of profits in a drugstore. He had assembled a well-oiled machine headed by capable executives, and his company, the Jack Eckerd Corporation (so named to differentiate him from the drugstores in two other states owned by relatives), was already a publicly held company and a high-flying stock.

And at the very moment in 1973 that Harold Simmons was reach-ing the conclusion that the time had come to look at moving on and selling Ward's, Eckerd called again.

"I like what you're building up there in Dallas, Harold, but I'm very interested in keeping my expansion going in Texas. If you're interested in a deal for Ward's, maybe we should talk."

The lawsuit in Illinois was dangerous, but it was a background issue best left to the lawyers, and Harold had no trouble compartmentalizing the problem and focusing his entire professional attention on the potential sale to Eckerd.

The negotiations began innocently enough, with Eckerd dealing directly with his younger counterpart. The initial sketch of a deal seemed to fall into place quite easily: an exchange of Eckerd's stock to pay for the Ward's Cut-Rate Drug Store Company stock held by Harold through Contran and the public. But the amount of stock—and thus the amount of money to be paid for Ward's—hinged in part on Ward's achieving their stated profit goals on the upcoming quarterly report. When the profits fell considerably short of the mark, Jack Eckerd seized on the shortfall as leverage to lower his original offer.

For a month, phone calls, memos, letters, and meetings whirled back and forth with the outcome uncertain. Harold was under no immediate pressure to sell, but the time for cashing in on all he'd created seemed ripe. The fact that the stock market was high and the business climate in general was good pushed a pinprick of urgency in his backside, spurring him on whenever the deal looked shaky.

"He wants to pay too little," Harold had told Robert Wall, his financial vice president, late in the negotiations. "I think we'd better . . . we'll, maybe we can counter with something better."

In the end, the deal was struck at just under $50 million of Eckerd stock at the current market value, with a major proviso: Harold and his companies would have to hold the Eckerd stock transferred in payment for one year, in order to protect Eckerd against an adverse tax situation.

"I can do that," Harold had told Eckerd. After all, the investment climate, the market, and the economy were all strong, and in a year Eckerd's stock might go up from the current $30 per share to something even greater. Harold believed Eckerd was an unshakably strong company, and so did the stock market. Surely there was no danger, and besides, Ward's weak performance in the eleventh hour had done nothing to strengthen Harold's bargaining hand.

As Fred Bartlit of the firm of Kirkland and Ellis labored to defend Harold's interests against the Chicago lawsuit, the final papers were drawn and signed, and Contran Corporation became the owner of nearly $30 million worth of Jack Eckerd's stock, plus Clyde Campbell's Men's Stores.

■   ■   ■

Sandra had seemed incensed that Dr. John Whitaker did not agree with her bill of particulars against her husband. She had begun supplementing the sessions with another psychologist, apparently finding one who reinforced her conclusions that all her problems were related to mistreatment by her rich and famous spouse.

And tonight, again, she was a no-show.

How do I feel? Harold caught himself thinking. After all, moving out of the Ward's offices and giving up the role of chief executive of a growing, healthy company did mean a rather radical change had occurred. Not only that, the Chicago lawsuit was an ongoing concern, and now there was a very real possibility that the Texas insurance commissioner was going to file a separate suit. The legal difficulties were serious, but they were overshadowed by Harold's quiet elation over successfully concluding the Eckerd buyout, which he he considered a huge win. After all, Harold mused, from the position of barely owning a single store with perhaps a net worth of $50,000 to having a net worth (after loan paybacks) of perhaps $25 million meant that he was, in fact, both a millionaire and a success on his own—though an adverse legal judgment in Chicago could wipe it all out in an instant.

CHAPTER 28

CHICAGO, ILLINOIS: 1974

*T*he flight from Dallas to Chicago had been a joyless affair, given its purpose. Fred Bartlit had phoned with the news that Harold, Glenn, and Robert Wall would have to come to Chicago the following week.

"Why, Fred?"

"Harold, remember when you were in that deposition several months ago and the other side's attorney warned you that you fellows were under criminal investigation and you had the right to remain silent, and so on?"

"Yeah."

"And remember, I told you they were running around trying to get the U.S. attorney interested in making a criminal case?"

"Yes."

"Well, they succeeded, Harold. It's a totally ridiculous action, but they've handed down a federal criminal indictment against you, Glenn, and Bob Wall, and I've got to have all three of you come in to formally plead to the charges."

The idea of being indicted for trying to do the right thing with three insurance companies that had essentially been made insolvent under prior management before he bought them was surreal. Hadn't it been Harold Simmons who *volunteered* to spend hundreds of thousands of dollars in legal and administrative fees to shift around the ownership of his companies on the suggestion and approval of the Texas insurance commissioner? In effect, he had *given* Texas Consumer Finance Corporation to his insurance companies to buttress their value, and TCFC was worth over $5 million. There was no way he could have known from the financial statements that Texas Consumer Finance was insolvent and that investors—including Harold Simmons—had sunk real money into what was actually a bankrupt company. But now *Harold* was being accused of being a crook.

Fred Bartlit informed Harold that the indictment was the political act of an ambitious United States attorney in Chicago named James Thompson, who was trying to secure a reputation for himself as a zealous prosecutor of white-collar crime. Thompson was openly preparing for a run on the governorship of Illinois and was viewed by some as a dangerously ambitious man with a reckless disregard of the facts in search of easy targets.

Fred Bartlit was convinced that Thompson's ambition—and the unfounded allegations of a former head of Fidelity General Insurance Company dismissed by the Simmons brothers—had sparked the outrageous indictment. The fired insurance company executive of Fidelity General had alleged that the Texans who'd taken it over had stripped the company of its assets, when, in fact, the assets of Fidelity General had been depleted over many years through improper accounting practices and his own ineffective management.

Stung by his firing, the insurance chief had urged his lawyer to take his embellished story to big Jim Thompson, demanding criminal prosecution of the raiders from Dallas, and Thompson had taken the bait.

"Well, one thing positive I can say is that we've got Judge Prentiss Marshall."

"That's good?"

"Probably the best judge in the area."

CHAPTER 29

DALLAS, TEXAS: 1974

*H*arold stood in the living room of his home and sighed, rubbing his forehead, and slipping again into the endless process of re-viewing where things stood with Contran and his business world.

The picture wasn't pretty, but his constant re-examination wasn't grounded in apprehension, rather in the constant suspicion that he might be missing a solution somewhere which would pop into his mind if he just thought hard enough.

He had a lot to review. There were the basic nightmares of the law-suit and the separate criminal case against him in Chicago, both of them arising from the same insurance company collapse, and both of them approaching trial dates and costing incredible sums in legal fees and bad publicity. And there was the new Texas lawsuit filed by, of all people, the very Texas insurance commissioner Harold had tried so hard to please. With no law forcing him to do so, Harold had inno-cently used what he thought was a very profitable ownership stake in Texas Consumer Finance to shore up his insurance companies. *He* had voluntarily moved the assets around to remove any appearance of shaky capitalization, and he'd done so in complete consultation and with the complete approval of the commissioner. The suit demanded $25 million in damages, a sum that, if awarded, would wipe him out completely.

That, of course, will never happen, Harold reassured himself.

But the mere possibility of such a Draconian result was scaring the people who worked for him and distracting them on a daily basis, as well as confirming in the minds of bankers and financiers the idea that lending money to Harold Simmons or his companies was a bad idea.

In addition, an irritating lawsuit by a disgruntled Contran stockholder named Gaston Shumate had been filed, demanding that Contran be placed in receivership because Harold Simmons was spending too much money being the head of Contran. The filing had almost been amusing at first. Shumate claimed *he* could do the same job for no more than $20,000 a year with virtually no management or financial experience.

"What's this guy mad about?" Harold had asked his local attorney.

"He doesn't like you having Sandra as a copilot on business trips in the jet. He saw the article last year before she went with Braniff about how she flew with you. Since he doesn't have a jet, you shouldn't either."

"It saves us money, for heaven's sake, having Sandra as copilot."

"Welcome to the wonderful world of derivative stockholder nuisance suits, Harold. It goes with the territory. He wants you to settle and pay him money to go away."

A gust of wind rattled the windows, causing his mind to snap back to the living room. Harold looked around at the fireplace and wondered if he should put another log on the fire. Firelight always relaxed him, but even the flickering light and the soft heat couldn't soothe away the increasing galley of specters lurking in the dark corners of his future.

He would prevail, of course. There was no gut-level feeling of impending doom, just ... well ... *fatigue.* Dealing with all the problems and making good decisions and staying ahead of everyone else had always been fun. But bit by bit the fun seemed to be going out of it.

The wind had picked up outside the house and Harold heard the windows rattle again and a tree branch tap the side of the structure. He made a mental note to get a ladder and trim the offending Chinese elm on the coming weekend.

He thought of his mother in Austin, and how long it had been since he'd seen her.

He thought about Colorado and how much he'd like to be back in Aspen for a few days of skiing.

■   ■   ■

"Did you hear about Harold?"

The question was becoming common among those who knew two basic facts: First, Harold Simmons' entire fortune was locked in the Jack Eckerd stock he had contractually agreed to hold for a year, and second, the 1974 rout in the American stock market had led to previously unsinkable stocks being "taken out and shot" one after another, including Eckerd's. Suddenly, Contran Corporation was worthless on paper, and with it, most everything Harold had worked to build for the previous fifteen years.

For more than a year, a small number of stock analysts had been predicting a significant "correction" in the stock market, but when it came, the so-called correction rapidly cascaded from a sell-off into a major disaster, scrubbing more than one-third of the market's worth from the books.

The Jack Eckerd Corporation resisted at first, dropping only a small percentage, but as the depth of the disaster betrayed something between a loss of confidence and a complete Wall Street panic, even the Eckerd stock declined dramatically. From a previous high of $38 per share, Eckerd bottomed at $10 per share.

Yet, in the new Contran offices near Hillcrest and LBJ Freeway, Harold Simmons refused to waver. There were decisions to be made on what to invest in when the market came back, and, after all, it wasn't a loss until the stock was sold. There was still money in the bank, and Contran's various loans were still being serviced. Why panic?

Every week a procession of letters emanated from Harold's office to a wide variety of public corporations asking for copies of annual reports and public financial filings, information he could interpret like few others. Since the world of corporate finance and corporate takeovers knew little of Harold Simmons, the requests almost never triggered corporate concern at the other end. He could still sit quietly at his desk and examine the profiles of interesting companies in anonymity, looking for hidden values and spotting significant facts where others saw nothing.

And even in the dark shadow of multiple lawsuits and a criminal indictment, he persevered, seemingly unmoved and unaffected both in public and in the privacy of his inner circle, a steadiness that significantly calmed his brother and his employees.

Those around him took his words on faith that the stock market would eventually recover and that Eckerd stock would eventually climb again to reflect in direct value the strong corporation it really was. But how much time that would take, and whether such a recovery would come too late to save what he'd created, were questions no one wanted to ask openly. Instead, they looked to his example and found steadiness and strength beyond his forty-three years.

Contran's people, from Glenn Simmons to the receptionist, became very good at reading the latest Eckerd stock quotes, but they, too, kept their emotions under control, primarily because Harold remained unaffected and confident.

In Harold's mind, there could be no thought of closing the office and returning to the role of employee in someone else's company. There was simply too much opportunity out there, and, after all, weren't Texans legendary in their ability to ride the boom-bust-boom cycle back to wealth? Dallas, in fact, was knee-deep in such stories, from tales of wild men such as H.L. Hunt and the indefatigable gambling in oil that had made his fortune, to the real estate developers who seemed to be able to absorb monstrous bankruptcies one year and be back on top building giant shopping centers and office towers the next. Honesty was the key, and Harold knew that, above all else, he was a straight-shooter who dealt honestly with everyone, even those who were dishonest with him. It was far more than some jingoistic code worn on the sleeve of his daily dealings; it was the bedrock element of all his assumptions and decisions, a sort of solid faith in the essential worth of human integrity.

And it was wholly consistent with being a Texan, although there was never any indication such considerations entered into Harold's thinking. But those around him knew. After all, part of the lore and legend of being Texan bespoke an inheritance of quiet strength and resilient confidence, and Harold was unconsciously adding to that legend each day, as the steadiness of his resolve overrode the very real perils that lurked in all directions. He was not denying reality, but merely redefining its meaning—and that was the key. It was, in other words, not the best of times or the worst of times until the tale had been fully told and the last option closed, and he was far, far from being painted into that corner.

■   ■   ■

In the relative silence of a Sunday afternoon, a day and time normally devoted to the girls, Harold unlocked the door to his office suite and moved quietly into his carpeted office, barely seeing the sweeping view of North Dallas.

He felt his chin, regretting that he hadn't shaved. But no one was coming in anyway on Sunday, and he could be scruffy and unkempt for a few hours if he wanted.

Dropping heavily into his desk chair, he sighed, wondering how much time it takes for a man to recover from the assault of being ordered to leave his own home.

Being served with papers for formal separation in a pending divorce action, in the final analysis, had not been terribly surprising. After all, he could not help but feel that in her eyes he was broke, finished, and probably going to jail, and it was the perfect time to land one final kick and get it over with.

But it was the part about wanting sole custody of the kids that made no real sense to Harold. Hadn't it been Sandra who secured the airline pilot job and began spending nearly twenty-one days a month on the road?

How, then, could she seek sole custody?

He was returning each evening to a faceless apartment complex and a generic set of rooms, devoid of the voices of his girls, and while he could take almost anything else, this was the toughest test of all.

Calls to Lisa in college—and occasionally to Scheryle—became more frequent, but Serena and Andrea were his, too, and not having them around in the evening to talk to and read to and sing to was intolerable.

Weeks passed, and the demands for monetary maintenance intertwined with the fury from Sandra and her lawyer as Harold reluctantly called in Kirkland and Ellis, Fred Bartlit's Chicago firm, which Contran had begun using for almost all legal needs. Frank Cicero, another top-flight young attorney, was promptly dispatched to Dallas to handle the matter.

"She wants to break the trust, Harold," he was told.

"But, she *signed* the trust!"

"Yes, but if it holds, she gets very little of anything, since all your income and assets are owned by the trust, and she has no interests in it. So she's going to try to break it, and the tax consequences could be serious."

In Chicago, the battle was dragging on, and all attempts to get a dismissal of either the civil or criminal action had failed. The trials, Harold was told, would apparently occur as scheduled, and until then, in the eyes of the media and the business community who read their stories, he would remain "Dallas financier Harold Simmons who was recently indicted in Chicago for mail fraud."

Stoic or not, confident or not, it was increasingly difficult to see the horizon.

BOOK SIX

The High-Wire Act ...
Before Annette

CHAPTER 30

CHICAGO, ILLINOIS: 1974

*H*arold glanced at Fred Bartlit, who nodded in confirmation. After nearly six weeks of complicated, mind-numbing testimony, convoluted examination, and exhaustive cross-examination, the government attorneys had just rested in their marathon attempt to send Harold Simmons to prison.

Federal District Judge Prentiss Marshall called for a recess, and Bartlit motioned to Harold, Glenn, and Bob Wall to follow him. Two other Kirkland and Ellis lawyers tagged along, one of whom was the case's self-proclaimed "gopher," a newly minted attorney named Lanny Martin. Martin was assigned to assist Bartlit and take the clients to dinner each evening after trial while the primary team worked late into the night.

With the door to a conference room shut behind him, Fred Bartlit sat and studied his clients for a few seconds before speaking, his penetrating eyes and distinguished countenance so suited to his role of trial attorney that someone had joked that he must have come from Hollywood's Central Casting.

"Well, you see now why I said we should try this before Judge Marshall without a jury? They'd be hopelessly confused by now."

There were nods around the room.

"All right," Fred Bartlit continued. "We have a very important decision to make, right here, right now."

"What, Fred?" Harold asked.

Bartlit leaned forward, his right hand poised on the surface of the table, his eyes moving with deliberation from one man to the next.

"They haven't sustained their burden. They have *not* proven their case."

"Okay."

"And I think the defense should simply rest at this point, making it clear to the judge that we're well aware that the government has failed to even come close to proving the existence of a criminal act."

Fred Bartlit could see the idea sinking into the mind of each of the three men. He watched Harold in particular as the realization dawned and his eyes flared somewhat.

"You mean, abandon all the witnesses and testimony and depositions we've lined up—"

"All of it. And why shouldn't we? The government had to prove their charges beyond a reasonable doubt, and they absolutely have not done so. In other words, we have a very strong case without even putting it on. We can accomplish everything we need to accomplish in my summation."

"How ... risky is that?" Glenn asked.

Bartlit carefully explained the options, and the hazards, and the probable effect on a very reasoned, very experienced federal judge. It would be a dramatic affirmation of the defendants' belief that the government's case amounted to nothing, and a powerful affirmation of their own faith in their innocence.

"We'll shock him, in other words?" Harold asked.

"We'll impress him. It's a gutsy move, Harold, but I believe it's the right one. Only you guys can make that decision, however ..."

Judge Marshall reconvened his court fifteen minutes later, unprepared for Fred Bartlit's straightforward statement that due to the failure of the government to prove the existence of a crime, the defense rested.

When all the exchanges and final arguments were finished, the judge sat back in his chair for a moment before replying. "I'm going to need a while to think about this," he said.

■　　■　　■

"All rise!" The now-all-too-familiar call of the federal court's bailiff rang once again through the paneled courtroom as the federal judge took his seat and looked at the parties.

"Will the defendants please rise."

Harold, Glenn, Bob Wall, and Fred Bartlit got to their feet, their faces impassive, the stakes impossibly high.

"This ... case began as a civil case," the judge began, "and it should have remained a civil case. This should never have been prosecuted as a criminal matter, because there is no evidence of criminality here. The defense is correct. The government has failed to establish any credible evidence of a crime on the part of any of these defendants, let alone meet the burden beyond a reasonable doubt. These indictments are dismissed in their entirety, and the defendants are discharged."

The gavel came down hard as large smiles broke out on the faces of Harold and Glenn Simmons and Bob Wall.

Harold turned and shook Fred Bartlit's hand as he fought to hide his feelings.

But Lanny Martin, the young attorney-come-gopher, could tell he was thoroughly exhilarated. After so many evenings with Harold Simmons, he knew he was seeing something rare: pure elation in the face and the mind of a man who seldom showed the world his feelings.

Not only had they been vindicated, but the dangerous calculated gamble that Fred Bartlit had recommended and Harold had endorsed had worked.

Once again, in other words, Harold Simmons' judgment was right, his confidence in his own convictions correctly placed. And this time he had the ruling of a federal court to endorse that fact, a ruling which embarrassed and excoriated the government lawyers as well as the ambitious U.S. attorney, Jim Thompson, who had brought the case to begin with.

Not that Jim Thompson would be concerned. With his eyes focused on the governorship of Illinois, Thompson simply marked the defeat off to the luck of the draw and forgot the matter.

For Harold and Glenn and Bob Wall, however, the months of living under the shameful public assumption that they were guilty as charged would never be forgotten.

■   ■   ■

The criminal trial had cost Harold and Contran nearly a half million dollars in legal fees and months of time. But it had been more than a victory: it was a turning point.

There was a new bounce in his step on return to Dallas, a new focus, and a new optimism that only experienced Harold-watchers could discern.

Bob Wall, with Harold's blessing, put together a financial package to buy out Contran's ownership of Clyde Campbell Men's Shops and began happily running the chain of stores. The sale left Contran owning little more than Eckerd stock.

But the market was climbing again, and investors were rediscovering the bedrock fact that the Jack Eckerd Corporation was neither a loser nor deserving of such a low stock price. While the Olympian heights of the pre-crash values were out of reach, the stock began climbing from its low of $10 a share to reach almost $20.

The negative net worth of Contran resulting from the crash of 1974 had been weathered because Harold had arranged long-term debt and had short-term cash to service it. There had been enough cash left in the accounts for that purpose when everything began falling apart, and since the loans were being serviced on time, there were no grounds for the banks to call any. While most of his smaller credit lines dried up in the panic to get away from "Harold Simmons, who has been indicted for mail fraud in Chicago," as the papers had continuously reported, the loss of those credit lines was merely an inconvenience.

Now, however, cash *was* growing short, and some of the major loans were coming due in the near future. Harold had to pick the right moment to sell Eckerd's recovering stock, though the choice was an agony. At one time their holdings had been worth $50 million, and his share more than $30 million. What if he sold now and lost $15-20 million over the stock's high mark, and then had to sit on the sidelines and watch the price recover to $40 a share or more?

Nevertheless, practicality had to rule. Waiting in the hope of a better price when there were loans to be paid off constituted an unwarranted gamble because what Harold knew he needed the most was an instant restoration of his credibility. Certainly there were two major insurance-related lawsuits still pending, but he had been totally exonerated and confirmed an honest man, and the partial recovery of the Eckerd stock had chased the buzzards away from Contran. The company had a positive net worth again, and that had to be re-solidified. In addition, poorly crafted federal laws passed in 1940 had risen up to ensnare Contran for merely holding the Eckerd stock. Since the value of the stock exceeded 40 percent of Contran's worth, the law branded them as an investment company subject to a restrictive slew of federal laws and procedures. The sooner they could unload the stock and escape the investment company designation, the easier life would be.

Over a period of weeks, Goldman Sachs found block buyers to purchase close to $20 million worth of Eckerd stock, much of which was banked after repaying loans. Raising fresh cash positioned Contran Corporation for renewed acquisitions, and revitalized the investment engine Harold had created.

■　■　■

The plaintiff in the Chicago civil trial who sought to recover millions from Contran for the self-engineered collapse of Fidelity General had bragged to friends after the acquittal in the criminal trial that the government lawyers had "screwed up the case." This time, for the civil trial, the plaintiff crowed, they would do it right and get a heavy verdict against the raiding Texans.

A jury had been empaneled, and to help read the jury's thinking, Kirkland and Ellis assigned an employee named Joe Gallo, a man of limited education who had always wanted to be a lawyer but whose great worth *to* lawyers was his ability to think like the ordinary juror. Harold and Gallo had already spent a pleasant evening in conversation during the early stages of the case, and his advice to Fred Bartlit about the jury's reaction had proven invaluable.

The civil trial in Chicago was not a foregone conclusion, but after the scathing dismissal of the government's criminal charges, the momentum was clearly with Harold and Contran against the plaintiffs. When the case finally went to the jury, they came back quickly with complete vindication for Contran, and the matter seemed closed.

The judge, however, had other ideas. Elderly and disengaged throughout the trial, the judge had proven a major impediment, and it was about to get worse. The young lawyer who had represented the plaintiffs in the trial had blown it badly, but he was well connected as the son of a respected politician who, in turn, was a good friend of the judge. The judge decided to rescue him, and a week later suddenly set aside the jury's verdict and ordered a retrial, a move which stunned both sets of lawyers and spurred a $250,000 settlement—less than the cost of retrying the case. As a part of the settlement, the judge agreed to enter an order of dismissal that wholly exonerated Harold, wiping away at last the second of three major courtroom challenges that had loomed on the horizon.

Harold returned to Dallas and promptly retained the jury-watching expert who had called it right in Chicago. Jerry Gallo would help with the impending Texas insurance commissioner's lawsuit, one that held the possibility of becoming an even greater agony with far more potential for damage—and one that would involve far more expense since an entire legal team from Kirkland and Ellis would have to deploy to Dallas for many months.

Having spent the better part of a month with Lanny Martin during the criminal trial in Chicago, Harold had come to understand two things about the young lawyer: He loved securities law, and he had an extremely sharp, facile mind.

Kirkland and Ellis, Martin's firm, now had all of Contran and Harold's significant legal business, and a major focus of their services had become the monstrous lawsuit by the Texas insurance commissioner against Contran. Another senior attorney for Kirkland and Ellis, Frank Cicero, was the lead lawyer on the case, and as his third assistant, Lanny Martin was assigned to begin preparing Harold for the depositions and in-court testimony that would follow.

Morning after morning Lanny would leave his hotel room and appear in Harold's office, only to be both frustrated and fascinated by the fact that Harold wasn't at all interested in the lawsuit. He was only interested in the next deal, the one that could relaunch everything he had worked to accomplish.

"We'll get to that later," Harold would say, brushing aside Lanny's sincere attempt to focus his client on trial preparation. "Right now, Lanny, I'd like to know what you think about this idea." A cascade of facts and figures and stock information regarding one public corporation or another would pour from Harold, and within minutes Lanny would be captured by the process and knee-deep in analyzing the legal and financial aspects right along with Harold.

"Harold, I can't give you an immediate answer on this," Lanny would, often as not, demur. After all, he was just out of law school and into a wonderful job with a powerful firm. The last thing he wanted to do was shoot from the hip and give bad advice.

"Yeah, but, what do *you* think, Lanny?" Harold would prompt. "Can we do a deal like this?"

"Well, I *think* we can, but I'll have to do some homework." Lanny would dive for the phone during the lunch hour and call the firm back in Chicago, sending a small army of fellow associates into action to assemble authoritative answers to Harold's questions before returning to his office to resume the attempt to prepare his testimony.

"That's great, Lanny," Harold would say. "Now, what about *this* idea?"

"Harold, forgive me, but don't you have a corporate lawyer locally?" Lanny asked one morning in complete exhaustion.

Harold smiled. "Sure, Lanny, but I like your answers better."

CHAPTER 31

DALLAS, TEXAS: 1975

*W*ith a stack of reports on his desk, Harold sat back one after-noon in early 1975 and decided that he needed to know more about an increasingly attractive company in Colorado, a state he loved to visit.

Since public corporations *had* to file a snowstorm of certified and essentially sworn-to reports each year, the ability of a careful analyst like Harold to discern a great deal about what the company really did and what it really owned was extensive. The advantage of never needing inside information to evaluate a company meant that he wouldn't be tempted by the inevitable flow of rumors and tips that become a form of background noise in corporate life: who's going to merge with whom, who's going to unload what. With the quiet addition of his own foot-work—the occasional personal visit to the site of a property owned by a target company—coupled with his native knowledge of the art of business, Harold's expertise was akin to that of a seismologist who studies how to draw a schematic of the earth beneath his feet by analyzing the arcane medium of reflected compression waves as read by seismographs, something which can be accomplished in the privacy of the office.

And Harold knew the Vail area as one that would someday probably become the world-class chic resort it already pretended to be. The Vail company was stuck, having bought the adjacent Beaver Creek area without the money to develop it.

"We're going to tender for the majority of the shares," Harold had announced. "It's dropped to six dollars per share, and we're going to offer ten a share, and if we get it, selling Beaver Creek will pay for it."

But the stock had merely trickled in after the offer had been published, and within a month it was painfully obvious that there were two choices left: raise the tender offer price, or abandon the idea of taking control.

Harold made his decision swiftly. "It's only worth ten. I know we'd probably get enough if I raised it to twelve, but I don't like to overpay for anything. Therefore, we're out."

The offer was withdrawn, the stock already tendered was returned, and the other files in the growing pile of possible acquisition targets on his desk were opened once again.

"Lanny, look at this! Here's a local investment trust trading for half its net *asset* value!" Harold announced on a Monday morning as Lanny Martin once again began trying to go through the upcoming deposition testimony Harold would have to give.

"What's the company?" Lanny asked in resignation.

"It's an investment trust," Harold said with a big smile. "Should be selling at twice the price."

"Yeah, I can see that from your figures," Lanny said.

"If we can get just fifty percent of this, we can take it over, and realize the true value."

"Sounds like a great value, Harold."

"Okay. So how fast can we get together the legal paperwork to make a tender offer on this one?"

"Oh, within a week or two," he said.

"Fine. How about Friday?"

"Fri ... Friday?"

"Yes."

"I, uh, suppose we can."

"Good. I'll count on it. We've got to move fast."

Lanny flew back to the Chicago offices of Kirkland and Ellis and began leading a group of fellow associates in a mad dash for the goal line of bringing Harold Simmons a ready tender offer in three days. An incredible number of papers had to be drafted, vetted, checked, researched, and then printed, all of them bearing all the requisite information and filling all the statutorily required squares that the Securities and Exchange Commission required of anyone mounting such an offer for a public corporation.

Tuesday, Wednesday, and Thursday's workdays all extended into the wee hours of the following mornings, but early Friday, a bleary-eyed Lanny Martin was able to board a Braniff Boeing 727 at Chicago O'Hare bound for Dallas with a briefcase and suitcase stuffed full of the legal instruments that would initiate the offer to buy the company.

"Mr. Simmons, Lanny Martin is here to see you," Harold's secretary announced late Friday morning as Harold smiled back. "Send him in."

Lanny moved through the door carrying boxes of legal papers which he unloaded onto the edge of the desk. He was smiling. This was the payoff for a week of hard, long effort.

"Well, we made it, Harold! We're ready to file."

"Everything's set, Lanny ... except for just one thing."

"What's that?" Lanny replied as he glanced proudly once more at the completed piles of paper.

"We've changed the target. We're going to make a tender offer for another company."

Lanny looked around, his eyes studying Harold's, wondering if the wry, subtle sense of humor he'd occasionally seen during the long evenings in Chicago had kicked in again.

"Excuse me?"

"We're going after a different company," Harold repeated with a smile, moving energetically around behind his desk to retrieve a sheaf of papers. "This one's even better, Lanny! You won't believe it."

"That's the truth. You've ... changed the *target?*" Lanny asked, his eyes going back to the product of three sleepness nights of work.

"This is the best company I've ever found in terms of hidden value! I mean, this one's amazing. It's a little thing called Valhi down in Houston."

"Val ... hi ..." Lanny repeated absently, trying to follow Harold's narrative as the fruits of his labor seemed to evaporate on the edge of the desk.

"That's right!" Harold was saying. "Let me show you the figures. There's incredible value here!"

"I'm sure."

"Oh," Harold said suddenly, stopping to look up at Lanny's

stunned expression. "You can just change the name on the papers, can't you?"

"Yeah," Lanny replied, glancing down and trying to imagine the work ahead. "I'm sure we can do something like that."

"Great!" Harold had already turned back to the folder full of exciting figures. "Because we need to move real fast."

■   ■   ■

Doyle Mize was a man Harold admired. A Houstonian, Mize had purchased a small oil drilling company named Zapata from a future U.S. president, George H.W. Bush, when Bush was ready to retire and turn to politics. Slowly and smartly, Mize built Zapata into a very large and successful conglomerate, a firm with a habit of acquiring other companies, including a sizable land company based in New Orleans, Louisiana, named Southdown Corporation, which Mize bought in a hostile tender offer.

The executive vice president of finance for Southdown Corporation at the time Zapata acquired control of it was a man named Hugh Roberts, whom Harold had come to know in Houston during the Mading-Dugan days. The fact that the two men kept in touch after Harold returned to Dallas gave Harold a vicarious view of an unfolding oddity after something unique occurred in the corporate executive ranks of Houston's business community: Doyle Mize had suddenly resigned his job as chief executive of Zapata, the *parent* company, to take the chief executive position at Southdown, a *subsidiary* company of Zapata.

Why on earth? Harold had wondered when he read about the self-demotion. CEOs never demoted themselves without a substantial reason, but there *was* no apparent reason. Something was clearly motivating Doyle Mize, and Harold made a mental note to watch what unfolded as best he could in the following years.

Southdown was a land investment company, and anything but the larger diversified corporation that Zapata had become. True, its assets were all over southern Louisiana, including hundreds of thousands of acres with mineral rights intact, lands which might have more value than anyone realized.

Harold began hearing that Mize had struck a deal with Zapata to separate the two companies by spinning off Southdown to its share-holders. Then Southdown, under Mize's control, had apparently bought back Zapata's controlling stock from Zapata by trading them a large block of Louisiana land, and as soon as the deal was complete, Southdown had become its own independent company again—with Doyle Mize as chief executive officer, and all the stock publicly owned.

Once again Mize turned to conglomerate building just as he had with Zapata, making numerous diverse acquisitions. Within a few years, Southdown had also found a major supply of oil on its lands in Louisiana and was reaping a windfall of oil money. Mize expected the stock price to rise, but conglomerates had begun to fall from favor in the investment community.

Tarred with the same image as a conglomerate acquiring dissimilar companies that had little cooperative potential, Southdown's stock price began to sink, and with it, Doyle Mize's prospects for great wealth based on his stock options.

A routine phone call between Hugh Roberts and Harold Simmons had transmitted the seed to Harold that would rapidly grow into the best takeover idea he'd ever had.

"We're getting ready to spin off a little company down here called Valhi," Hugh Roberts had mentioned. "It'll take with it a lot of Louisiana farm land and some large farm lands in California. Mize will become chief executive officer of Valhi and resign his position with Southdown."

When the deed was done and a routinely requested prospectus arrived, Harold casually flipped through it one afternoon in Dallas as he checked on the latest over-the-counter quote for the new stock.

The juxtaposition of stock price and apparent value of the properties reported caused him to sit forward suddenly in his chair on a Wednesday morning.

Good Lord! This thing is worth $50 a share, and it's started trading at $5 a share!

During the three days Lanny Martin worked away in Chicago preparing the papers to launch a tender offer for the targeted real estate company while in Dallas, Harold had snapped to high alert as he rapidly dug for more facts and made the decision to launch a tender offer at $15 a share for 50 percent of the company called Valhi.

"So what do you think, Lanny?" Harold asked on Friday after dropping the bomb that he'd abandoned the real estate firm and explaining his reasons.

"That's incredible," Lanny agreed. "I think you're right. I think this is a much better deal."

"So, how soon can we go?"

Lanny took one last look at the stack of useless papers he'd just hauled in from Chicago and sighed through a tired smile.

"We'll be ready to go on Monday. We'll publish in the *Wall Street Journal* on Monday." It would cost the weekend and mean no sleep for several more days, but Harold was clearly right. The opportunity was unprecedented, and the principals, including Mize, apparently owned a little of the new stock.

CHAPTER 32

DALLAS, TEXAS: 1975

$\mathcal{T}$he extremely dangerous case against Contran filed by the Texas insurance commissioner had been moving slowly, and all indications were that it would be early 1976, if at all, before it went to trial.

But suddenly an early court date was set, and Frank Cicero, as lead attorney, was under extreme pressure to prepare the case and his client.

Harold seemed to have unblinking confidence that he would win, and complete confidence in Kirkland and Ellis and Cicero, but there was no question that in theory a judgment for $25 million would destroy him.

There was, however, far less confidence on the part of Cicero's legal team, who knew they had a substantial battle ahead against a state officer who was determined to recoup the losses of the Fort Worth insurance company from Harold Simmons on the theory that he must have known that Texas Consumer Finance Corporation was worthless when he used it to shore up the company's capital base.

There was cash in the Contran treasury, but it was earmarked for acquisition of a new business, without which Contran would rapidly cease to have a purpose. Yet litigation was costing rivers of money, and in this case those costs included expenses for a small army of lawyers flown in from Chicago, not only in fees, but in the basics of hotels and cars and food and clerical support as well. Fred Bartlit realized that his Texas client, while on his way back from the corporate equivalent of the biblical Valley of the Shadow of Death, had insufficient funds to pay Kirkland and Ellis' growing bills and still make the corporate moves necessary to survive and prosper.

"We've got to cut this guy some slack," Bartlit argued to his partners in Chicago. "We don't bill him now, we bill him later. This man is going to be a very loyal client, but if we take our money up front, it could be a Pyrrhic victory."

Reluctantly, the senior partners agreed.

Where the offer of less-than-first-class accommodations might have been rebuffed by many firms, Harold's suggestion that three of the lawyers move into his apartment and share a couple of rented vans was accepted. When Sandra was out of town flying Braniff trips, Harold stayed in the family home while day after day most of the legal team working on the trial, including Lanny Martin, used the apartment as a slightly upscale dormitory.

The level of activity competing for Harold's attention reached a fever pitch just as the trial got under way. The tender offer for Valhi had triggered a strange response in the Houston offices where Mize had set up the company. Although they had owned almost no stock in the spun-off company of Valhi, Southdown CEO Doyle Mize and the two brothers from California who managed the company's farmlands under a lucrative management contract suddenly popped up with a $17.50 per share tender offer themselves, this one for *all* the Valhi stock!

"They've offered *what?*" Harold exclaimed when he found out. "That means they're trying to take the damn thing private, which also means there's even more there than meets the eye."

The Mercantile Bank of Dallas, Harold's first local employer after he left government service and once the most hidebound and conservative bank in town, now under new management, Gene Bishop, CEO, and Jim Gardner, president, had taken solid notice of Harold's Chicago vindication and the successful sale of his Eckerd stock. They agreed to back his takeover run at Valhi. With some of his cash pledged in the deal and the rest borrowed from Mercantile to buy control, it seemed a safe bet.

But now the stakes had been raised, and Harold had to return to Mercantile Bank for a significant increase in the borrowing needed. He had a little over $5 million in the bank from the Eckerd sale, but outbidding the competition would cost around $7.2 million, and the Mercantile agreed to provide the majority of the money.

As Harold was called to testify in the insurance commission trial for what would be nearly two weeks on the stand, he authorized the launch of a new tender offer for $22.50 per share for 51 percent of Valhi's stock.

The trip to the downtown Dallas courtroom every morning became a distraction and a grind from the beginning. Since cellular phones had yet to sweep into being as the mainstay of corporate America's communication link, Harold rapidly located the nearest bank of pay telephones and instantly honed the habit of heading for them on every break from the courtroom. For hours he would be on the stand recalling the most arcane minutiae, all of it potentially critical to the case, and during the interims he would be hunched over a pay phone balancing a notepad.

Several days into the ordeal, word came during one of the courtroom breaks that Valhi's management had matched the $22.50 price for 100 percent of the Valhi stock.

"I hate to tell you, Harold," Lanny said, "but the stock's flowing into their depository, and we're getting almost nothing in ours. This isn't going to work if we don't do something."

"What do you suggest?"

"Well, from what you told me, I suspect they haven't disclosed everything in their prospectus."

"You're saying we should sue them?" Harold asked.

"I'm suggesting that if we're sure they're holding back information and we sue them for securities violations based on failure to disclose, once we get into depositions and start looking at their documents, we'll probably find out what we need to prove it. We may be able to get an injunction then to stop them from actually buying the offered stock."

"I *know* they're hiding something. Go ahead and file. Let's see if we can stop this."

"Harold?" one of the trial attorneys said, having been sent to retrieve him. "They're reconvening."

"Just a second," Harold replied as he hunched down with the pay phone, making a few notes as he balanced the receiver on his shoulder.

"We have to go—now," the associate said.

Harold held up a finger in a "wait" gesture as he addressed the lawyer on the other end of the phone. "Same drill. I'll call you on the next break."

■   ■   ■

The financial gunfight between the forces of Doyle Mize and Harold Simmons reached the showdown stage. The period for stockholders to deposit their stock in either Harold's depository or that of Mize's forces was drawing to a close over a weekend, and with the Texas trial still hanging in the balance but winding down, the tension all around was building.

A separate team of Kirkland and Ellis lawyers, in Houston fighting the Valhi battle, conducted a number of rapid depositions and used discovery motions to obtain a small storeroom full of documents, all of which contained the clues that were now coalescing into a clear picture of what Mize had been up to and why Valhi had been allowed to languish quietly.

Doyle Mize hadn't wanted the newly public Valhi's price to rise. In fact, he and the McCarthy brothers, who ran the California farms owned by Valhi, had expected it to sit and languish while they honed their plans to buy up the stock quietly, knowing full well that the properties listed for the company were not only understated but failed to enunciate a very important point: Much of the new and nonproducing farm properties in California were about to begin production of grapes, olives, pistachios, and almonds, and when the upcoming profits were realized, they would be immense.

With time running out and Mize about to grab the stock through his 100 percent tender offer, Harold authorized his attorneys to go to a federal district judge in Houston for an injunction against Mize's offer, on the grounds that a conspiracy existed to defraud the Valhi stockholders through nondisclosure of the imminent harvest.

"If you permit the managers of this company to purchase their own stock," Contran's lawyers argued, "without disclosing the probability of the near-term increase in profits, it is a clear violation of their fiduciary duty and security laws."

The federal judge agreed and, on the day the tender offer expired, issued a temporary restraining order against Mize's forces, enjoining them from buying any of the offered stock.

Mize's lawyers flew to New Orleans with the Kirkland and Ellis team in hot pursuit and filed an emergency appeal with the Fifth

Circuit Court of Appeals in an attempt to reverse the decision and vacate the district judge's restraining order.

The weekend was upon them, and Monday was the day purchasing of stock could begin. If the Fifth Circuit reversed the Houston-based district judge, the fight would be over and Mize would snap up the offered stock by Monday noon at $22.50 a share.

"They'll issue a decision tomorrow, on Sunday," Harold's team relayed to him from New Orleans. "Where will you be?"

Harold gave them his phone number, and the following evening—still in the midst of the war with the insurance commissioner's lawsuit—called a Sunday board meeting to give instant final approval to the offer if the news from the court was positive, and if not, to consider making a higher offer. Harold and the Contran board members milled around and waited for the critical call, all of them essentially watching the phone.

Lanny Martin could feel the nervousness in the room. It was precisely like waiting for a major verdict in a long trial, since the tender offer he'd put together on Harold's orders had been under way for weeks and consumed an immense amount of financial, professional, and emotional capital.

Harold, Lanny noticed, was amazingly calm. He sat with a Coke and chatted with other directors or occasionally immersed himself in reading something, but there was no pacing, or nervous behavior, or sharp words betraying frayed nerves.

When the phone would ring, others would leap for it, not Harold. When someone injudiciously brought up serious worries in the Dallas trial, there was no indication of concern.

Lanny watched him at one point and wondered how he'd learned to remain so calm. His entire professional life, his empire, however miniature, was literally on the line. If the trial went against him, regardless of appeals, he stood to lose everything, although Harold had lectured Lanny gently on the real potential loss he would face with a verdict for the commissioner. "My credibility is everything," he'd said. "If I lose this trial, they will have proven what just isn't true, and that's the allegation that I somehow knew TCFC was corrupt and worthless and used it anyway. If that happens, I'll have no credibility, and everyone will say, 'Well, you just can't trust that Simmons guy.' That, Lanny, is what would destroy me. Not the money."

The trial appeared to be going well for Harold, Lanny knew, but no one could ever really be smug about what could happen in open court.

The one phone call they were all waiting for was uppermost on everyone's mind. One phone call to tell Harold Simmons whether he'd snagged a prize worth tens of millions in instant additional value, or whether he had to begin looking for something else to buy after dumping hundreds of thousands in legal fees and expenses into the effort to acquire Valhi. All that, and he was the calmest man in the room.

The phone rang in midafternoon, the fourth time that day it had shattered the group's collective nerves. This time, however, it *was* the call from the Kirkland and Ellis team in New Orleans.

Lanny took the call, listened for a second, then turned to the assemblage with a big smile. "They denied the motion!" he exclaimed. "The restraining order stays!"

Relief, applause, and shouts from everyone except Harold filled the room. As Lanny watched, a large smile took over Harold's features, but when the other shouts of victory had died down, there was only one reaction from the new chairman-to-be of Valhi.

"Ya-hoo!" he said quietly.

■   ■   ■

The Valhi stockholders—already in a frame of mind to sell and sell quickly—withdrew their stock from Mize's depository on Monday morning and sold it to Harold. By midweek, control of Valhi was his.

Meanwhile, in the Dallas trial the defense finally rested, and after a short period of deliberation, the Dallas jury returned with a resounding judgment for the defense and a complete rejection of the Texas insurance commissioner's claims.

Having won all three trials in a twelve-month period, and suddenly free of the $25 million damage claim, Harold Simmons turned his attention to taking actual control of Valhi. The attorneys representing Valhi and Doyle Mize were notified that Harold had elected his own board of directors to replace the previous one, and that the executives of the company were expected to immediately vacate their Houston offices.

Harold traveled to Houston within a week to look at the offices and the operations of Valhi, unexpectedly finding that the spoils of cor-

porate war included a new Cadillac Seville the company had just purchased for Doyle Mize to use.

"If the car's for the chairman and I'm the chairman, then I think I
want that car," Harold said, mindful of the imagery as much as the substance. The Mize team had tried to pull a fast one and had been vanquished. The Seville would serve as a sort of symbolic scalp of victory
on his belt and as a reminder to him as well that the trappings of corporate position in a public company are just that: trappings.

Valhi was still a public company, but the majority of the stock was
in Harold's hands, subject to the money loaned by the Mercantile.
When the immense value of what Valhi owned began to become apparent, however, the bank loan was quickly retired, and Harold began
probing with amazement the wealth of the lands the company owned
and controlled.

Some of them, however, were beyond the reach of daily control,
even for the owner. The McCarthy brothers in California, controllers
of the vast farm lands under a management contract with Valhi, were
highly resistant to direction or change, especially since they had lost
their ownership bid along with Doyle Mize.

"There's no reason I can see," Harold told his staff after examining
the Houston offices, "to maintain Valhi down here. Let's just pack the
whole thing up and bring it to Dallas."

"How much do you think the company's worth, Harold, now that
you've had a chance to see the files?" Lanny Martin asked a week later,
before returning to Chicago.

"I don't know," Harold replied, "but it could be as much as fifty million, or who knows, maybe much more. It's incredible what Mize was
sitting on."

"And the final price was what? Eight million?"

Harold nodded with a smile.

"Harold, I think the nightmare is over."

Harold nodded again. "I hope so, but I don't have time to sit
around and think about it." He turned to a far corner of his desk and
pulled over a folder. "By the way, on the flight back to Chicago, why
don't you take a look at this and tell me what you think?"

"What is it?"

"Another company we may want to try for. I've got an idea
sketched out in there on how we could do it."

CHAPTER 33

DALLAS, TEXAS: 1976

*F*or Jim Ling, being fired as the chairman and wunderkind of LTV had been a seismic embarrassment only a deposed monarch could thoroughly appreciate. Dallas in the seventies had been to some degree *defined* by Ling and his success, and to see the high-flying company he'd built tottering, and Ling himself corporately disgraced, quickly chilled the practice of the very game Ling had seemingly perfected: corporate takeovers, corporate acquisitions, and the building of corporate conglomerates whose various subsidiaries bore absolutely no operating resemblance to each other. Suddenly, caution became a watchword, a concept which had seemed virtually foreign to everything Ling practiced.

But Jim Ling refused to be broken. He took what cash and resources he had—which were considerable—and turned his attention to finding another corporate vehicle to use in re-creating his stunning LTV success. After all, Ling essentially told himself, he had committed an act of corporate financial genius in building LTV, and he could darn well do it again, proving in the process how wrong his detractors were and how dumb the LTV board had been to fire him. It shouldn't take more than a few years, he reasoned, to wheel and deal his way back to the ranks of one of the most powerful men in America.

To carry out his plan, Ling formed a company called Omega-Alpha, but by the end of 1975—as Harold Simmons was completing his takeover of Valhi—Ling's would-be comeback conglomerate Omega-Alpha had gone bankrupt and tumbled into receivership.

Jim Ling the empire builder was out in the cold once again, *this* time without the fortune.

Before his final fall, Ling had opened an office in the same North Dallas building that housed Contran corporation, and on an otherwise unremarkable afternoon at the start of the Valhi battle, the formerly mighty conglomerate builder had dropped by Harold's office to chat.

"How much do you have in cash to spend on that company, Harold?" Ling had asked, aware from the *Wall Street Journal* of the Valhi tender offer.

"About eight million."

"Really?" Ling had seemed amazed. "Well, you better perfect your ownership on the first try, because eight million isn't much to work with. I'm in a transitional period here myself, and I'd be willing to join you as a junior partner at Contran on a half-time basis. I think you're at a point where I could help you greatly with new ideas."

"Jim, I . . . think an advisor position would work better."

"Okay, then hire me half-time as a senior investment advisor."

"Half-time?"

"Yeah. I need time to work on my own investments and recovering Omega-Alpha. We've got some real opportunities there, even in bank-ruptcy."

Harold agreed to a two-year contract at $90,000 per year, and Ling became, in effect, his employee. Harold forced himself to ignore the irony. Here was the man he had approached with some degree of awe in the early sixties now working for *him,* and grateful for the job. The contrasts were too great to ignore, and after all, to have *Jim Ling* on the team would mean a new and brilliant perspective on every possible deal from the guru who had all but invented the genre of corporate acquisition.

Harold returned to the apartment that night in a state of mild, reflective confusion. The sliding back door of his apartment—the entrance to the deck—was hardly a place for a corporate titan to stand and think grand thoughts, but Harold permitted himself a few moments of quiet satisfaction as he reminded himself to heed the eternally repeated lesson that even the mighty can fall.

When he'd approached Jim Ling in 1963 as a supplicant, Ling had treated him with dignity. To be able to return the favor now in Ling's hour of need was more than satisfying. It was the right thing to do and made perfect business sense, all rolled into one.

Harold stepped back inside and pulled the glass door closed with a rueful chuckle. Ling had no corner on the market when it came to close encounters with financial ruin. Business at his level was, truly, a high-wire act.

■   ■   ■

Jim Ling began pitching a major investment recommendation the moment he came aboard.

"Harold, I'm not kidding you. Buying Omega-Alpha out of bankruptcy would be a very profitable move! I know what's there. After all, I put it together."

"I don't know, Jim," Harold replied. "That's a lot of money for a dead company."

The lawsuits were flying around the collapse of Omega-Alpha like Kansas thunderstorms in April, but Ling had his eye on several of the companies he'd purchased while running the failed conglomerate. While his ill-advised acquisition of a secretly troubled, Hollywood-based record company provided the final straw to break his corporate camel's back, another of his acquisitions was purring right along. While its stock was tied up in the Omega-Alpha bankruptcy proceedings, the wire manufacturer continued churning out high-quality copper wire and turning a healthy profit.

Ling urged that Valhi offer to buy the wire company from the bankruptcy trustee, and Harold was listening. He'd already begun researching the possibilities while trying to contain Jim Ling's obviously self-interested enthusiasm, but at least one aspect of Omega-Alpha was in fact beginning to look like a good investment: the bonds of the bankrupt company.

In the midst of analyzing and reporting on other potential deals, Ling's constant return to the pitch that Harold Simmons and Contran should buy the main asset of Omega-Alpha began to solidify Harold's growing, somewhat uneasy impression that the foremost consideration for Jim Ling would always be the personal interests of Jim Ling, who had most of his remaining assets invested in Omega-Alpha bonds.

Harold reached a decision one morning before calling Ling into his office. "Instead of buying the company, Jim, what we need to focus on is the fact that it's the *debt* that's the best investment at present prices. You've been buying the Omega-Alpha bonds, right?"

"Yeah. As much as I could. I couldn't afford much."

"So, let's buy up some bonds in the open market, then make a tender offer for the majority of them so we can become a major influence in the bankruptcy process. I figure, from what you've told me, we could eventually get back maybe three times our investment when the company is liquidated and all the parts are sold."

It wasn't the solution Ling had hoped for, but it was better than nothing.

Before paying for the Valhi acquisition, Contran had barely $8 million in the bank. After buying Valhi, Harold was immensely pleased to find that he now had enough Valhi cash and liquidable assets to buy the Omega-Alpha bonds. In fact, most everywhere Harold shone the flashlight of internal audit within Valhi's accounts and holdings, more hidden value showed up. It was a small gamble at best to use some of that cash reserve on the Omega-Alpha deal, and Harold proceeded to make history by making a tender offer not for the stock, but for the *debt* (bonds) of a bankrupt company at approximately thirty cents on the dollar. The move was based both on Ling's personal assurances and Harold's own analysis that there really *was* far more value in the various parts of Omega-Alpha than were reflected in its open market price during the bankruptcy proceedings.

The minute the tender offer was made, bondholders who had watched in dejection as the market traded their bonds for only fifteen cents on the dollar suddenly found themselves being offered partial salvation by Contran at the rate of thirty percent of the face value. The response was rapid, and within days enough bonds were surrendered and sold to make Contran the largest creditor of the corporation.

Ling was becoming as much a part of each prospective deal as a corporate senior officer would, understanding more and more of what Harold was assembling in Contran, and understanding as well the continuously growing value of Valhi's properties. It was the sort of inside information corporate leaders are very careful about disclosing, but in Harold's thinking, there was a personal and professional honor among such men, as well as federal laws governing who could have inside information, and what could happen to those who misused it.

There was no longer any question what Doyle Mize and his friends had been trying to do. The extensive farm properties in California were about to start producing after years of buildup, and while control of the operation was temporarily vested in the McCarthy brothers under a management contract, it was obvious that these properties had great potential value. It would take several years to sell, reorganize, recapitalize, or dispose of all the various parts of Valhi, but in the end what had cost $8 million to buy (and another $12 million to secure the remainder of the stock from the other stockholders) was going to pay back over $100 million. That value wasn't reflected in Contran's stock price yet, but it would come, and Ling had noticed.

There were other deals in progress, of course, some of them involving Jim Ling's advice and counsel, but as 1977 came to a close, Harold was becoming uneasy about relying on Ling.

"I'm telling you, Harold," Ling said one morning before a critical meeting, "that isn't going to be a problem."

"How can you say that, Jim?" Harold asked.

"Because I know this guy and I know the situation and I absolutely guarantee you he won't go off in the wrong direction. Just follow my advice and he'll fall right into our hands."

When the meeting was over and the man Jim Ling had promised would make a decision favorable to Contran had done precisely the opposite, Harold confronted Ling.

"Jim, you stood there and told me ... no, you *guaranteed* me ... that he'd agree with us."

"Well, he *should* have agreed with us," Ling said indignantly.

"What do you mean, 'should have agreed'?" Harold asked.

Jim Ling got to his feet and paced Harold's office in an agitated state. "What I told you was exactly right, Harold. He would have agreed with us if he'd done the right thing. He should have agreed with us. I told you precisely the right thing."

"But, Jim, it didn't work. Why did you guarantee me it would work if you weren't sure?"

"Well, hell, I can't be responsible for someone doing something illogical."

It was, Harold later told Glenn, as if Jim Ling couldn't see reality the same way the rest of the world viewed it.

"Was he lying to you?" Glenn asked.

"No, I don't think so. I think he really believes what he says, even when it's obvious he's changing the story from telling to telling."

"He sees what he wants to see, in other words."

"No, he tries to make everyone else see exactly what he wants them to see. He's a master salesman, Glenn. You know what he said to me last year? He said, 'Look, when I talk to one guy, I'll put on one hat and tell him what he needs to hear to get the deal done, and then I'll go see someone else and put on another hat to get him to do what I want him to do. So I just change with the circumstances.'"

CHAPTER 34

DALLAS, TEXAS: 1978

*L*anny Martin was in Dover, Delaware, working on the settlement of a complicated case Contran had filed during another acquisition attempt, when he received a note to call Harold Simmons in Dallas.

"What's up, Harold?" Lanny asked when he found a phone and made the connection.

"Well, you remember that Jim Ling's contract was up last week and I told him I wasn't going to renew it?"

"Yes."

"Lanny, you won't believe what he's pulled."

A kaleidoscope of strange scenarios flashed across Lanny Martin's mind in the space of a heartbeat. Even the name "Ling" carried a small electric charge, a mixed jolt of caution and distrust. Lanny had lost count of the times over the previous two years that he'd discovered a major flaw in one of Jim Ling's glib recommendations. The response from Ling was usually the same: rolled eyes and the unappreciated title of the "Ayatollah Martin" for being, in Ling's view, too stern, too disapproving, and far, far too conservative.

"Ling and his lawyer just came in my office," Harold began, "to notify us that he's going to be making a run at us."

"I'm sorry, *what?*"

"Ling's going to make a tender offer for Contran, and he said he hopes 'I'll just sell him the company.' He's going to tender to our shareholders at thirty-five a share to try to buy control. I own thirty-five per-cent, for heaven's sake! I can't believe he's dumb enough to think he can get control when we own that much. A lot of the rest of the stock is with friends of mine. There's no way they'd vote with him. This is typical Ling. You know, overlook the details that'll kill you."

Lanny flew back to Dallas the next morning with a small knot in his stomach. In his few years around Harold Simmons, he knew Harold had a propensity to sometimes initially underestimate external threats. It was Harold's way of guarding against overreactions and hasty deci-sions, but the soothing words Harold would utter when some new cor-porate torpedo hit the water were not always the best assessment of the threat. And in this case, Harold's having anything less than 51 percent voting control—or outright ownership—gave Ling a chance of success.

But Harold was right, too, about Ling's fatal flaw: his ability to con-veniently ignore vital details. Highlighting the holes in Ling's reason-ing on some deal or other was all too familiar a task, and one that had sometimes ended with Lanny making a trek to Harold's office to brief him on precisely why Ling's assessment was off target.

Yet, Ling's advice during his two-year stint had not always been worthless to Harold and Contran, and Ling, better than most, had learned how much value Harold had already built into his growing company. In particular, the Omega-Alpha bond purchase had proven an excellent investment. Although picked up at thirty cents on the dol-lar, when the smoke had cleared from the Omega-Alpha bankruptcy process and the known assets of the conglomerate were evaluated, it was obvious the bonds would be worth at least their face value, either in direct payments or in the distribution of assets, reaping an eventual profit of over 300 percent.

But the fact remained that Jim Ling had been privy to the inner de-tails of Contran and Harold Simmons' strategic and tactical plans. In the view of Harold's people, Ling's run at Contran was, at the very least, an egregious breach of faith.

"I cannot believe the audacity of the man!" Lanny had told one of his law partners by phone before he left Delaware. "Ling came hat in hand to Harold two years ago, and Harold bailed him out, gave him a great salary for only half-time work, loaned him a lot of money, helped him buy some of the Omega-Alpha bonds, even helped him buy a house, treating him like an honorable, trusted insider. Now he's trying to use all the inside information he's gathered to buy Harold's company? Unbelievable! He's convinced his partners that Contran is worth a hundred dollars a share even though it's only trading for twenty. His initial offer is for thirty-five a share, and you know he's going to up that, so the loyalty of our friends had better be iron-clad."

Convinced that Ling had a remote chance of success, Harold put Contran on a wartime footing and began moving to shore up his voting control, calling friends who held significant numbers of shares as he made his own purchases to counter Ling's.

"Absolutely I'll stand with you, Harold," one acquaintance from Fort Worth reassured him. Six days later the same individual quietly abandoned his pledge and sold his critical five percent stake in Contran stock to Jim Ling and Danco, the new company formed by Ling to wage the takeover battle.

Within a month, Danco was filing lawsuits at a frightening rate as they shopped for the most favorable courts in various parts of the country— some in state court, some in federal court, all of them seeking to tie Harold's hands from buying, or voting any shares. Thirteen suits were in progress by late spring, an onslaught which kept Fred Bartlit and dozens of the Kirkland and Ellis lawyers busy. The scope of the threat was beginning to become clear.

"If Ling succeeds," Lanny explained to Harold's secretary one afternoon while waiting for a meeting, "what he'll do is sell off the different companies Contran controls, then make it *his* personal investment company to pick up where Omega-Alpha left off."

Once again a small army of Kirkland and Ellis lawyers migrated to Dallas from Chicago, and once again Harold's apartment became the unofficial bunkhouse.

The battle with Ling accelerated, raging back and forth through court actions and shifting strategies, as injunctions were granted one minute, only to be dissolved within days or hours by higher courts. As Contran's legal bills climbed and the legal battle oscillated around a draw, Ling's forces were working overtime to find ways to entice more stock into their voting control. For all the men and women fighting the battle on both sides, the overt rules of the game were all too obvious: When the appropriate moment came and all the stockholders were asked to vote at the rate of one vote per share, whoever gathered more than 50 percent of the votes won the battle and took over the company.

No one had to sell stock to do so, just vote the shares for Harold or for Ling's side.

Prior to starting his quest for Contran, Ling had purchased a convertible note held by a local insurance company. The note could be converted into ten percent of the company stock. Ling was working hard to find ways to control a majority of the shares, whether by owning them outright or by having a proxy fight—a battle for signed authorizations from the shareholders giving the holder of the proxy the right to vote in his or her place. Ling's group purchased the convertible note immediately, adding more control to his portfolio, which, despite the uphill battle of having to go from a 27 percent ownership to 51 percent, was increasing. In spite of all Ling's efforts to get control of the stock, he realized he wasn't succeeding, and raised his tender offer price to $50 per share.

It was obvious Harold needed more stock to counter Ling's efforts, and the most logical purchaser under his complete control was Flight Proficiency. The company quickly took out a loan of $1 million and used the money to buy Contran shares with the intent to vote those shares in favor of Harold Simmons' management team. The move would spark yet another Ling lawsuit, but the extra votes would be critical to Harold in the upcoming proxy contest.

By midsummer the battle had taken a toll on Contran and Harold, diverting his attention from most other pending deals and investments and catching the imagination of the business press, which was enthralled by the image of a fallen master titan trying to wrest control of a younger titan's own corporate empire from his grasp. The fact that Elvis Presley's ex-wife, Priscilla Presley, was one of the Ling investors made the story even more colorful.

In early July, Harold had firm control of 43.6 percent of his company, while Danco claimed control of 41.2 percent and confidently crowed to the *Dallas Morning News* and *Wall Street Journal* that it would easily secure the rest.

Contran stock, however, was not flowing into the Danco camp, despite the pricey $50-per-share offer. By late July it became inescapably apparent to Jim Ling and his investors that they had lost the battle. When the ballots in the proxy contest were cast, Ling and Danco were no shows, failing even to cast their own ballots. There was no point.

Harold, in the meantime, collected more than 50 percent of the votes, and the battle was over.

The day after the end of the proxy contest, some of the Danco investors appeared in Harold's office offering to sell the Contran stock they'd amassed for $50 per share now that there was no hope of getting control.

"Well, you know what, fellows?" Harold said. "You can just keep that stock forever, because I'm not interested." After letting the Danco investors twist in the wind for a few weeks, he decided to offer a buyout at the original tender price of $35 per share, a move that would all but take the company private. In return for buying back all the Contran shares still held by Danco, Ling's company agreed to drop all of the fourteen lawsuits they had ignited around the country. Ling also agreed to drop his desperate post-proxy lawsuit seeking to invalidate the shares voted by Flight Proficiency.

The victory called for a celebration dinner. Old Warsaw, a superb restaurant in near North Dallas, was becoming a favorite place for such a celebration, and on September 7, 1978—the day the *Dallas Morning News* and *Dallas Times Herald* announced Ling's latest failure—a smiling, relaxed, and expansive Harold Simmons sat with his brother Glenn, Lanny Martin, and many of the executive and legal team to raise a few glasses of wine to the win.

The decks were clear once again to resume the business of doing what Harold did best: find the hidden values in companies others had missed, and he was anxious to get back to work.

■　　■　　■

Sandra had reined in her lawyers for the time being, but many believed that the reason for the delay had less to do with Sandra trying to make up her mind whether or not to divorce Harold than it had to do with the possibility of finding a way to defeat the family trust.

Texas was one of the nation's most ardent advocates of marital community property, the civil law concept that any assets (other than gifts of money or property or an inheritance) brought into the "marital community" during a marriage belong equally to both husband and wife on a fifty-fifty basis. But both Harold and Sandra had agreed in writing that all money and assets they earned or acquired over the years through their companies (with a few exceptions) would become the property of the trust. Without a trust, half of everything Contran was worth would belong to Sandra. But as long as the trust owned Contran, Sandra could make no claim on its multimillion-dollar assets, all of which were essentially being held and preserved for the benefit of the four girls. And as long as Harold was the trustee with complete authority to determine who received a salary from the trust, leaving the marriage meant leaving the beneficial umbrella of the trust.

Therefore, the only way out of the marriage with any substantial funds required finding a way to declare the trust invalid, which would then make the money and stock within it community property, half of which would be Sandra's. Other than the massive assets locked in the trust, there was little community property left to be divided. While Sandra's lawyers claimed that a terrible injustice had been done, the original reason for creating the trust had been to protect them *as a family* with no thought to a future divorce. And Sandra herself had signed the trust instruments of her own free will.

"Harold, Sandra's lawyers are going to find a way to allege that you never told her what the trust instrument contained, or what it meant," one of the attorneys advised Harold. "She may even develop selective amnesia and testify that she never signed it."

"But, we can disprove that, right? Because that *is* Sandra's signature on the paper creating the trust, and it *was* explained to her, by our lawyer as well as me."

"We can probably get a handwriting expert to confirm the signature."

"What else?"

"Well, you need to decide whether we fight for custody of Andrea and Serena, or let Sandra have them."

"Yes, we fight for custody. I'm a better dad than she is a mother, with all her time away from home."

"That's it?"

"Nothing else to consider," Harold replied sadly, his mind wandering to the unwelcome solitude of the apartment and the difficulty of maintaining frequent contact with Serena and Andrea.

He hadn't wanted the divorce, but Sandra did, so now that it was to be a fait accompli, it was time he let go of it emotionally. Despite the scars, there were other women out there. Perhaps someday he'd find the right one, a woman who would strike the right balance—the girl he should have found the first time around.

BOOK SEVEN

The World through Different Eyes

CHAPTER 35

TEXAS STADIUM, IRVING, TEXAS: 1978

*A*nnette Fleck smiled at her host as he handed her a Coke from the bar of the sumptuous Texas Stadium skybox.

"Why, thank you!"

A surge of noise from the crowded stadium rolled over them for a second, blocking his response as the Cowboys completed a spectacular pass play on the gridiron below. When the roar of 60,000 approving fans had subsided, a male voice could be heard from the direction of the corridor outside.

"Hey, Blake. Someone's here with a phone message for you from his box down the hall."

Blake waved an acknowledgment and got to his feet as Annette turned around to look, spotting a familiar figure in the doorway of the Skybox.

It's Harold Simmons! she thought.

She remembered how her husband and his friends had always spoken of Harold Simmons with awe. "The guy's incredible," they'd say. "He can look at a balance sheet and tell you in sixty seconds whether a company's doing well or not."

"Smartest guy I've ever met."

"A real genius."

Harold delivered the phone number and was preparing to leave when Annette stood and caught his eye. She waved then, approaching him with a smile, and noticing how he smiled back.

"Why, Harold!" she said. "How *are* you? It's been a long time."

His smile broadened. "Yeah, it sure has, Annette." *She's even more beautiful than I remember,* he thought. "How's Larry?"

"He's fine, I suppose, but we divorced about five years ago."

"Oh. I'm sorry to hear that," he replied.

That same lovely voice, Annette thought to herself. *I remember his East Texas accent. Just like mine, but more distinctive.*

"It's good to see you," she continued. "What have you been doing with yourself lately?" She had heard he was separated again, perhaps for the third time, and the incongruous mental image of Harold Simmons with Sandra Simmons returned, as she remembered seeing them at one of the breakfast club evening parties so many years ago, back when all Harold owned was a single drugstore.

Wait. Hadn't he asked her to dance that one time? Yes, he had, she recalled. And the invitation had shocked her, since he was obviously not a very outgoing man. A consummate gentleman, certainly, a good dancer, and cute—but shy in a way that had interested her as much as his marital choice of Sandra perplexed her. She'd heard stories about Sandra's exploits, as well as her flying, and it had been no surprise in the early seventies to hear rumors that the marriage was in deep trouble.

Another memory competed for her attention as she studied his face: an evening of poker years back with her then-husband and seven others from the breakfast club. Before that get-together she hadn't known that Harold Simmons even had a sense of humor, but he'd made her laugh that night and she'd found him to be quite charming.

All the other wives had been a bit intrigued by him, too. Perhaps it was because their husbands held him in such esteem. Or perhaps it was his reserve, which seemed to obscure a deeper, more interesting personality. An aura of mystery surrounded him.

And now he was here, talking easily, pleasantly, catching up on the previous decade.

"You have a few minutes to come see *my* Skybox?" Harold asked.

"I didn't know you had one," Annette replied.

"Yeah, about three doors down. You sure look beautiful, Annette," Harold said.

"Why, thank you, Harold."

"What are *you* doing these days?" he asked her as they walked slowly down the passageway.

"Interior decorating, mainly, and I'm really enjoying it."

A cacophonous roar of vocal support for something the Cowboys had just done on the gridiron below all but shook the stadium, but neither was paying attention.

"You have your own decorating firm?"

"No, not really. I work with several furniture stores on a commission basis. I like doing this kind of work for friends, and it's kept the kids and me comfortable."

"You've got how many?" he asked.

"Two. A girl and a boy. Amy's fifteen, and Andy is nineteen."

"Sounds like you have a good life."

"Most days, yes." She paused, watching his smile. "I was very glad to hear that you won that battle against Ling." She'd followed the newspaper reports of Ling's unsuccessful attempt to take over Harold's company, and she knew through friends just how dark a betrayal it had been.

"We were rather pleased to beat Ling, too," he chuckled. "Otherwise I might be out here with a paper hat selling peanuts and hot dogs."

"Somehow, I seriously doubt that, Harold. Owning the company that *hires* the people who sell peanuts and hot dogs, maybe."

"Say . . ." Harold began, pausing in midthought.

"Yes?" she replied, cocking her head ever so slightly.

"Well, I was just wondering if you'd like to go out to dinner with me sometime."

A kaleidoscopic range of thoughts crossed her mind, culminating with an image of Sandra, who—separated or not—was still his wife and in the process of waging a bitter battle in her divorce action. Without thinking further, she answered quietly, "When you get your house in order, Harold, I'd love to."

After the game was over, Harold climbed behind the wheel of his Cadillac and paused for a few seconds to pull out and re-read the card with Annette's number on it—an act, he told himself, that was good executive discipline. That was all. He would have his secretary enter it in the Rolodex that next day.

He started to put the card away, then stopped to look at it again. It was an insignificant gesture, but silent evidence that somewhere in

the recesses of his psyche, a small, distant ember of possibility was beginning to glow.

When he had his house in order, she'd said. But when would that be?

The irretrievable finality of the break with Sandra suddenly came
in focus, as if he'd never seen it clearly before. He hesitated, then put
Annette's card carefully in his pocket and started the car.

Maybe, Harold thought, *it already is in order.*

■   ■   ■

The call took Annette by surprise. She had assumed the divorce
from Sandra would take much more time. Perhaps years. But suddenly
Harold had invited her to dinner.

So, it's all over now with Sandra, Annette thought. *Good.*

Five years had passed since she'd made her own break from her
marriage of twenty years.

"We were awfully young when we married," she explained to
Harold. "You know, college sweethearts. He felt it was time to get married and I thought all girls should be married by age twenty-one, and
there we were."

Annette returned from their first dinner together feeling an odd
mix of anticipation and excitement. He was fun to be with, she concluded, and she could tell there was far, far more to Harold Simmons
than anyone else seemed to notice. Perhaps it was feminine conceit, or
maybe the subtle signals he'd sent in being so open with her, but she
expected him to call again.

And he did. Promptly.

"If you don't mind," he said on the phone, "I've got a good friend
in town, one of my principal lawyers named Lanny Martin, and I'd like
to bring him along rather than just let him forage for himself tonight."

"Wonderful," Annette replied. "I'm looking forward to meeting
him. Where are we going?"

"Well," he answered, hesitating, "I'm kind of fond of a little place
called the Vineyard."

"That's perfect," she replied, slightly unsure of why a lawyer named
Lanny Martin was going to essentially chaperone them on their second
date. There were several possibilities, some of them as funny as they

were unlikely. She had no way of knowing that Harold, armed with her approval, was now calling Lanny to issue the same invitation.

"Now, Lanny," Harold was telling him by phone, "there's this wonderful woman I've met, and I'd like you to meet her, and join us for dinner tonight."

Lanny Martin treasured the fact that Harold had become his close friend as well as his best client. And he knew Harold well enough to know that his involuntary loneliness needed to end.

"That's great, Harold," Lanny said, acknowledging the pickup time.

"She has a townhouse not far from here," Harold explained, when Lanny met him at the front door of the hotel and climbed in. Harold spun a quick narration of where they'd met over the years, and the serendipitous encounter at Texas Stadium, finishing the story just as he turned into her parking lot.

Annette was stunning, Lanny thought, as they took their seats at the Vineyard and began perusing the menus.

"Do you like wine, Annette?" Harold asked.

"Yes, I do. Well, I mean, I'm not a connoisseur of fine wines or anything like that, but every now and then I try different wines."

"Well, what kind of wine is your favorite?" Harold asked, as they balanced menus and wine lists.

She smiled broadly. "Since I see it here, I'll tell you. I've fallen in love with a little California wine called San Martin. It's really wonderful. One of my friends knows quite a bit about wines, and San Martin is what he serves."

Lanny kept his expression neutral as he watched a big smile slowly capture Harold's face.

"Well, I think San Martin is just about the best wine around," Harold affirmed with a bit too much enthusiasm.

"You *know* that wine?" Annette asked, slightly puzzled at his reaction.

"I *own* that vineyard," he said. "I own the San Martin Winery that makes it."

"You ... own the winery?"

"Yes, I do."

"The ... San Martin Winery in California?"

"That's the one. I bought it a couple of years ago when I acquired a company called Valhi."

"I see." *We've hardly gotten here,* Annette thought, trying to keep an even expression, *and already he's trying to impress me with wild stories!*

The realization some time later that Harold Simmons really *did* own the San Martin Winery was even more confusing, but happily so. Harold was a man of substance, a man who built things steadily over time.

We're only dating, Annette cautioned herself. *This is just exploratory.*

But there was a basic recognition she couldn't ignore: She truly enjoyed being around him, and that, in itself, was a rare pleasure. She refused to conjecture beyond that point.

CHAPTER 36

DALLAS, TEXAS: 1979

"*L*anny? This is Harold."
          The distinctive voice on the other end of the phone had a tone of enthusiasm Lanny Martin well recognized. Harold had found another undervalued company.

"You know anything about an airline out in California named PSA?"

"No, but I have the distinct feeling," Lanny replied with a chuckle, "that I'm about to."

PSA and Southwest were cut from the same philosophy: high-speed intercity transportation using aircraft instead of buses or trains, and beginning with service only to high-density markets within a single state.

California, in PSA's case.

The young air carrier had been successful at first but had made the mistake of diversifying into hotels, radio stations, and rental car companies—all of which were unsuccessful. Most of these other businesses had already been sold or shut down, except for a small, money-losing hotel venture.

The effects of heavy-handed state regulation of fares by the California Public Utilities Commission had locked PSA into a set of velvet handcuffs. Although guaranteed a small profit by the commission's rate setting, the profit was insufficient to support new growth.

In California, with the double whammy of fare controls and badly performing subsidiary companies run by an unimpressive management, PSA's stock was in the cellar—which is where Harold found it.

"We know what their jets are worth," Harold explained to his key people, who now included a financial vice president named Mike Snetzer. "Those are Boeing 727 two hundreds, which is just about the most popular airliner out there, and they own most of their fleet outright. They've got almost no debt and a great cash position. You figure their twenty-six 727s at six million apiece and total up the rest of the assets, and PSA's clearly worth two to three times what the stock's selling for. Also under the new airline deregulation act of 1978, I think there will be a wave of large airlines acquiring small ones like PSA. Any way you cut it, it's a low-risk investment."

Contran began quietly purchasing PSA stock on the open market, raising its stake to just over 20 percent for just under $13 million. As the news—and the requisite SEC disclosures—hit PSA headquarters, the team at Contran braced for the inevitable broadside.

The reaction wasn't long in coming. In the Los Angeles headquarters of PSA, the frightening news that a Texas financier named Harold Simmons—a man with a history of taking over undervalued companies—had purchased 20 percent of *their* company caused an immediate panic. After all, PSA was a *California* airline, and no such creation should be owned by a Texan, or for that matter by anyone who might take management jobs away.

Following the script of endangered management everywhere, the lights began burning into the night at PSA's headquarters as its leaders raced to build an anti-takeover defense system on the spur of the moment. The age of mature and effective corporate defense systems had yet to arrive, along with a device the business press would later dub "poison pill amendments," which were catastrophic provisions (also called "porcupine amendments") planted in the corporate bylaws of public companies that would cause ruinous things to happen to the stock values of any would-be purchaser who dared amass stock without management's permission. But in 1979, there were few tried and true defenses, and PSA's version required a special stockholders' meeting to enact a revision to the bylaws.

Once again Harold assembled Lanny Martin and the Kirkland and Ellis forces, this time launching them to San Diego. Instead of waging a fight for outright control of PSA, Contran decided to stage a proxy contest on the question of whether PSA's porcupine amendments should be enacted, and Harold intended to win.

PSA countered with a public relations campaign specifically designed to vilify the "raider" from Dallas and build both fear and loyalty among its shareholders. The campaign sparked corporately xenophobic articles in local papers and coined the epithet "Texas Gunslinger" to falsely paint Harold as a ruthless destroyer of corporations and jobs.

"Gunslinger?" Harold asked incredulously when informed of the title. "What guns am I supposed to be slinging? That's about the dumbest thing I've heard yet." However, PSA had forged the perfect bone to throw to the media, a juicy reference which fit perfectly into headlines: "Texas Gunslinger Simmons in showdown with PSA."

Despite the invective, a significant number of shareholders took Contran's position seriously. Those who did their homework soon realized that Harold had a positive track record of building companies, and no history of buying just to liquidate ongoing operations, and that realization led a significant number of stockholders to conclude that Harold Simmons intended to make the company more valuable by concentrating on the possibilities deregulation provided. Besides, the upcoming proxy fight was not over control of the board but over implementation of the amendments which would discourage a merger or acquisition.

As the date for the pivotal stockholder meeting and the end of the proxy voting approached, Contran's campaign seemed headed for a tight win.

And that called for last-ditch action at PSA. Management could read the vote trend as well. They had one chance, and that was to suddenly postpone the stockholder meeting at which the final showdown was supposed to occur.

The move apparently gave them just enough time. Within a month, a block of stockholder "votes" suddenly materialized which put PSA management over the top against Contran. With PSA unable to give a satisfactory answer about where the new block of votes had come from, or why they should be treated as valid, Contran sued for illegal manipulation of the election.

CHAPTER 37

DALLAS, TEXAS: 1979

*A*nnette had spent the previous three hours absorbed in cata-
logs and sample books, trying to find the right combination of
colors, furniture, rugs, and drapes for a client. She was standing at her
kitchen counter trying to visualize yet another ensemble when the
phone rang, the bell almost failing to crack through her concentration.

She picked it up almost absently. "Hello?"

"Annette, this is Harold. What would you like to do that you've
never done before?"

Annette straightened up and tried to focus on the unexpected
question.

"I beg your pardon?"

"Remember when we were having dinner several weeks ago and we
were talking about what we wanted to do?"

"I ... guess so." She closed one of the sample books and rested her
hand on the counter.

"Okay," Harold replied, a chuckle in his voice. "Well, what haven't
you done that you'd like to do?"

Annette shook her head, the palm of her left hand held aloft.

"Have you ever been to the dog races in Juarez?"

She shifted the phone to her other ear and sat down.

"No," she said, carefully, "I've been to the horse races, once, but no
dog races."

"Well, let's go."

"When?"

"Today. We can hop in my plane and get out to El Paso in an hour and a half and be back tomorrow."

A flurry of images filled her head like a sudden explosion of cotton. She had work to do, but she hadn't heard from him in a week, and the work could wait. Couldn't it? But he'd said they would return tomorrow, which meant overnight, which meant . . .

"Harold, I'm not sure I—"

"I'm not going to take no for an answer, Annette."

There was a pause as she ran through the possibilities, deciding what to do.

"Okay," she said.

"Good. I'll be by to pick you up at two o'clock."

She toggled the phone and almost instantly dialed one of her best friends, Sandra Tucker.

"So I'm going to El Paso with him, and I want you to know, because I'm not telling anyone else, and someone needs to know where I am."

"Annette!"

"I'm not even telling Amy or Andy until I get back. They're with their father tonight."

"What are you going to El Paso for?" the friend asked.

"Dog races," Annette said.

"Okay, but why?"

"Why? Because . . . I've never seen dogs race."

■　　■　　■

Annette had already let herself get excited over the spontaneity of the sudden trip when Harold added another shock.

"Just climb in the right seat there," he said when they arrived at the aircraft. She realized he was pointing to the cockpit of the Cessna Citation.

"The copilot's seat? But where's the copilot?"

"I don't need one on this airplane. I can fly it by myself."

"Oh."

"So, you're going to be my copilot."

"Okay. What do I have to do?"

Harold laughed, more easily, he thought, than he had in a long time. "Just sit there and look beautiful and enjoy the view."

The flight was exhilarating, from the rush of the takeoff and the expansive view from the Citation's wide cockpit windows to the thrill of watching him handle the machine so effortlessly, setting it down smoothly at El Paso's international airport.

The dog races, she discovered, were not what she'd expected, nor was the crowd at the racetrack. The people around her were far more focused on the betting than the fun of the various races, and even though she'd seen the same behavior among horseracing patrons, it was different somehow.

But definitely fun. Just being in Harold's company was fun.

They'd talked all the way to the racetrack and all the way back to the hotel in a running conversation of shared goals and dreams and ideas.

Harold returned from the front desk of the hotel. "Here's the key to your room, Annette," he said, reading the room number off the metal tag, "and I'm down the corridor a ways. What time would you like to meet for breakfast?"

■　　■　　■

By midspring, 1979, Annette's picture had appeared in a small frame on the desk of Harold's North Dallas office. They were seeing each other regularly, to the delight of their friends, who were already spending a lot of time discussing how right Annette was for Harold, and vice versa.

The effect Annette had on Harold was obvious. His excitement at new ideas and potential deals, his understated sense of humor, and his overall zest for life (that had been dampened by the deteriorated relationship with Sandra) were all back in spades. Even though the divorce battle continued and included a bitterly contested fight over the custody of Serena and Andrea, Harold's horizons had brightened and broadened with the arrival of Annette in his life.

And if Annette was a tonic for him personally, the tonic was equally good for Contran. The timing, in fact, was perfect.

The tempo of activity and the excitement at Contran was building, even as the chairman himself retained the same ordered and focused style of doing business. The heart of what he did best, Harold knew, was quiet study of balance sheets and corporate reports that would have numbed most people into a coma. But from such documents he could divine with increasing accuracy and sophistication truths about company assets that even the sitting management might not know.

Wall Street as a community seemed increasingly oblivious to the core values of American public corporations. Something was changing in the psyche of the American investor, led by stock market analysts, investment bankers and advisors, and the managers of mutual funds. Corporate dividend payments to shareholders—the traditional heart and soul of corporate performance—seemed not to matter. The potential for consistent future growth became a more important concern than the amount and consistency of paying a dividend from a corporation's stable earnings.

As he did with PSA, Harold found undervalued companies all over the map, although not all of them were desirable investments or takeover targets. But in addition to the eternal search for new companies, Contran was becoming very sophisticated in its equally important function of managing the investments it had already made. Valhi, for instance, had yielded a never-ending string of surprises, some of them worrisome. But with the sale of the more troublesome California properties and the sorting out of the Louisiana land and oil holdings, Valhi's components were yielding more and more cash.

In addition to the ongoing battles which were becoming both common and expected, new investment possibilities seemed to emerge literally every week, many of them failing Harold's initial examination of their financial profile, though just as many passed.

Interesting patterns were emerging from Harold's tireless research, including a tendency for the more basic and unexciting industries to produce the more attractive investment opportunities. It wasn't exactly an axiom, but it was becoming obvious that Wall Street was least likely to discover a corporate bargain when that bargain company was engaged in some nonglamourous industry.

Following Harold's PSA investment, and even while Contran's $13 million stake was tied up in court, he spotted the substantially undervalued stock of Ozark Airlines of St. Louis, which was similarly well positioned as a takeover target. Acting quickly, Harold directed Contran's broker to buy ten percent of Ozark's stock on the open market.

Once again a sitting management overreacted. Ozark's leaders openly threatened him, declaring that if Contran bought a single, additional share of the company, Ozark would start a legal war that would be large and costly. The utter absence of any substantive grounds for such a threat was apparently irrelevant to Ozark's leaders, yet the intensity of the reaction from St. Louis meant that moving from a relatively small investment position to any greater degree of ownership would undoubtedly spark a very intense and expensive legal battle at a time when the PSA fight was still in progress.

It wasn't worth it, Harold decided. He knew Ozark was a good takeover target—an airline quite dissimilar to PSA, but one whose fleet was worth more than the total price of its outstanding stock by quite a margin. However, picking the right fight for the right reason was as important as finding the right target, and Ozark was not worth the battle.

Harold had expected Ozark to be gobbled up by a larger airline rapidly, but as the months went by following his stock purchases, nothing was happening. The regional carrier had not turned a profit in two years and had taken two employee strikes in the previous eight months.

But suddenly the pressures of deregulation began to buoy Ozark's stock, and the price started rising. While foregoing any more purchases and making no attempt to influence management, Harold hung on to his 9.9 percent, biding his time.

Day after day, week after week, the happy whirl of activity kept Harold completely engaged during the day as his growing relationship with Annette made it all worthwhile on a different level. With Sandra effectively gone from his life, two of his daughters grown, and the younger two growing fast and predictably unaware that their father was so unusually successful, there had been something substantial missing from his daily existence: someone to cheer him on. It wasn't that the people of Contran who were serving him so well didn't count as an extended family who appreciated and reveled in his successes. They meant more to Harold than he would ever admit, as he proved constantly in *his* loyalty and generosity to them.

But the missing element was akin to the plight of a successful musician who nonetheless has no one at home to applaud him and appreciate the magnitude of his achievements. Sandra had rejected that role. Penny, before her, had been incapable of understanding that role.

But Annette!

Here was a woman—a cultured, beautiful, exciting, educated woman. A graduate of SMU. Not only had she been selected once of the top ten beauties on campus each year she was there, she was also the ROTC Sweetheart, a member of Kappa Alpha Theta, and a woman of substance as well as a woman of faith. She wasn't afraid of work, and had supported her two children.

They were only dating, but he could feel her understanding and appreciation of what he could do, and what he had done. Not the money. It had never been the money that drove him, or impressed her. Money was merely a barometer of how well he was doing. No, he already knew what was important and what mattered, and that there could be no one in the world more perfect for him. What more could he ask than for Annette to be by his side while he pursued his dreams?

And into the portal of his heart opened by that knowledge flowed the beginnings of a trust that he feared was lost.

CHAPTER 38

LOS ANGELES, CALIFORNIA: 1980

*T*he PSA litigation was moving slowly. Clearly, PSA's leaders had tried to rig the proxy contest by manufacturing votes at the last minute, but PSA's legal team was having success at delaying a trial to determine the accurate results.

It was obvious to PSA that the litigation was further hurting their stock price and diverting the company from the recovery steps it should be taking, and there was a stern warning from their legal team that Harold Simmons could end up winning regardless of what they did.

Suddenly, the climate seemed ripe for settlement.

"We'll buy back your stock, Mr. Simmons," PSA's leaders finally offered, "but we'd like you to take your payment in hard assets instead of cash."

The wholly owned fleet of Boeing 727s were on the table as Harold and Lanny and two others flew a Contran jet to Los Angeles to take a closer look.

"I'll take some of your aircraft in exchange for the stock," Harold offered.

PSA's men exchanged glances and looked back at Harold. "Well, we'll trade you three 727s."

"Not enough."

"Well, we have another property that's really got a lot of promise and value, and we'll include that as well."

"What is it?"

"Three Boeing 727s and the *Queen Mary*."

"Excuse me?" Lanny had said.

"The *Queen Mary*. In Long Beach. The grand old Cunard liner. You know, she's known all over the world. Carried queens and kings and presidents, went through World War Two as a troop ship. Great history. She's a hotel now right here in Long Beach, and we own her."

Harold had glanced at Lanny and raised an eyebrow before looking back at them. "Okay, we'd better have you take us out there and show it to us," Harold said.

But no one moved. It was obvious that none of the leaders of PSA arrayed around the table wanted to make the trek to Long Beach. The day was cloudy and rainy, with thunderstorms marching across the L.A. basin, but there were other reasons. Perhaps a contributing reason was their reluctance to be in the company of the detested man they had tried to label a "Texas Gunslinger," or perhaps—as Harold opined later—the real explanation was the embarrassment of having to show off the old, retired ocean liner, which they knew was threadbare and too poorly turned out to really be a successful hotel.

"Okay, tell me how to find it and I'll drive out there myself."

Armed with directions, Harold drove the thirty miles through bumper-to-bumper Los Angeles freeway traffic and out to the special quay constructed to be the final floating place of the once-proud, retired flagship of the London-based Cunard Line.

They're trying to sell this thing to me and they can't even provide a free admission ticket! Harold thought with a chuckle as he parked and braved a downpour to board the ship.

The *Queen Mary* was being advertised and used as a grand hotel, but to a minor extent it was also being held out as a tourist attraction—the physical embodiment of luxurious ocean travel—and people were charged a fee to come aboard. Yet the grand furnishings that had made the *Queen* an opulent floating palace were long gone. The carpets, the elaborate chandeliers, the gold and silver doorknobs and accessories, and the hand-turned furniture had long since been carted away, leaving a tawdry, barely floating shadow of what the ship had been. The exterior was in need of paint and deep maintenance, and the interior was simply depressing.

From a phone booth, Harold placed a call to Annette.

"You interested in owning the *Queen Mary?*" he asked, listening carefully to her cautious reply.

"The *Queen Mary?*"

"Right."

"The ship?"

"That's right," he said, filling her in on the details. "So, do you think I should buy it?"

"Well, only if *you* do, Harold. I mean, it could be fun to be able to tell your friends you own the *Queen Mary*, but you have to decide if it makes sense."

"Well, you're right, and it really doesn't. Make sense, that is."

■   ■   ■

"That ... was an experience," Harold reported a few hours later as he met his team for dinner at Le Orangery Restaurant and began giving a wide-eyed description of his self-guided tour. "I asked to see a stateroom, and the guy behind what passes as a front desk looks up like a deer in the headlights and says, 'A what?' I said, a stateroom, you know, like they used to have on big ships. Like, for instance, the *Queen Mary.*"

"Is all the staff that poorly trained?" one of them asked.

"He *was* the staff. At least as far as I could tell. I didn't see anyone else."

The group had started shaking their heads and chuckling at the beginning of Harold's oration, but now each new observation he made was punctuated by several seconds of laughter. The heads of the other patrons increasingly turned in their direction as they strained to hear what on earth the man with the East Texas accent was saying that was so hilarious.

"Anyway, he finally hands me a key and points to a corridor that looks like some sort of passageway in an oil tanker. No carpet. The paint's peeling on the walls."

More laughter.

"And I go down there and open up this broom closet. I mean, the thing was tiny! For instance, the bathroom was so small, you could barely get in it. And it had a shower stall that was so narrow, I figured you'd have to soap up the sides and spin around to get clean."

"So what could we do with it?" Lanny asked.

"Well, let's see," Harold said, feigning deep thought, then smiling and raising an index finger. "Now, we need to put our heads together and really think about this, because there are probably a hundred beneficial uses. For instance ... we could sink it, and sell tickets to see the spot where she went down. That would save on maintenance."

More laughter.

"Or we could tow it back to Europe and make a casino out of it. You know, free admission, but you have to pay to leave."

The others chimed in with even more ludicrous ideas.

The dinner became progressively funnier at the *Queen Mary's* expense as Harold and the team spun wilder and wilder uses for a ship whose usefulness as a PSA bargaining chip was obviously nil.

"I saw your ship yesterday," Harold began the next morning.

"So what'd you think of her?" the PSA men asked cautiously.

"I don't want her," Harold replied. "Instead, I'll take four of your 727s ... *five,* if I ever have to go out there again."

The deal was concluded with Contran taking ownership of the four Boeing 727s, then leasing them back to PSA for eighteen months for $13 million in advance, which covered the cost of the PSA stock. This meant the PSA deal would end up profitable no matter what happened.

CHAPTER 39

DALLAS, TEXAS: 1980

*T*en-year-old Serena Simmons pushed through the front door of her North Dallas home and stopped. It was too chilly, she decided. Better get a coat. She turned and entered the hallway again just as her fourteen-year-old sister Andrea rounded the corner.

"So where are *you* going?" Andrea asked, already aware of the answer.

"I told you," Serena mumbled, dodging a half-hearted glancing blow from Andrea's right fist. "Dad's picking me up. You want to come, too?"

"NO!" Andrea snapped, rolling her eyes. "Why would I want to see a new house? We already have a house."

Serena watched her sister push through the front door and purposefully slam it behind her for emphasis. The news that their father had purchased a new home not too many miles distant had sparked an outburst from Andrea that frightened Serena, but she refused to be intimidated. Her father was excited. He wanted to show it to her, and Serena wanted to please him.

Andrea could just be mad.

Serena moved quietly into the living room and checked the clock. He wasn't due for another twenty minutes, but she wanted to be ready. He was always on time. It had been that way her whole life. When Dad said he'd be there, he was there.

The constant turmoil of the previous months threatened to roil her stomach again, but she tried to suppress the memories of how angry her mother was every time she came home from flying. Andrea got mad right along with her mom, agreeing that Dad was a terrible person, and using bad words that Serena was quite sure a fourteen-year-old shouldn't use.

Serena closed her eyes and tried to imagine what the new house would be like. She loved it when her father got excited about something. He got excited about small things, neat things, like new gadgets and devices, as well as new places. He was always so much fun to be with. Some of her earliest memories flooded back, and she smiled to herself now as she sat primly on the sofa with her eyes closed tight, remembering the wild tales he used to tell as they'd walk through the woods somewhere, or stop suddenly at the side of a road to see some beautiful sight.

"Daddy's full of stories!" Andrea had exclaimed once, the older sister teaching her sibling the basics. "But I don't think they're always exactly true."

"Serena, come here!" her father would say as he motioned her down a leafy trail they were hiking. "See that rock over there?"

"Yes."

"There was an old Indian chief around these parts who used to come here and sit on that rock a hundred or more years ago and just think."

"Really?"

"Really. He was a Comanche. That was his tribe, and they were powerful, scary warriors capable of doing terrible things to their enemies in battle. But the old chief had a daughter just like you that he loved very, very much."

"Like me?"

"Just like you."

And Harold would go on to spin a tale of heartbreak and sadness, then joy and recovery, all of it allegedly occurring right there in front of her, the images coming alive as he talked. He'd adopt voices, gesturing with enthusiasm and a storytelling showmanship that would have astounded those who knew him in the business world.

Serena never cared whether the stories were true or not. She just loved the way he told them, and how they made her feel.

She opened her eyes and checked the clock again. Only three minutes had passed. Her eyes roamed across the living room, taking in the picture of her mother in the Braniff pilot's uniform. She wondered where her mom was right now. In a cockpit somewhere, probably, flying over some distant city. She was proud of her, but mad at her at the same time for being gone so much. So was Andrea, although lately she was just mad at her father. Somehow it seemed more comforting to know her dad was just a short distance away. She could call him anytime from school if there was a problem, and he would come. It would take hours to get a message to her mom. And then, when Mom came home, she and Andrea would fight terribly and Serena would try to hide.

"Serena, honey, where are you?" a woman's voice called from the kitchen.

"In here, Jackie," Serena answered.

Jackie Campbell rounded the corner with a dishtowel in her hand and stood for a second in silence, studying Serena's face with a practiced eye.

Her friends used to be puzzled when they'd see the older woman pick her up at school or drop her off at a girlfriend's house. "Who *is* that, Serena?" they'd ask.

"That's my nanny," Serena would answer—unless she was mad at her mother. Then, sometimes, she'd say Jackie was her mother. Or her grandmother.

Jackie put her hands on her hips, her face taking on the kindly look of concern Serena knew so well. "Are you okay, Serena?"

"Yes!" she said brightly. "Dad will be here in a few minutes."

"Okay." Jackie turned and disappeared into the kitchen. She'd been with them six years now, living at the house most of the time, taking care of them, and they treated her badly sometimes—even calling their mother in some distant layover city when Jackie tried to enforce what were loosely called "the rules." Serena thought about all the times she and Andrea had hurt Jackie's feelings.

Harold believed that Sandra's attempts at disciplining and controlling the girls were far too inconsistent to be effective. Andrea rapidly learned that no rule her mother laid down was absolute, especially if Sandra was confronted with a protest while on the road. "Oh, that's okay, Jackie," she'd say. "I know I said they couldn't do that, but go ahead and let them."

Serena shifted her gaze to another family photo, this one of her half sister Scheryle. She wondered where Scheryle was today. Scheryle seldom came around anymore, and the last time she had, she'd been angry, too, yelling something about not wanting her father's money and not caring about it. Serena had heard the whole thing, and watched in confusion when her dad came in the door an hour later and Scheryle started asking for money as sweetly as ever.

The sound of a car approaching sent her to the window, and an involuntary smile spread across her face as her father's Cadillac pulled into the driveway. As he got out of the car, she leaned toward the glass and waved, then dashed for the door.

"See you later, Jackie!"

"Wear your coat!"

"I am!"

The drive to the new house took only ten minutes, and Serena was leaning forward as they turned into the circular driveway of the stately brick home.

"Wait 'til you see this, Serena. This is so great. Look at how big it is in front! Impressive, huh?"

"Yeah," she said.

He hurried her in the front door and stopped in the expansive foyer with a sweeping staircase climbing from the right to the floors above.

"Isn't this beautiful?" he was saying. "This is a really big deal, Serena. I managed to buy this place for a good price, but it's still over a million dollars. How about that?"

"That's neat."

"Come here. Look here!" He led her quickly down the hallway, pointing out various features, including control panels and electrical appliances, moving too fast for her to really take it all in. He opened the back door and stepped out to the brick patio, pointing out features on the property.

"Well?" he said at one point, turning to watch her expression.

Serena smiled as broadly as she could. "It's sure nice."

"Sure nice, huh? It's better than that! Come on. There's an elevator."

"An *elevator*? In a house?"

"Yep." He pointed the way and opened the door. "Let's ride it up."

"Where does it go, Dad?"

"Second floor."

They turned to go, but out of habit Serena turned back. "Wait, Dad. You forgot to turn out a light."

It was a small gesture, but it gave him hope. He'd always taught her such things. Turn out the lights. Conserve. A wasteful hand will come to want.

It was hours later lying in her bed that Serena remembered the light switch and the smile that had spread across her father's face when she'd turned to snap it off. The memory of the house came back to her just before sleep overcame her resistance. She wished she'd pretended to be more excited for him. It was a pretty house.

■　　■　　■

Annette couldn't recall a particular moment when she realized she had, indeed, fallen in love with Harold Clark Simmons. It was more of a recognition that the milestone was long past, and she was hopelessly committed.

By the middle of 1980, Harold had asked her to marry him.

"Why?" she'd asked.

"Why what?"

"Why do you want to marry me?" She was working to stifle a smile.

"Because you're stable and dependable."

"That's it?"

"No. But it's a good beginning," he said with a smile that told her clearly she was adored.

On June 14, 1980, Harold and Annette were married by an assistant pastor in a parlor of the Highland Park Presbyterian Church. Harold paid the pastor and drove his new bride to Brennan's at One Main Place in downtown Dallas for a sumptuous lunch which doubled as a private reception. Annette's lifelong friend Paul Bass, Harold's brother Glenn and his wife, Dee, John and Patsy Roach, Blake and Sandra Tucker, along with Lawson and Fran Ridgeway, joined them for a honeymoon sendoff as they motored away to DFW airport to board the first-class section of an American Airlines 747 bound for Paris. The office, Harold had decreed, could take care of itself for a few weeks—a declaration Annette had been greatly relieved to hear.

■　　■　　■

Harold had always believed he knew how to relax, but in Annette's opinion, he had a lot more to learn. She was determined to teach him an advanced course in enjoying life, and travel was a good place to begin. She also determined to love him enough to make up the years he had not been loved. Removed from phones, daily stock quotes, hourly market updates, and the quiet but constant drone of business, she knew the honeymoon would be more than a personal shakedown cruise for two lovers. It would also be lesson number-one in the school of broadening horizons that Annette was determined to hold for Harold, and the prime directive of that curriculum was learning to relax and explore and enjoy each other.

While Harold had been to Hong Kong and Tokyo in years past, and had made a quick trip to Europe, this experience was entirely new.

They started with two days in a small suite at the Bristol Hotel, exploring Paris during the day, then heading for the wine country in a rented car and staying in Beaune in the heart of the Burgundy region, where they ate dinner in one of the most impressive restaurants Harold had ever experienced. "The way they served the food was amazing," Harold told Glenn weeks later. "Every dish was a production, brought out with pomp and personal flourish, and I've never seen so much silverware on a table. They changed it with every dish."

The itinerary had been planned so well, the trip felt almost spontaneous. They ended their honeymoon with a self-driving tour of the Bordeaux area using Harold's huge wine encyclopedia full of maps of the area to track down various châteaus. Little more than a week had passed since the wedding, but the smile on her new husband's face as they flew home told Annette what she wanted to know: Beyond just enjoying the honeymoon itself, he'd enjoyed exploring a new area together, and he wanted more of it.

Annette did not set out to transform Harold into someone else. Her quiet mission from early in their relationship was to ease him into the world of friendships and social interaction that had been essentially foreign territory for him. Until their marriage, his world had been defined by work and the necessary relationships and human interactions which went with the world of corporate management and finance.

But learning how to *enjoy* such social interactions was a process he had yet to experience, and she slowly and lovingly began to plot a course that would bring out the Harold Simmons she knew was there: the fascinating, funny, charming man whom so many respected, and so few really knew.

CHAPTER 40

DALLAS, TEXAS: 1980

*A*side from the bragging rights that ownership of four 727s might bring, there was little reason for Harold to do anything but put them on the market. The planes, after all, were assets, and they had stopped earning their keep.

For the first eighteen months PSA had kept the four 727s flying in their system on the lease-back agreement with Contran. But when the lease ended and PSA decided not to buy them back or extend the lease, the 727s became tied-up capital.

At the precise moment the four planes were turned over to Contran, the market for used 727s all but collapsed. Suddenly, there were too many empty seats flying in the airline business and too many airplanes in the various fleets, partly due to a catastrophic rise in fuel costs and interest rates. Dallas' own Braniff International, for instance, had already been embarrassed by huge losses and an inability to pay Boeing for four 727s just out of the factory—one green, one orange, and two red. The multi-colored aircraft would spend more than a year parked at the south end of Boeing Field in Seattle as mute testimony to Braniff's problems. Suddenly, Harold found himself having to park *his* four 727s while he searched for a buyer, bypassing the costly services of a broker to make many of the phone calls himself directly to various airline vice presidents around the country.

Mike Snetzer soon found himself flying to Miami in response to such a call to discuss the four 727s with Eastern Airlines. A series of meetings with Eastern's leaden bureaucracy ended with a surprise handshake between Snetzer and the Eastern CEO, Frank Borman.

"I accepted their offer," Snetzer told Harold on returning to Dallas. "All four for a total of nineteen and a half million."

Harold said nothing, his silence raising alarm bells in Snetzer's head.

The good news was bad news, in effect, since Piedmont Airlines had decided to make an offer on the aircraft while Snetzer was in Miami, and Harold was expecting the formal figure at any time. When it came, Piedmont had placed $22 million on the table.

"I need to take Piedmont's offer," Harold told Mike Snetzer, who was sitting in some degree of personal agony on the other side of Harold's desk.

"Harold," he began, "you can't do that. I shook hands on the deal."

"Well, you call him back and tell him it was premature."

"You mean that I didn't have the authority to shake on it?"

"That's right. You thought you did, but I hadn't endorsed it."

"No. I can't do that."

Harold sat in thought for a few minutes before nodding. "Okay. You're right. I'll call him."

Chairman Borman came on the line within minutes and Harold introduced himself, explaining that his representative had jumped the gun on concluding the deal.

"I'm sorry to have to tell you this, but basically Piedmont has offered us twenty-two million for the airplanes, and here's what's going to happen. Mike, now, is going to go to our board and uphold his obligation to you by recommending we accept your offer. But I'm going to recommend we accept Piedmont's offer, and I'm the chairman, so I feel sure they're going to take my recommendation."

"I see," the Eastern executive said. "Are you going to give us a chance to . . . to raise our bid?"

"Well, sure, if you want a chance."

"What'll it take to get those planes?"

"Well, you match the Piedmont bid and I'll let you have them."

"Twenty-two million?"

"That's right."

"I'll get back to you."

A half hour later the man was back on the phone accepting the new price. "You've got us over a barrel," he said. "We're going to lose a lot of money if we go into the summer market with too few airplanes. I have to have those planes."

The cost of the PSA stock had been just under $13 million, with the cost of the proxy contest and litigation less than a million more. However, with the $13 million derived from leasing the aircraft to PSA and the $22 million sale to Eastern, Contran's total profit from the PSA deal stood at almost $21 million.

■　　■　　■

When Harold bought their beautiful new house on Deloache Avenue in North Dallas, he realized that many new pieces would need to be purchased, along with drapes, floor coverings, and paintings, before the house truly became a home. So they agreed that Annette would do the decorating.

Within weeks a growing gallery of family pictures began to appear around the sumptuous Georgian interior, pictures of Amy and Andy, Annette's children, and pictures of all four of Harold's daughters, as well as pictures of Harold and Annette in various places over the prior two years. It was becoming a home—*their* home—with the understanding that it could become Andrea and Serena's home as well if they ever changed their minds about living with their mother.

The divorce had ended badly for Sandra. Unable to break the Simmons trust that she, herself, had agreed to and signed, the settlement came to a fraction of what she'd sought. After more than six years of litigation, her attorney ended up with more money from the deal than she did. Even the custody issue had gone against her. Due to her constant need to be on the road and other evidence examined by the court, Andrea and Serena were awarded to Harold.

But the girls wanted to stay with their mother, and Harold agreed, permitting them to stay with Sandra in the family home, which was also given to Sandra in the settlement.

"Even though you live there, this is your home, too," Harold had told both girls, referring to the new house on Deloache.

BOOK EIGHT

Master of the Game

CHAPTER 41

SAN ANTONIO, TEXAS: 1980

*H*arold who?"

Steve Watson, a company vice president, sat at the conference table in the National City Lines offices in downtown San Antonio watching his leader. Mr. Pratt, the chairman, was seventy-two years old, but his thinking was still crystal clear, and the fact that he wasn't upset by the news they had just received was a calming influence.

"Harold Simmons, Steve," Pratt said. "He's a very successful, very sharp businessman up in Dallas, and he's spotted the rather substantial differences between our book equity and our price."

"And ... he's going to mount a takeover bid?"

"Hard to say. But the man called me this morning and wants to come in and talk. I told him 'by all means.' After all, he may already be our largest single shareholder. Anyway, here's the date he's coming, and I want you to be in the meeting." He handed a slip of paper to Steve, who looked at it glumly before folding it and slipping it into his shirt pocket

Steve Watson returned to his office in a mild state of alarm. He'd never heard of Harold Simmons, but he knew what takeover artists did, and the aftermath was seldom comfortable for an established corporation.

"What did we do to attract his attention?" Steve had asked the executive who brought the news.

"Well, apparently he's been buying our stock for several years because we have a lot of cash, a lot of real estate you can solidly value, and our stock price doesn't come anywhere close to the reality of what we're worth as a company. Add to that the fact that Mr. Pratt only owns about one percent of the stock, and there's no one but Harold Simmons who holds even five percent, and there's your answer."

Steve Watson had grown up in North Dakota, trained as a CPA, and joined National City Lines in 1976 before the corporate move to San Antonio from Denver. He knew the company was bogged down with difficult problems, especially the ones plaguing the huge Time-DC trucking operation based in Lubbock, Texas. Truck deregulation, rising interest rates on equipment purchases, and a stranglehold by the Teamsters Union on labor costs had a negative impact on Time-DC's profits. Wall Street was, as usual, focusing on the operational results of National City Lines and ignoring the inherent value of its assets.

Because of all this, even if he owned less than 20 percent, the arrival of an investor in the home offices of a targeted corporation such as National City Lines was usually a tense affair. Harold had grown used to the too-often injudicious overreactions of established managements who triggered lawsuits, proxy contests, the aid of investment bankers, and frantic searches for "white knight" alternate buyers, supposedly to preserve stockholder value but too often to hang on to the power and perks that come with running a company they didn't own. Many times such defensive campaigns were driven only by self-interest, but there were also instances in which the reactions were fueled by a seriously misguided belief that the sudden presence of Harold Simmons at their gate meant a true threat to the company's very life. There were, after all, corporate raiders out there who *were* simply looking for undervalued companies to break up and sell off without regard for the employees or the business momentum of the corporation. Harold Simmons was not one of them; nevertheless, he had been called a corporate raider. Therefore, those less informed assumed Harold Simmons would automatically dismember a company and sell off all the parts, regardless of the human cost to the employees.

But Skip Pratt viewed the call from Harold and his new stock ownership quite differently. At the end of his long business career and used to running his corporation with a firm hand, Pratt nevertheless well understood that with only one percent of the stock, it wasn't his province to decide unilaterally whether National City Lines should be liquidated, continue in business, or merge with someone else. He also understood that his turn at the helm was all but over, and the matter of who his successor would be was as much a current concern as his worries over what to do with the company and its employees. National City Lines, Inc., was clearly in need of help, and if Harold Simmons could bring new ideas and new, workable solutions to the table, then they all should welcome his growing ownership and interest with open arms.

On the day and hour that Harold Simmons was to appear in the offices of National City Lines, two men entered the waiting room. Glenn Simmons, with his full head of silver hair and engaging smile, passed his name and that of his companion to the corporate receptionist, and within minutes, several of the National City Lines executives who had been waiting nervously in the wings made their appearance.

"Mr. Simmons, welcome," one of the men said, walking over to Glenn and pumping his hand as he introduced the other key vice presidents.

"Jim, this is Harold Simmons. Mr. Simmons, this is ..."

"Well, excuse me, fellows," Glenn interrupted, his smile broadening as he turned to gesture to the other man in the reception area, a slim, business-suited figure sitting quietly in a chair and watching with amusement. "I'm *Glenn* Simmons. *Harold* Simmons is our chairman, and he's the one sitting over there."

The confusion on the faces of the three men was visceral. They had gravitated to the man who *looked* the part of a corporate takeover baron and just assumed the quiet one was the other brother. It was an embarrassing moment for them, but the feeling soon dissipated as both Glenn and Harold smiled warmly and shook hands all around.

The meeting began and ended with a degree of cordiality and receptivity Harold had seldom seen. While Pratt's lieutenants, including Steve Watson, were correct and reasonably friendly, Pratt himself seemed visibly relaxed, and by the end of the meeting he made it clear he was ready to anoint Harold as his heir apparent, the next CEO of National City Lines.

On return to Dallas, Contran's attorneys thought through the new developments and made a routine recommendation to Harold: "We need to tell the Securities and Exchange Commission."

"What, file it with the SEC?"

"It's the safe way to do it," the lawyers said. "He's indicated you're to succeed him, and that's a significant change in business and senior management for a public company."

"But ... it was a private conversation," Harold countered. Yet the weight of their arguments and the inherent need to be careful where public corporate matters were concerned led him to approve the filing, though against his better judgment.

Within a week, the *Wall Street Journal* had plucked the story from its close watch of public filings and the board of National City Lines— with the obvious exception of its newest member, Harold Simmons— all but exploded in fury. "We are not accustomed," one board member sputtered in the process of chewing out the longtime chairman, "to being given formal notice of a major management change through the medium of a newspaper!"

Pratt and Harold had a small, smoldering revolt on their hands, as well as an expression of sudden alarm from the Teamsters, who were also watching carefully what the corporation intended to do.

An outstanding aspect of National City Lines' balance sheet was its unusually large cash balance. But now a majority of the board members—many of whom had considerable money invested in the corporation's stock—decided to pay out most of the cash to the shareholders in a special series of dividends—a move that would have seriously changed the equation for Harold and Contran. National City Lines had been slowly liquidating some of its marginally performing subsidiary companies for several years, and as properties were sold, the cash balance grew. There had been a feeling for some time among the stockholding board members that maybe the time had come to distribute those dollars, especially if all that cash was becoming a magnet for takeover artists. The recognition, and the intended distribution, were far too late.

In November 1980, a special meeting of the board was called in San Antonio to discuss and approve the massive payout, and with Harold in place as the sole defender of Contran's interests in stopping the move, the subject of the first special dividend came to the table— an issue that, if approved, would cause a quarter of the company's cash reserves to evaporate.

Harold had a split-second decision to make. The board was clearly ready to approve it. The company's entire stock value at present market price was only a little over $20 million, which was just above the amount of cash in National City Lines' accounts. If a quarter of that cash was discarded in a dividend, the master plan Harold had brainstormed for using the cash to leverage new investments and create new profits would be crippled or destroyed.

"Now, wait a minute, gentlemen," Harold said, taking the floor. "Before you act on this, I want to discuss my purchasing all of the publicly held stock, right here, right now. You've got two million shares outstanding with a market value today of about twenty-six million, and I'm going to offer you twenty dollars per share for all of it, which comes to about forty million, provided you don't do any of these dividend distributions."

There was a momentary silence in the board room before the men around the table began to exchange glances, then comments, then open discussion.

In the weeks that followed, increasingly frantic meetings were held in San Antonio, New York, and Dallas, where one all-day marathon session took place in a rented meeting room at DFW airport. Investment bankers and lawyers and senior executives briefed Pratt, board members, and each other on the wide range of defensive maneuvers that could be mounted to counter a takeover attempt, painting the outlines of an all-too-familiar campaign which, whether successful or not, would certainly succeed in making millions of dollars for the professionals who ran such operations.

But in the end—sitting calmly in the corner of every major discussion—Mr. Pratt had kept to his course. "I just think," he said, "that we should negotiate as good a deal as we can get with Harold. After all, he has a sterling track record as a businessman. He makes good decisions. He may well have answers we can't generate. And it's time for me to go."

To Pratt, throwing away the company's capital on a possibly doomed corporate cat fight to hold on to control of a company already under financial siege made no sense whatsoever. He had listened to the arguments and concerns and worries of his people, and in the final analysis it came down to one thing: Starting, for no valid reason, a costly war he couldn't win was not an acceptable choice.

He sent the professional gladiators packing.

Within months, Harold Simmons emerged with the board's support for a Contran tender offer which eventually brought in 92 percent of the corporation's outstanding stock.

As plans were formulated to move NCL's offices to Contran's headquarters in Dallas, and executives such as Steve Watson were asked to stay on and make the move north, Harold turned his attention to Lubbock, Texas, and the amazingly difficult problem of how to convince the Teamsters not to commit professional suicide. Time-DC, National City Lines' problem-child subsidiary, was being strangled to death by truck deregulation and its own unions.

CHAPTER 42

ST. LOUIS, MISSOURI: 1981

*W*hen the battle began in 1978 for control of St. Louis-based LLC Corporation, Harold had assumed that no more than a year would be required to bring the acquisition to a conclusion. Yet the battle dragged through 1981. By November, a Contran tender offer which should have provided a solution was obviously failing, and a proxy contest for additional board seats was being hotly resisted by the entrenched president, former ITT executive Steven Friedrich. Friedrich was clinging to leadership of LLC with stubborn tenacity and throwing every roadblock he could muster in Contran's path, while at the same time worsening the corporation's performance.

Harold, in fact, had become alarmed at Friedrich's investments of LLC's funds, including the millions he'd thrown into mining interests that had nothing whatever to do with either the corporation's core consumer loan business or the fast-food business that LLC had also pursued for years with puzzling rationale.

Meanwhile, Harold continued buying stocks in other companies and actively pursuing one of them in particular. It was another under-valued corporation called Keystone Consolidated Corporation of Peoria, Illinois, a longtime maker of wire and steel products.

On November 16 Harold flew into St. Louis for an LLC board meeting. He had learned that a Florida investor named Maurice

Halperin was also in town for the same board meeting. Harold arranged a meeting with Halperin, hoping to strike a deal to buy his ten percent.

But Halperin also owned a 25 percent block of Keystone stock and already had a deal in mind. If Harold would sell him all the Keystone stock Contran held, Halperin would in turn sell Harold his LLC stock.

In Harold's view, Halperin's offer for the Keystone shares was far too low. Harold decided to turn the tables and offer to buy both Halperin's LLC *and* his Keystone holdings, a deal that was sealed by the time the private meeting broke up.

Halperin snagged an instant profit of $3 million in the transaction, but for Harold and Contran, the purchase was far more significant. With his LLC holdings already at 40 percent, Halperin's shares meant solid control at last of LLC. At the same time, Halperin's Keystone stock would give Harold control of Keystone as well.

Within weeks, Harold was back at his desk looking over an annual report of a company that was becoming more interesting by the day: the Amalgamated Sugar Company. The figures were lining up nicely on Amalgamated, and the research he'd been doing indicated that once again an entire nation of investors had failed to spot the fact that Amalgamated's stock was vastly undervalued.

Harold had known little of the sugar industry until 1974. When two of the sons of the famous Texas oil wildcatter H. L. Hunt had suddenly bought into Great Western Sugar Company that year, Harold took notice.

The Hunts had purchased Great Western at precisely the right moment as the sugar market price was beginning to rise dramatically. The first year after their purchase, the company earned $100 million, which was roughly what they paid for the stock.

For Harold, Great Western was out of play, but there were a few other sugar companies, and the best one seemed to be a very steady beet sugar operation headquartered in Ogden, Utah, called Amalgamated. Very quietly, Harold began buying shares of both Holly Sugar and Amalgamated as an investment, later selling both stakes for a profit when Wall Street's valuations hit their next high.

But there would be another downturn, Harold knew, during which Wall Street's inability to understand the business would lead to misreading their financials and scaring investors away from the industry stocks, leaving them to fall to vulnerable lows. Perhaps by then he'd have the cash to go after more than a limited amount of shares. Timing would be everything, and he intended to be ready.

The sugar business presented a unique combination: sufficiently small and specialized (and sufficiently unglamorous) to escape the attention of most Wall Street professionals, yet great profits resulted in good years, and never a loss in the worst years. In Amalgamated's case, each year was a repeat of the last: buy the sugar beet harvest with cash on hand, process the sugar, and sell all of what had been produced, using the proceeds to replace the cash. It was elegant, and it was simple, and—Harold realized—uniquely wasteful. There was a better way to do it than spend six months of every year sitting on a cash reserve of $100 million at low interest rates.

In 1980 the sugar cycle peaked once again. In the months that followed, stock prices began to decline with the help of Wall Street's negative predictions. Sugar prices, the analysts said, would be sinking with the next crop, and investors should move away from stocks like Amalgamated.

Harold watched over the months as Amalgamated's stock price sank, knowing that this time he had enough cash to probably buy control of the company. All the signals were right. Amalgamated's balance sheet was strong, and as he re-analyzed the value of the company in terms of the stock price times the number of shares outstanding, it was hard to understand why no one else was making a play for the company.

In lieu of a product inventory, after all the sugar had been sold, Amalgamated stored cash. It was the seed corn for the next crop, and the company had long operated the same way. No borrowing, no danger, no question of having enough to buy the next season's sugar beets. But the United States government provided low-interest crop-purchase loans to such companies, and if Amalgamated used that system, it would free up the $100 million in its accounts for whatever its management decided to do with it.

And, of course, whoever owned the corporation outright, owned the cash.

Harold began buying the stock carefully and quietly on the open market, taking care not to alert the usual people on Wall Street who would rush in as soon as they sensed a takeover attempt was brewing and buy the same stock, running the price up in the process. When he reached 15 percent of the outstanding shares, he phoned the longtime chairman of Amalgamated, Art Benning, and arranged a personal visit to Ogden, where the headquarters were located.

Harold brought up the subject of a seat on the board of directors during his Utah inspection trip, but even though Benning rebuffed him in gentlemanly fashion, the message from Benning and his board was clear: They would rather not have Harold Simmons helping to run the company or having any control over its affairs.

In the background at the same time, Amalgamated retained a prominent investment banking firm known as First Boston, seeking immediate advice on how to beat away Contran's interest in controlling and, perhaps, owning them.

First Boston made much of its money from giving such advice and helping besieged companies mount a defense. They began immediately searching for another buyer for Amalgamated, but the very facts of financial life that had made Amalgamated so attractive to Harold in the first place as the sugar industry hit the bottom of the next cycle seriously discouraged most of the would-be investors First Boston contacted—especially since few of them had studied the sugar market enough to understand what was happening.

As Contran continued buying Amalgamated's stock, Harold realized that Amalgamated's grossly undervalued condition also gave him a golden opportunity to fix the terrible pension fund problem he'd inherited at Keystone.

"Fellows, look at this!" he said one afternoon. "This is a great chance for the fund to break even, because I don't know if I've ever seen a better deal! We'll just get all the pension funds in on this and we'll fix the underfunded problem right here, right now."

The move would have a double-barreled benefit. Not only would the investment be wonderfully profitable for the pension funds, but his control over those funds meant they would be added to the amount of stock whose votes he controlled.

Harold studied the laws and reconfirmed the limitation that no more than 25 percent of a pension fund could be invested in the same company. As the owner of Keystone and as chairman, he was the administrator of the pension fund as well, and directing investment of the maximum allowable percentage of the fund in Amalgamated stock was a logical decision, once the legal team confirmed its legality.

"How much, Harold?" Mike Snetzer asked him at the end of a pivotal meeting in Dallas on the subject.

"Twenty-five percent. The maximum."

Harold estimated that Amalgamated's total worth was in excess of $150 million, far above the stock price, which had been trading around $20 per share when he'd begun buying. But First Boston countered with a potential buyer ready to offer $60 per share, and Amalgamated's management quickly gave them a "lockup option"—an exclusive guarantee—to sell the First Boston buyer 15 percent of the company at that price.

Harold authorized an immediate lawsuit to stop the sale, alleging that the First Boston deal violated securities laws. But the request for an injunction in Utah was denied, and an appeal was initiated. Harold sat alone in his office one afternoon in deep thought thinking about the $60-per-share figure.

Amalgamated's chairman, Art Benning, was in his seventies and ready to retire. Many of his very loyal board were also in their seventies, and equally cautious and tired. They knew their company was amassing more and more cash each year, but they had no expertise in what to do with it or how to invest it, and according to Benning himself, they had been looking for ideas.

Harold returned to his desk determined to get deeper into the records the lawsuit had generated. There was something there, he concluded, that he needed to know, and after several hours of research, he found it.

The suitor turned up by First Boston was planning to finance his deal with a small amount of cash and a portfolio of heavy bank loans. But something else was needed to make the deal, and that "something" was buried in the figures: a one-half interest in a high-fructose corn syrup plant in Alabama which had resided quietly on the books for $30 million, and which showed no profits, to be sold to the other half owner for part of the purchase price. This additional asset added $15 per share to the value of the stock, and could be used to repay part of the acquisition costs.

After the information helped him overcome their offer, the problem followed him home in his Cadillac that evening and dogged his conversations with Annette. It lurked in their master bedroom as well, and nagged him in the shower the following morning. He *knew* that there was a solution lurking just out of reach, but it wasn't until he slipped behind the wheel of his car and headed for work that the previous twelve hours of mental concentration suddenly came together in a thunderclap of an idea.

"Here's what we're going to do," Harold explained to Mike Snetzer and Glenn with visible excitement. "If the other guys can do that deal, so can we. Here's how. What we'd normally do is offer, say, sixty-five dollars a share to buy all the outstanding stock. Then we'd wait to see if First Boston's guy upped the ante and offered more. If not, we'd use Contran's cash to buy all the Amalgamated stock, then—once we owned the company—we'd take the hundred million out of Amalgamated's accounts and sell the fructose plant for thirty million dollars to cover the funds we've used from Contran's cash to make the purchase."

Harold was sitting behind his desk, leaning forward, his eyes wide with excitement as he raised an index finger. "But ... why go around in that circle? Why don't we just cut out the intermediate part of that and just approach Benning with a streamlined, less expensive version of the same deal? We offer the same sixty-five a share, but *Amalgamated* itself announces a tender for their *own* outstanding shares at that price. Now we hold our stock, which is worth about what First Boston's guy was going to spend of his own money. Amalgamated pays for all those shares out of its hundred million cash reserve. With all that stock then retired, and only our stock outstanding, ours will represent almost a hundred percent of the shares, and we'll immediately take the company private. We follow that with a sale of the fructose plant for thirty million and leave the company soundly financed."

"You can talk them into that?" Glenn asked with a smile.

"I don't see why not. It makes sense."

The suitor First Boston had found refused to raise his tender offer price. Instead, he folded, leaving Harold and the Keystone pension funds in possession of Amalgamated Sugar.

Chapter 43

Dallas, Texas: 1983

$\mathcal{P}$am Phillips punched the telephone "hold" button and sat a moment at her desk in deep thought. The man on the other end was polite, but incredibly insistent, and this was his third call in what was obviously a determined attempt to reach the ultimate chief executive of the company that owned a particular Arby's Roast Beef Restaurant.

She pursed her lips, took a deep breath, and made a decision as she punched in Harold's extension number, then hung up the receiver and got to her feet to break into his meeting and explain it in person.

The chairman of the board of Contran and owner of LLC Corporation, with its chain of over one hundred Arby's franchise locations, looked over as she entered. On the opposite side of his desk sat another Contran executive, who looked over as well.

"Mr. Simmons? I hate to interrupt you with this, but there's a gentleman on the phone who called yesterday about a bad chicken he got at one of our restaurants."

Harold nodded. "Yeah, I remember. I told you to pass him over to Glenn, since he's president."

"I did, but he won't talk to Glenn. He's very polite, but insistent. Apparently he's read that you are the chairman, and he won't talk with anyone but you, and this is his third attempt, and I promised I'd at least tell you."

"So, he's a dissatisfied customer?"

"He is definitely that."

"A bad chicken, you said?"

"A bad chicken."

"Okay. I'll talk to him," Harold replied as he reached for the phone and punched on the speakerphone function, motioning for Pam to stay in the room.

"This is Harold Simmons," he said into the receiver, a trademarked greeting Pam had become used to hearing.

"Mr. Simmons, thanks for taking my call." The voice was gravelly with a heavy Texas accent. "I need to ask for my money back, Mr. Simmons, and I want to tell you how your people treated me about this. It's your place in DeSoto."

"Okay. Tell me what happened."

"I'm just a working man, Mr. Simmons," the man began, explaining how he had purchased a roasted chicken from the small deli section of the new Arby's. "My wife, you see, she was plannin' to fix it when I got home. For supper, don't you know. Well, sir, when she pulled out that chicken, that chicken was bad. You could see it and smell it. Wasn't fit for the dog, let alone for us."

"And you took it back?"

"No, sir. It was too bad to keep in my car while I was at work the next day, and I couldn't have gotten back to your restaurant until I was on the way home. So my wife, she threw it away."

"I see."

The man related how he had driven back to the new Arby's a day later with the receipt and been told by the manager that a refund wasn't possible.

"What'd he tell you?" Harold asked.

"Well, Mr. Simmons, he tells me I have to bring back his chicken to get a new chicken. I explained to him how the chicken was too bad for me to leave in my car all day, and how we threw it out. But he's not a-goin' to move. You want a new chicken, he tells me, you've got to bring back the bad chicken. Them's the rules."

"Well, that really is our policy, you know, since some folks will say anything to get a refund."

"Now, Mr. Simmons, it's just not right to be unreasonable. You give a man a bad chicken, you should replace that chicken without askin' him to haul around a smelly carcass all day for a refund."

"How much did you pay for that bad chicken?" Harold asked.

"Well, just a minute, let me go get the receipt," the man said. The sound of the receiver being placed on a counter was followed by several minutes of silence before the customer returned to the line with the answer. Harold wrote down an amount just under seven dollars.

"Tell you what," Harold began, "I know how you feel. I've been in the same position. I remember buying something years ago and being mistreated by someone who wanted to just quote me rules and not listen."

Pam stood watching and listening, internally fascinated with the fact that here was the chairman of what was now a billion-dollar corporation taking the time to defuse a seven-dollar dispute on a one-to-one basis, relating to the customer as if they were both sitting on the front porch of the Golden, Texas, general store swapping fishing stories. He wasn't in a hurry, she noted. The entire story of his frustration as a young man trying to return a bad product unwound into the room and the phone, bonding the two Texans together, his verbal hand on the other man's shoulder as he commiserated with him.

This wasn't a performance or an artificial act of shrewd customer service. It was merely Harold Simmons being himself, an unpretentious, unassuming fellow consumer vicariously righting the wrong he'd experienced so many years ago.

"So," Harold finished, "I sure do understand, and I'm going to write you a company check today to repay you, and you have my apology. We'll talk to our manager out there and impress on him the need to be much more responsive to reason . . . as well as to stop selling bad chickens."

"I sure do appreciate that."

"And . . . I sure hope you'll come back and visit us again, despite all this."

"Oh, I will, Mr. Simmons. I understand how these things can happen, but you're real nice to fix it. Yes, sir, I'll be back."

"I don't like bad chickens either," Harold added, ignoring the barely successful attempt of the executive across the desk to keep from exploding in laughter.

Ten minutes later Pam Phillips interrupted the chairman again with the check in hand. "I've . . . got to put something down on this check for the reason for the refund. You know. For the auditors."

"All right."

"So . . . what should I put?"

"Bad chicken."

"Bad chicken?"

"That's it."

"The auditors will love it," she said, chuckling all the way out of the office.

CHAPTER 44

DALLAS, TEXAS: 1984

*B*efore he'd turned into the driveway of their stately North Dallas home, Harold had removed the black bow tie from the shirt of his tuxedo. He was looking forward to being alone with Annette.

The dinner party had been all right, he decided, but by the time the elegant dessert had been served by their hosts, he'd found himself longing to retreat to the sanctity of their residence.

Annette, resplendent in a gold brocade designer gown, followed her husband of four years into the hallway and closed the door behind her. He turned then and looked admiringly at her with that sly smile that she loved so much. "You really are something, Mrs. Simmons," he said, his East Texas accent sharply in evidence, "if you don't mind me saying so."

"Why, I don't mind at all," Annette replied with a smile. "I'm glad you approve."

"I sure do. So did everyone else tonight. You were the belle of the ball."

"Well, your belle will be there in a minute, honey," she said before moving into the kitchen to take inventory for breakfast. That small duty complete, she wandered through the foyer to the foot of the stairs, but stopped, deciding to stroll through the den first just to admire it once again.

It was all so new, living in a house that was nothing less than a mansion. She felt a warm glow as she looked around the interior she'd decorated herself, and walked farther into the den, feeling a surge of pride in the way it had turned out—the array of elegant furniture and paintings she'd hand-selected, the carpets, the piano, and especially the galaxy of framed pictures of friends and family she'd placed on every available surface around the room.

Annette let her eyes wander over the shrubs by the rear wall marking the rear boundary of their property, glowing now in the soft lights placed throughout the garden. A stereo was playing softly somewhere in the house, and the music underscored the richness of the scene.

They had both longed for a bigger backyard, and now it was going to happen with Harold's purchase of the house just to the west. "We'll redraw the lines," he'd said, "then we'll incorporate all that property next door as our backyard, and then sell off that house with a much smaller lot." The landscaping plans were proceeding well, and she was delighted to see him so excited.

She turned now, aware she'd been daydreaming, and climbed the stairs to their bedroom, instantly warmed by his smile when she entered.

"Honey, can I talk to you a minute about the seating arrangement tonight?"

"Sure," he said. He was trusting her completely to guide him in learning to enjoy the social occasions they were attending more and more, but the thought of sitting at a dinner table with her on the other side had been very uncomfortable when he'd discovered what their hostess had in mind.

Annette had been in conversation and was unaware that he'd moved into the elegant dining room and rearranged the place cards. Suddenly, he was back at her side whispering conspiratorially in her ear. "They had us sitting apart," he said, "but I fixed it."

"Oh?" Annette had replied, suppressing the urge to say, "You did *what?*"

"Yeah, they had you on the other side, but I switched the cards and got us back together."

Annette smiled at her husband now as he sat on the edge of their bed waiting for her evaluation of his performance.

"I didn't want to be too far away from you this evening. Was that the wrong move, changing the place cards?"

"Well, darling," Annette began, "other than the fact we'll probably never be invited back ..."

"That bad, huh?"

She sat beside him. "Actually, I *was* worried, but our hosts thought it was cute. Otherwise, though, I thought everything went beautifully. In fact, did you see how that lady next to you responded tonight? Just as I've told you."

"Well, she was polite."

"No, Harold, she *listened* to every word you had to say. You were the most interesting man at that party tonight, and she knew it, and she was fascinated by what you were saying, as was her husband."

"You keep telling me that, and I keep thinking I'm boring them silly."

"Honey, aren't you enjoying these things just a little bit more? You seem to be. I even saw you smiling tonight."

"Well, I was smiling 'cause I was still sitting next to you."

"Come on, now."

"Yeah, I guess so."

"Good! Because you're becoming a real conversationalist and I'm terribly proud of you."

"Thanks," he said.

"But, honey, that's why Nancy originally had you sitting across from me with those place cards, so you'd be able to talk to more of her guests."

She chuckled, remembering the hard-won concession he'd made out of pure love and trust four years before: "Okay," he'd said, "you can take me to these dinner parties and social things, but no more than three nights a week, and only if we can leave each time by ten."

"Yes, we can still leave by ten. A deal's a deal," Annette had replied, feeling a glow of accomplishment.

Marrying Harold Simmons had been an act of love, but an element of courage had been required as well. The continued hostile presence of Sandra as a bitter ex-wife and the clear lack of acceptance by two of Harold's daughters were challenges Annette had thought through carefully. She knew instinctively it would be one heck of a ride, but she had fallen in love with him anyway, as he had with her, and with her love and trust had come an overriding mission to expand Harold Simmons' enjoyment of life.

Not that he was morose or incapable of joy and happiness, but there was something Annette knew that Harold did not: Life could be much more fun when you shared it with a wide array of friends, and someone you deeply love.

"I was socially retarded," he would say years later. "Until I met Annette, I really didn't know how to deal with social functions. I didn't know how to reciprocate socially and send thank-you notes or how to take a real interest in other people. Annette was my teacher, and she was great at it."

Harold's Arkansas property had been a wonderful beginning, a place to take friends for fun weekends. He'd purchased the first 1,600 acres northeast of Fort Smith in the Ozarks for $80 an acre in the early seventies, hiring one of Sandra's uncles to run the place—an arrangement that was to last for twenty-five years.

"It was the only good idea Sandra thought I'd ever had," Harold joked. But with Annette by his side, the encouragement to enjoy the beautiful rolling hills and heavily forested mountainside became continuous, and more and more they began to expand it, building additional houses and paving the roads as Harold added more acreage at the mid-eighties rate of nearly $2,000 an acre.

There were geographical horizons Annette was determined to broaden as well. Before Annette, Harold had traveled principally on business, but at her urging, they were increasingly taking trips around the country and abroad. Some trips were taken in their own aircraft, and others, such as overseas trips, were by commercial air. Sightseeing, exploring, and enjoying each other's company, Annette was relieved to find that her husband could leave the office behind without making daily phone calls or micro-managing from afar, trusting his highly capable people to run Contran and all its subsidiaries while he was away. In fact, the financial genius, whose ability to stay focused on business had built an empire valued at $800 million, was beginning to relax.

"They're teasing me at the office, Annette," he said one day with a grin.

"Oh?"

"Yeah, they say that since I married you, I've been coming in later and leaving earlier and earlier."

"You've got a life, in other words. Good!"

"I'm not sure that's precisely what they're teasing me about," he said with a grin.

The acquisition of NL Industries had brought with it a vacation property on Padre Island along the Gulf of Mexico, and together they had purchased a house in Palm Springs, California, and a house in

Aspen as getaway properties. More and more weekends a year found them heading out of Dallas, often in the company of Annette's teenaged daughter Amy, whom Harold had all but adopted.

The qualities that Annette had seen in Harold Simmons had been immediately apparent to her daughter as well. Amy appreciated his wry sense of humor and depth of caring from the first, and she adored her new stepfather.

For Harold's part, Amy was an instant ray of sunshine, a daughter who easily expressed affection and appreciation. He felt instantly comfortable around her, and although Harold had immediately liked Annette's son Andy as well, their relationship grew at a much slower pace—a process impeded somewhat by the fact that Harold had no previous experience relating to a son. Nevertheless, the bond between them grew, and as the years went by, Harold often told Annette of his admiration for her son—a sentiment he expressed directly to Andy as well.

Family outings in McKinney were filled with horses and four-wheelers, a fun means of scooting around the acreage that Harold and the rest of the clan thoroughly enjoyed. Staying active remained vitally important to him, and Annette cheered on his devotion to tennis and his daily exercise routines, which included a specific program of stretching to combat an inherited stiffening of the spine.

"I have these strange early memories," Serena would say with a chuckle in later years. "I'd walk into my dad's room as a five-year-old and find him hanging upside down from a bar in the doorway."

From Annette's point of view, even Andrea's continuous snubs and childish behavior couldn't dampen the satisfaction of knowing she'd made the right matrimonial decision. Harold had changed her life for the better in so many ways, but she'd changed his as well, as those around the office were well aware from such clues as the extra spring in his step and his expanded wardrobe.

"Harold had only one suit when I married him, and it was gray," Annette maintained.

"Not quite true," Harold would reply. "I actually had two suits. Both gray."

"We changed that."

"I liked gray, but we made a deal. You figure out what I should wear and I won't have to think about it, and that'll be great."

At Harold's invitation, Annette set about decorating his large corner office at Contran with an elegant, understated look of success well tailored to the chairman of a major conglomerate. Intriguing bronze sculptures were placed on desks and tables, and beautiful paintings appeared on the carefully coordinated wallcoverings that bordered windows which featured sweeping views of North Dallas.

Annette, in fact, was proving to be masterful at handling the details of maintaining, furnishing, expanding, and sometimes adding to the various vacation properties Contran owned, while keeping their social calendar with all the related details in her head. Harold had been awed by her smooth, seemingly effortless talent for organizing myriad details, especially parties and charitable fund-raisers, which often involved marshaling and motivating dozens of people. Even before *Forbes* magazine formally recognized Harold's stratospheric financial status by inclusion in the "Forbes 400" list of the nation's wealthiest men, Annette had successfully landed Harold on the "A" list of Dallas society.

Not that the Dallas business community wasn't already respectful. Harold was a unique breed of financial cat, especially for a man the newspapers were fond of calling a "corporate raider." Far from the stereotypical pattern of corporate takeovers, once Harold gained control, the fortunes of the acquired companies almost always improved—sometimes dramatically. Moreover, he was earning widespread respect in the corporate world for sound management and responsible treatment of both the rank-and-file employees and entrenched managements alike, something that could not be said for the majority of so-called corporate takeover "artists." Harold Simmons' brilliance was not just in spotting an undervalued corporation, but in having the ability to run it better once he'd plucked it from the old management, the majority of whom had little or no real investment in their company.

"That's one thing you can always say about Harold," one of his Dallas admirers remarked in the mid-eighties. "He risks his own money. When he controls a company, it's his financial posterior that's on the line."

But it had been the 1981 masterstroke of spotting the immense hidden value of the Amalgamated Sugar Corporation (and acquiring it so adroitly) that had not only earned Harold an entirely new level of respect but catapulted Contran at the same time to new financial heights. By the end of 1984, Amalgamated was cranking out a regular profit of at least $30 million annually and had become Contran's star performer. Due to the success of Amalgamated and Harold's other galaxy of companies, Contran was looking for new acquisitions at the very moment the rest of Texas was languishing in an oil and banking collapse.

Not every deal had gone smoothly, of course. The long battle for LLC Corporation of St. Louis had been bruising and draining, as had one startling aftermath of the Keystone Consolidated Industries takeover. The Illinois maker of steel and wire products, saddled with aging plants, a legacy of poor management, and a very expensive unionized work force, had a financial bomb hidden that neither Harold nor his team had discovered until they'd taken over: a pension fund underfunded by at least $100 million.

Harold determined to even out the fund by investing a quarter of its resources in his newly acquired Amalgamated stock. With the assurance of the legal staff that such a maneuver was legal and appropriate, Harold reached for the phone and gave the order that made the Keystone fund part owner of Amalgamated Sugar—a deal that would have eventually earned the fund a little over $100 million.

At the same time, the Reagan administration—on the hunt for someone to make an example of among companies suspected of abusing pension funds—latched on to the fact that, at a pivotal moment, Harold Simmons and Contran had benefited greatly from Keystone pension's investment in Amalgamated. Regardless of the fact that the investment had been spectacularly successful, the Justice Department couldn't see beyond what they construed to be a conflict of interest and filed suit against Harold and Glenn Simmons. Although a sympathetic federal judge in Peoria openly praised Harold's efforts on behalf of the pension fund, he nevertheless assigned it to an independent trustee who urged Harold to buy back the Amalgamated shares at somewhat above the price the fund had paid, a massive mistake which ultimately transferred more than $100 million in profits from where Harold Simmons had attempted to put them (in the pension fund) into the coffers of Contran. The repurchase (and promise by Glenn and Harold not to violate any technical pension fund rules for four years) nearly doubled Harold's overall profit from the Amalgamated deal, as well as the net worth of the trust he alone controlled, which by the mid-eighties was reported to be over $300 million.

BOOK NINE

The Measure of Success

CHAPTER 45

SANTA BARBARA, CALIFORNIA: 1985

*P*alm Springs wasn't working out.

What had been Harold and Annette's California getaway—a newly built resort home on a golf course purchased in 1979—had never had the feel of home. The heat was horrendous in the summer, and the house, although beautiful, seemed too isolated.

By contrast, the McKinney farm and the Arkansas property were constant lures, beckoning to them even in hot summer weather. But the heat of a Southwestern July was mild compared to the blast furnace that Palm Springs became in the summer months, and with all those negatives arrayed against it, Harold and Annette were spending very little time in the desert.

Yet, being in California from time to time was still an enticing idea, and Harold had long heard that Santa Barbara was different: ten to fifteen degrees cooler than L.A. in the summer, spread on the lush seaside slopes of the California coastal range, and under luxurious blue skies most of the year. Santa Barbara, friends confirmed, was an idyllic spot, and this was enough to prompt Harold and Annette to plan a special two-day trip there to look at thirteen different properties.

From the first, it was the one on Cold Springs Road that stood out, a twenty-four-acre estate in Montecito, just next to Santa Barbara. Owned by actor Gene Hackman, who had already moved out of the beautiful two-story Mediterranean Villa home, the property had originally included an entire hillside to the northeast where a masonry tea-house still stood perched several hundred feet up on the ridge. On the grounds that were to be sold with the house, there were lemon and orange trees, a creek flowing past a lovely three-bedroom guest house, and a breathtaking view of the Santa Barbara channel to the south. The weather was mild, the sky was blue, and the Simmonses were hooked. Harold purchased Piranhurst for $5.5 million, the highest price paid for an estate in Montecito to that date.

Annette immediately set out on a mission to furnish the baronial home with furniture and art befitting its sweeping central staircase and stately dimensions. Making the process seem effortless, she measured the rooms and researched the myriad pieces she would need for the interior. But before leaving, they walked around the property from front to back and hatched plans for landscaping what was an overly barren front lawn and drive.

On the first of July, they took possession and moved during one of the hottest spells in Santa Barbara history. The hot Santa Ana winds were howling from the north, and the electricity went off, leaving them without lights or fans. The house was not air-conditioned, as few were in Montecito. Amidst problems with water and bathrooms and lights, they were forced to retreat into town, where they found the only air-conditioned hotel around, and where they remained for several nights, seriously worried that they might have made a terrible mistake.

Within days, however, the local power company turned the lights of Montecito back on, and a contractor soon air-conditioned the entire 12,000-square-foot home. Immediately afterward, there began a procession like none other Harold had ever witnessed: a convoy of trucks loaded with goods began rolling onto the Piranhurst property from the four corners of the compass, their arrivals carefully coordinated. In addition to furnishings, they bore paintings, rugs, curtains, dishes, linens, and cutlery.

"How on earth did you coordinate all this, Annette?" Harold had asked, well aware that his wife was in her element and enjoying the moment. "How do you keep it straight? I don't see you using any notes."

"In my head. After all, this is what I love," she replied, smiling, as she turned and moved off to supervise yet another item coming through the elegant glass and metal double doors from the courtyard.

Within two days, Piranhurst became a sumptuous home, and the level of curiosity around Montecito began building, as the locals pre-pared get-acquainted dinner invitations for the couple who had just single-handedly raised the town's average property values.

"Are you retiring?" Harold was asked at one such gathering.

"No. I see no reason to retire. My people back in Dallas can run things just fine and I'm at the other end of the telephone if they need me when we're here. We're just looking forward to spending as much time out here as we can."

The local Federal Express office quickly learned to match Harold Simmons' name with Piranhurst's street address as Pam Phillips back in Dallas pioneered the practice of sending a daily "pouch" of correspon-dence, important papers, or anything else that absolutely positively had to have the chairman's personal attention. The pouch was usually small, since members of Harold's inner circle at Contran already had plenty of experience in how to guard the chairman's time by making their own decisions whenever possible.

But when they needed him for a specific decision, he was there.

"Harold, this is Steve," a typical call from senior vice president Steve Watson in Dallas would begin. "Two items. First, I'm ready to make a recommendation to you on the Houston matter, and second, Mike (Snetzer) and Lanny (Martin) are ready to send you that analy-sis you wanted, if you still want it out there."

"Okay, go ahead," Harold would say, and Steve would crisply lay out the alternatives and give him the decision points: "Of options A, B, and C, Harold, I like C the best."

"I like B," Harold might reply.

"Okay ... well, let me tell you why I think you should like C more than B," Steve would continue, going into greater depth and then wait-ing for the silence to end on the Santa Barbara side.

"What does Lanny say?"

"He likes C, too."

"Okay, then I agree," Harold would reply at last. "Option C's the best one. And, yes, tell Lanny to send me the analysis. That it?"

"Yes, it is."

"Okay. Thanks a lot," and the daily conference would be over.

Together, Harold and Annette spent the summer happily following the recommendations of many of the Montecito neighbors they were meeting, exploring the local restaurants and the surrounding countryside. On one such evening they drove, as usual, up Cold Springs Road and through the automatic gate at the front of the new estate. The sun had disappeared over the rim of the Pacific behind them, leaving a cobalt blue sky overhead. Harold stopped the car halfway up the drive and the two of them got out and walked a few dozen yards up the road before stopping to look at the house. Their home sat at the crest of a rise above the gardens, its light-colored masonry exterior glowing golden in the residual light, the grandeur of it all the more impressive against the ruddy hues of the mountainside to the northeast and the deep green of the trees on each side. It stood like a beautiful image at the focal point of a masterful painting, and it was theirs.

Harold reached for Annette's hand as he looked at the house.

"Amazing, isn't it?" she said.

Harold nodded, his eyes following the outline of the trees to the east, then finding her. "Can you believe we really own a place like this?" he asked.

She laughed and shook her head. "No! It's so incredible . . . so magnificent. I've had to keep pinching myself all summer."

He was quiet for the longest time before replying. "We're so very, very fortunate, Annette, you know that?"

"I know."

"I guess I just don't understand why I'm so blessed."

She squeezed his hand.

Harold Simmons, she thought, *the feared corporate raider. But I know his soft heart.* He was a man who understood forgiveness and charity, and a man who could fully appreciate what he'd been given.

Harold turned to her and smiled, his eyes glinting. "It's just that . . . having this wonderful place, and having you . . . Annette, it's like going to heaven without having to die."

CHAPTER 46

DALLAS, TEXAS: 1986

*S*pring had exploded as usual in North Dallas with a profusion of green, yellow, blue, and pink as trees awoke from winter and wild-flowers peppered the freeway medians. The annual metamorphosis was framed by the margins of Harold Simmons' office windows, like a beautiful landscape painted by a master of southwestern art.

But on this particular day, Contran's chairman was too deep in thought to pay much attention to the scene, as he flipped through a stack of reading material and focused on the task of looking for his next takeover target.

The time had come, Harold knew, to put his sights on an even larger acquisition target, if he could find the right company. As always, the right company would have strong asset value not reflected in the stock price, and it should be stable with not too much of the stock held by any one individual or entity, and the price per share of the voting common should be at the bottom of whatever current cycle was depressing its particular industry.

There was a substantial sum of money in the bank again since Contran's sale of Sealand Corporation stock. Harold had liquidated his 40 percent share of the company and cleared $90 million in profit and recovered the nearly $200 million in cash originally invested.

Some of the business writers around the country had created the illusion that Harold Simmons was looking for a billion-dollar deal simply for the sake of bragging rights, but in fact the war chest was big enough now to require shopping in precisely that arena. It was amazing, he thought, how things had worked out. Going after a billion-dollar acquisition wouldn't have been possible before the windfall of Amalgamated Sugar and the string of profit-making moves he'd captained over the previous three years.

Harold leaned forward to re-read the first sentence of a small article in the *Wall Street Journal* that had snagged his attention. It was a report about a substantial old-line New York-based corporation called NL Industries that was in the process of restructuring. Nothing unusual in that, he thought, but there *was* something substantially unusual in the partial tender offer just made by NL management to buy back some of their own stock for $15 per share. When managements tried to buy back their own shares, it was a red flag that the stock might be undervalued.

Harold summoned Pam Phillips into the office and dictated a request to NL for current financial reports, just as he'd done with hundreds of other corporations over the years. That accomplished, he moved to the next task and pushed the NL item to the back burner—where it sat until the reports arrived several days later.

There was a century of history behind the NL corporation, a company formerly known as National Lead. It had expanded over the years into two major businesses, one providing oil field equipment and services for the volatile oil market, and the other producing specialty chemicals. In mid-June, a day after receiving the reports, Harold sat at his desk and studied them.

NL's oilfield business was hemorrhaging dollars while the chemical division remained strong and profitable. Harold turned around to his Quotron terminal and keyed in NL's New York Stock Exchange symbol. A bid price of $10.75 per share popped up with an asterisk, indicating an important note or explanation. He hit the appropriate key and read carefully a small news clip that made little sense: NL management had suddenly *withdrawn* their $15 per share buyback tender offer, citing poor business conditions.

The New York investment house named Coniston Partners, Harold discovered, had made an unfriendly attempt to take over the company earlier in the year, and that, he figured, had probably triggered NL's attempt to buy back up to 12 percent of the stock to minimize future takeover attempts. But to the shock of management, their quietly stated desire to purchase no more than 15 percent of the stock had triggered an incredible tender of 80 percent by stockholders eager to get out of their investment in the collapsing oilpatch, as the oilfield business was being called. The spreading recession in oil was creating a stampede, but with NL's market value now well below the $15 NL's leadership had offered for the shares they wanted, NL chairman Ted Rogers and his board canceled their buyback. The management team was deeply concerned about both paying too much and draining their remaining cash during a recession.

But their sudden retreat had just left NL "in play," in the parlance of Wall Street, and Harold had noticed. In addition, he'd spotted the crown jewel no one else seemed to be looking at: the fact that NL's chemical division was very profitable and growing.

Harold picked up the phone and called his broker, giving the order to buy NL stock at the current price and to call him if any significant size was available. Over the next ten days he ended up buying about 19 percent of the stock.

The required SEC filings of Valhi alerted the NL board and started the predictable war. NL had already adopted an early version of an anti-takeover "poison pill" in the form of a corporate charter amendment which would make it prohibitively expensive for any outsider to buy more than 20 percent of the stock without NL's permission. If anyone were so foolish, NL management had figured, the poison pill provision would immediately issue all *other* existing stockholders a two-forone share bonus, cutting the value of the raider's investment in half. The pill also had other complicated restrictions on the corporation if 15 percent of the stock were acquired by one party.

But Harold and Lanny and the Contran team began studying NL's poison pill, and decided it had several flaws. The pill, Harold believed, was illegal, and if they could convince a judge of that, the 20 percent trigger point could be swept away.

Harold knew that Rogers would be looking frantically for some other device to preclude a takeover. Valhi then announced and began a tender offer for NL stock at $15 per share, subject to removal of, or overturning of, the poison pill. Contran would have to move rapidly, and Harold had figured out a way to use NL's own provision against them.

If the poison pill provision was triggered before some special deal could be reached exempting a white knight from the pill's effects, *any* stock purchaser of 20 percent of the outstanding stock, friendly or otherwise, would instantly lose 50 percent of their stock value the moment the stock was acquired, because only the stockholders as of the date of the poison pill activation would get the two-for-one issue of new stock. Therefore, triggering the pill would make a white knight rescue all but impossible, and would give Contran time to take the pill to court and try to get it thrown out.

NL management, knowing that the chemical division was what Harold really wanted, announced its intention to sell it in a public offering. However, Harold pointed out in a letter to the board that this would trigger their own poison pill because it would involve selling more than 50 percent of the earning power of the corporation. The NL attorneys immediately agreed and canceled the sale.

NL's next mistake, this one fatal, was to create a new issue of preferred stock which would have the right to receive dividends of all of the chemical division's pre-cash flow, and to pay the new stock out as a dividend to all common shareholders. The new preferred stock began trading immediately at $12 per share, while the common stock dropped to $3 per share. Valhi immediately dropped its offer price from $15 to $3.50 per share for the common stock, greatly reducing the total cost of control, if the pill could be removed.

With the tender offer about to expire, Contran argued the case in federal court in the Foley Square Federal Building in New York as NL's management paid for full-page ads pleading with its stockholders to refuse to tender their shares to Harold Simmons' interests for any price. "We believe your shares are worth more than Contran is offering to pay," the ads proclaimed, ignoring the extreme irony that the price Harold was offering was slightly above the $15 per share that management had refused to honor a month before.

Before the court handed down a decision, Ted Rogers had flown to Dallas to offer Harold and Contran the entire chemical division for a little over $1 billion. The stakes were high, and the offer substantial, but as Lanny Martin watched with great admiration, Harold calmly held his course, believing firmly that the poison pill was thoroughly illegal, and that once ruled so by the federal court, he could easily acquire the entire company for far less.

Rogers flew back to New York empty-handed and angry.

On Wednesday, August 6, 1986, Federal District Judge Vincent

Broderick ruled NL's poison pill an "illegal device," just as Harold had predicted. But the following morning, NL's legal team secured an injunction from a federal appeals court barring Contran from purchasing any more NL stock under the provisions of its tender offer.

"Okay," Harold decided, "we'll drop the tender offer and just buy control in the open market."

Learning of Contran's intentions, NL made a frantic attempt to secure a second injunction to prevent any open market purchases, but on the following Monday morning the appeals court refused. Lanny stood in the hallway outside the courtroom with a huge smile on his face as he punched in the number of Harold and Annette's Santa Barbara home on his new cellular phone.

Twenty-five hundred miles away in the master bedroom and upstairs office Harold had established at Piranhurst, the chairman of Contran answered.

"Harold? Lanny. We did it. The court refused their injunction."

"Great!" was the singular response.

Within thirty minutes, Lanny phoned back to report that NL was scrambling for a rehearing.

"Well, that's interesting, Lanny," Harold said, referring to the still-belligerent attitude of NL management and their stated determination to keep fighting. "Because we already own fifty-one percent of the company."

"Already?"

"Done deal. Just since you called, Boyd Jefferies of Jefferies and Company 'swept the street' and sold me the remaining thirty-two percent we needed to take control at four dollars per share."

Harold's clear, calm decision-making had won the day and secured a multibillion-dollar NL corporation with an investment of just a little over $200 million.

By mid-August, Harold became the chairman of the board of NL Industries and secured control of a majority of the board seats. One of the board positions went to Lanny Martin, who now had the assignment of learning as much as possible about NL, and making recommendations to Harold on how to improve its performance and its structure—as well as find out precisely what they'd just purchased.

And contrary to the dire predictions of the entrenched management that had fought so ineptly to keep the terrible Texan at bay, jobs did not disappear, divisions were not shut down or liquidated, and the human condition of the people of NL Corporation remained essentially unaffected.

The image of Harold Simmons as a ruthless, heartless takeover "artist" intent on acquiring companies for the purpose of destroying them as operating entities had become a very useful image for frightened corporate officers to invoke when news arrived that Harold was buying their shares. The greater the degree of alarm management could raise with such imagery, the greater the number of political and sometimes legal roadblocks that could be thrown frantically in Harold's path. But the business press had followed Harold Simmons long enough by the mid-1980s to begin to understand that a Simmons takeover did not automatically mean that workers were in trouble, and in fact—as more and more financial writers pointed out, sometimes grudgingly—the opposite was usually the case. Working conditions for those employed by companies acquired by Harold Simmons often improved dramatically, and that was the second half—the hidden half—of the story.

While divisions of companies were sometimes spun off or sold or merged with another company, what was clearly *not* a Harold Simmons trait was the eradication of jobs. His stewardship of almost any business resulted in a realization of the hidden values he'd spotted in that company to begin with, a reality that corporate leaders such as Skip Pratt of National City Lines had been shrewd enough to spot while others were running for cover.

In fact, if Harold had a fault in the way he handled the immediate aftermath of a successful takeover, it was that he was far too gentlemanly in his treatment of existing management—even those who had been guilty of vilifying him during the takeover battle. His tendency was to retain everyone on the vanquished management team until he had solid reason to do otherwise.

In NL's case, that tendency was becoming worrisome to Lanny Martin as he learned more and more about the workings and structure of NL Industries. He became increasingly convinced that NL chairman Ted Rogers should be fired as soon as possible.

CHAPTER 47

DALLAS, TEXAS: 1986

The tactical and strategic brilliance of Harold Simmons' acquisition of NL Industries had been carefully tracked week by week in the nation's financial press. But once NL was completely under Harold's control, the media quietly added net worth of the company to the previous total of Harold's net worth, and realized they had a new billionaire on the block.

Harold had always been wary of too much media interest in him personally, preferring to do business with as much anonymity as possible. But major takeovers of public companies inevitably generate major publicity, and too often, the absence of someone on staff to guide and assist the press in understanding who Harold Simmons *really* was had handed the competition an unfair advantage. Corporate leaders with full-time public relations representatives had always been able to paint a false image of Simmons the destroyer without fear of contradiction, and it was time, Harold realized, to put an end to the practice. After all, he was an acknowledged and accomplished investor and business leader, not a wild-eyed Attila, and he needed someone aboard who could communicate that reality by getting some good, positive press for a change.

In the months before Harold spotted NL Industries and began buying its stock, a highly complimentary magazine article crossed his desk, one that praised his business career. The piece had been published in

Southwest Airlines' inflight magazine, and the author was a Dallas public relations man named Largent Parks. Harold met with Parks and decided to hire him.

After Parks joined Contran, he began looking for effective ways to improve Harold's image. One idea in particular really appealed to him: writing a book-length business biography about Harold.

"I can write it myself," Parks assured him.

"No, Largent," Harold replied one afternoon in his office, "I don't want you to write a book about me. That's not what I hired you to do."

"But—"

"I don't think this is the right time."

Parks pressed the issue over the following months, urging Harold to, at the very least, let him conduct tape-recorded interviews about his entire business life for future reference—just in case he changed his mind about a biography sometime in the future. And in the spring of 1986, Harold decided the recordings would be a reasonable idea. He began making time on his calendar over the next twelve months for dozens of hours of taped interviews, which were to belong to no one but Harold Simmons.

The sessions were straightforward: Harold would sit at his desk while Parks asked questions about every aspect of his life and career, questions which, in some cases, triggered memories he'd almost completely forgotten. Since the tapes were his, and the interviewer his own employee, the remembrances were frank and candid and often peppered with his extremely sharp and wry sense of humor.

In other cases—such as the highly successful business deals of the early 1980s—the remembrances were far easier, and the words flowed onto the tape recorder and later onto paper transcripts. The stories of that decade alone were compelling. The aftermath of the National City Lines and Time-DC acquisition, for instance, had been a brilliant turnaround which snatched financial victory from the jaws of impending financial defeat.

Not long after taking over the San Antonio-based company, Harold had discovered that what appeared to be National City Lines' disastrously unprofitable national trucking unit—Time-DC—in fact had a silver lining. Over the decades, Time-DC had routinely purchased and run large truck terminals across the country, many of them consisting of substantial tracts of land in downtown locations acquired originally at modest cost, but now worth tens of millions. While the trucking operation itself continued to lose money, Contran spun off the real estate holdings into a separate corporation just before the Teamsters Union called a major strike in 1981.

The strike was an act of suicide, as Harold had tried to warn Teamsters officials, but they had a national agenda, and the potential loss of one company didn't impress them. The financial reality was that it would be impossible for Time-DC to compete in the deregulated long-haul trucking market under the old levels of driver compensation under the Teamsters national contract, but the union flatly refused to negotiate a separate agreement. Nine months of warnings and wrangling went by, with Harold making it exceedingly clear that, without a separate, lower cost agreement, Time-DC's life as a national trucking company was about to come to an end. The Teamsters, however, were immovable, and reluctantly Harold gave the order to pull the plug and liquidate the company—while permitting the completely separate corporation holding the valuable real estate to start selling off the old terminals. Time-DC ceased national operations and became, instead, a small southwestern operation. Thousands of heavy trucks were put on the used market, and thousands of jobs evaporated.

"We couldn't shut it down completely," Harold told Parks and his tape recorder, "because we would have owed an incredible amount of money to the Teamsters pension fund." Congress had made trucking companies liable for any shortfall in union pension funds even if they had no control over who was managing—or mismanaging—the pension investments, and the Teamsters fund was hundreds of millions of dollars short. Time-DC, when completely liquidated, would be liable for a share of that shortfall.

While the sell-off of the majority of the operating company earned little, the proceeds of the real estate sales netted returns of just under $100 million over the next several years, adding tremendous value to the National City Lines deal, and adding to Contran's war chest for more acquisitions.

At approximately the same time, a small *Wall Street Journal* article alerted Harold to a proxy contest for control of a major chemical manufacturer called GAF Corporation, which he also judged to be an undervalued stock. He bought nearly 15 percent of the stock and held on for a little over three years, selling it for a profit of over $135 million, an ultimate return on investment of over 80 percent per year. And thus armed with even more cash to invest, Harold set his sights on the largest containerized shipping company in the world, the SeaLand Corporation, just after it had been spun-off from the huge R.J. Reynolds tobacco interests. SeaLand, Harold decided, would be an excellent company to own and operate, and he went after it, buying 40 percent of the stock on the open market—only to lose the battle to a white knight bid from CSX Corporation. Contran's stock was eventually sold for an $83 million profit, leaving Harold to shake his head in wonder at the bullet he'd dodged when SeaLand promptly fell on hard times.

A steady drumbeat of great investments continued to pour profits into Contran's coffers year after year: a purchase of McDermott International stock earning a $20 million profit, a $19 million net gain from a run at Mustang Fuel, $7 million from a failed acquisition attempt at Kerr Glass, and a highly profitable success with the purchase of a timber company in Oregon called the Medford Corporation.

"Medford had a lot of undervalued standing timber, and several plywood plants, and made fiberboard and studs for walls. A pretty stable little company," Harold explained as Largent Parks' tape rolled. "It was controlled by a Chicago-based company called Baker Fentress, which was a closed-end fund that managed investments. But Medford was seriously undervalued, I thought, so I approached the Fentress family, and the head of the company invited me to come up to Chicago and meet with him. In fact, he invited me to lunch. Well, I guess I scared him to death. I talked with him about an hour and said, 'You know, if you don't sell Medford to me, I'll just come buy the whole Baker company.' I was real brazen, and he got so shook up, he forgot all about lunch. Finally I said, well, I guess I better go, and I never did get that lunch. What I did get, though, was the chance to buy all their Medford stock and take control, and the company has been very, very valuable."

"What about the Muse deal?" Largent Parks had asked during one interview as the litany of the successful deals in the early eighties moved toward the present.

Harold recalled the Washington Redskins-Dallas Cowboy game on December 9, 1984, that had spawned an invitation to Southwest Airlines and Muse Air founder Lamar Muse to join him and Annette in their skybox at Texas Stadium. Earlier in the year, the fiery, iconoclastic Lamar Muse—once the head of Southwest Airlines—had stepped aside to let his son run the startup airline, but despite Michael Muse's best efforts, the company had reached the brink of bankruptcy. Herb Kelleher at Southwest was pulling out all the stops to kill the classy non-smoking Muse Air operation, which had been dubbed by wags in the Dallas area as "Air Revenge."

"Everything you touch seems to turn to gold," Lamar had remarked to Harold during a lull in the first quarter of the game. "How'd you like to make a big investment in Muse Air?" The suggestion was only half serious, but it was taken with complete seriousness. At halftime, Muse Air director Norman Brinker—also a guest—joined Harold and Lamar in an intense discussion, and by the end of the game the outlines of a deal were at hand. Three days later, a deal had been concluded in which Contran's Amalgamated Sugar Company would make a short-term loan of $12 million to Muse Air to keep it afloat, in return for Lamar Muse's getting back in the saddle as chairman to prepare it for a possible sale.

From Southwest's point of view, a Muse Air bankruptcy would have been more desirable, but with Harold's financial support, Muse Air stood to be a more expensive competitive thorn in the side than the cost of buying out the corporation. In a series of negotiations in Harold's office in January, the final deal was struck for Southwest to acquire all the assets of Muse Air, leaving Amalgamated—and thus Harold—with a profit of $9 million—all of which became part of the war chest that enabled the takeover of NL Industries in 1986.

As was Harold's custom after a takeover, he planned to let the existing managers and officers continue in their positions at NL. However, by late fall of 1986, Lanny Martin began recommending to Harold that the NL president, Ted Rogers, be fired. Lanny had noticed that Rogers, although cordial during the various board meetings following Harold's takeover, dragged his feet on implementing the changes he was being asked to make. In addition, Rogers seemed preoccupied with preserving his own perks and his own more-than-generous "golden parachute," and was strenuously recommending against closing the expensive New York offices of NL any sooner than a year, primarily because he wanted to retain his own office, his company car, and his other corporate privileges. Instead of the owner and the boss, Rogers was treating Harold Simmons and his representatives as slightly nettlesome board members who could ultimately be bent to Rogers' will.

"We simply can't leave New York that soon," he'd told Harold by phone when the suggestion had been made that the New York offices be closed the following year. Harold let the issue simmer. There were far more important decisions to be made regarding NL, and the planning for how to best reorganize the corporation led to several trips to New York.

On a rainy January Manhattan afternoon in 1987, Lanny accompanied Harold to the office of NL's chairman of the board in Rockefeller Center, a plush and beautiful corner office adorned by expensive carpet and fine paintings and furniture, and two huge windows forming two of the office walls, one of them looking out over Radio City Music Hall from the thirty-first floor. The glassed-in skyscraper had been the expensive downtown Manhattan home of NL for some years, and Ted Rogers was in no mood to leave it, takeover or no takeover.

There had been a long list of items to discuss with Harold, who was now not only a member of the board of directors but in complete control of the board and the undisputed owner of over 50 percent of the corporation. But the end of the meeting was at hand, and Lanny had noticed that outside, the intensity of the rain had increased to a steady downpour.

"Well, I guess we'd better be going," Lanny said, watching Ted Rogers' reaction. "We've got to get back to the Plaza Hotel, and it's really raining hard out there."

No response, other than a nod.

"So," Lanny continued, "I guess we should ask you where it would be best to catch a cab around here?"

"A cab?" Rogers asked casually.

"Yeah. It's raining really hard."

Rogers got to his feet and motioned Lanny over to one of the windows as his secretary entered the office and caught his attention.

"Mr. Rogers?" she said.

"Yes?" the NL chairman replied, turning.

"Sir, your driver is waiting downstairs to take you to Mrs. Rogers' cocktail party. You really should be leaving now."

"Tell him I'll be right there," he replied, turning back to Lanny and pointing to an intersection some three hundred feet below.

"Your best bet to catch a cab is right ... down there, on that corner," Rogers said, turning back to his desk to get his briefcase and bid them goodbye, before following his secretary out of the office, presumably heading for the dry warmth of the town car essentially owned by the man he was leaving behind in his office.

Lanny looked at Harold and rolled his eyes, incredulous that Rogers had failed to even offer them a ride.

"A cocktail party!" Lanny said.

"Well, I guess we'd better go find that cab," Harold replied, keeping his expression completely neutral as they descended the elevator.

Neither of them had an umbrella, so Lanny insisted Harold remain under the imperfect cover of an awning while he took the brunt of the downpour and stepped into the street to hail toward the passing river of cabs flowing past at breakneck speeds and kicking up small rooster tails of dirty water in their wake.

None would stop.

Lanny's suit was getting soaked and his shoes were awash. He didn't dare throw himself in front of the taxis, but there had to be some way to snag one. The majority were off duty and oblivious to his plight.

Suddenly, he recalled an old New York taxi trick, and fished through his pocket to find a twenty-dollar bill. He waved the instantly soaked twenty in the air, and right on cue, the next passing cab driver spotted the money and tromped on his brakes.

Soaked to the skin, Lanny squished into the cramped back seat and motioned to Harold, who dashed through deep puddles to dive into the cab and pull the door shut behind him.

When they'd relayed the address and sat back, Lanny caught Harold's eye and pointed up toward the corner office they'd occupied for the previous hour.

"May I ask you a question about Ted Rogers?" Lanny began, knowing Harold was well aware of his dump-Rogers recommendation, and the reasons behind it.

"Go ahead," Harold replied, his expression still unreadable.

"Are you convinced yet?" Lanny asked.

"Am I convinced?" Harold repeated. He looked down and began brushing some of the water off his suit coat before looking back up. "Yeah, Lanny," he said, shaking the water off his hand. "I think this has just about convinced me."

On return to Dallas, Harold launched Lanny Martin on a search for a new president and chairman for NL while negotiating the exit of Ted Rogers and the closing within six months of the New York offices. Rogers' protests were summarily overruled.

While the oilfield business was still abysmal and generating losses, even among the oilfield division of NL there were bright spots. Baroid Corporation of Texas, for instance, rapidly emerged from the initial melange of NL properties as a very valuable company that should be built up further. Baroid had become the world's preeminent supplier of the drilling muds, the slurry constantly pumped down drilling pipes to lubricate whirling drill bits as they churn through rock thousands of feet down.

It had been apparent to Harold from the first that rearranging NL Industries to produce the maximum operating values was going to take some time, and the need for choosing a new president was becoming a pressing matter by the time Lanny Martin was ready to offer his list of possible candidates.

"I've got five names on the list," he told Harold.

"Good."

"And my name's on top," Lanny said.

"*Your* name? Why, Lanny?"

"I've always had a . . . I guess a deep desire . . . to run a corporation, not just practice corporate law, for one."

"Lanny, I don't want to lose my lawyer. Who else is on your list?"

Lanny ran through the other candidates, summarizing their interviews and strengths before returning to his qualifications. "Harold, let me try it for a year, and if you aren't happy, I'll rejoin my firm and go back to being your lawyer."

Harold sat quietly for a few heartbeats before nodding his head.

"All right," Harold replied. "One year."

■   ■   ■

On an otherwise routine afternoon, after many months of work reorganizing the corporation as its new president, Lanny called Harold into his Dallas office.

"Harold," he said, "I just needed to get your approval for the transfer of that park land in upstate New York to the New York Parks Department."

There was silence on the Dallas end of the call for a few seconds.

"Park land?" Harold asked.

Lanny repeated the specifics.

Harold had leaned forward at his desk. "Lanny, what are you talking about? What property?"

"It's ... somewhere around the Adirondacks ... I thought you knew about this."

"No. No one's cleared that with me. We're trying to give it back?"

"Well, the deal was in progress I'm told, when we took over, and ... I guess they were just going to cede it to the state of New York for a park. It's some old mining property, and not listed as being worth much. You want to hold off?"

"Well, until I take a look at it, absolutely. How many acres?"

"Says here, twelve thousand acres."

"Good grief! We're not giving away thousands of acres of land to anyone until I see it in person."

Several weeks later, Harold and Annette boarded NL's Falcon 50, a three-engine intercontinental business jet, and flew to Lake Placid, New York, where they rented a car and drove to what turned out to have been a private playground for the corporate rulers of NL, an understated, undervalued estate of enormous proportions filled with forests and streams, lakes, and a private lodge maintained by a caretaker. It was a property that contained the headwaters of the Hudson River. A private railroad traversed the scenic beauty as well, crossing the upstream expanse of the Hudson at one point as it meandered from a still-operable ilmenite—a source of titanium dioxide, which had been a critical strategic resource during World War II, but had become trivial in the decades since. The mine, Harold discovered, could still make a small profit and was, in fact, being worked. Obviously, the immense value of the property had been overlooked.

Harold immediately canceled the giveaway and returned to Dallas.

CHAPTER 48

FORT SMITH, ARKANSAS: 1988

*H*arold looked out at the familiar airport ramp as he toggled the three engine start switches to the off position and listened to the Falcon 50's tail-mounted fanjets winding down. His copilot, Mike Bonnell, began reading the shutdown checklist items as Harold unsnapped his seat belt and glanced over at Contran's chief pilot. Mike loved the company's new jet, which had come from NL Industries, and he kept it immaculate—as well as serving as first officer for the boss whenever Harold flew as pilot in command.

The flight from Dallas Love Field had taken a brief thirty-five minutes, and Harold knew his guests in the main cabin would feel as if they'd barely left the ground.

He stepped out of the cockpit and entered the main cabin, where Annette and the three other couples were waiting.

"Beautiful landing, Captain!" one of the women said, leading a round of applause as Harold grinned somewhat shyly.

"Well, it's all pretty simple," he explained with a mock-serious expression. "I just aim at the runway and hold a steady decent rate until Mike up there gasps real loud, and then I pull on the control yoke and it seems to work out okay every time."

More laughter, and Annette began gently herding them to the forward entry door Mike had just opened, its built-in stairs leading to the

Fort Smith ramp where the vans were waiting for the forty-five-minute ride to the Simmonses' 3,000-acre property to the north.

As the group climbed into the vans, Harold turned for a second to glance back at the Falcon, allowing himself a small moment of pride. Flying was demanding, but it was very satisfying to be able to operate such a craft, and especially to do it well.

Harold turned and smiled at Annette, who was motioning for him to join the others.

The weekend would be fun, and Harold was looking forward to it, even though the basic plan was the same whenever they brought guests to Arkansas. He'd narrate their trip north through the Ozark hills, and as soon as they rolled onto their private road, he'd begin pointing out the lakes and the creek, the forest and pathways as they approached the family compound. They would give their guests time to settle into the guest houses and freshen up, and then take everyone over to a nearby hillside and his four-story, control-tower-like observation lounge, where Harold would mix cocktails and host a breathtaking view of the sunset across three different sides of the Arkansas River valley.

How incredible, he thought, to be able to share such things with fun and interesting people. He knew there were those who would dismiss any display of such an extraordinary place as merely showing off, but he wasn't showing off. This was entirely different. He'd worked and planned and added to the Arkansas property specifically to make it a place people would enjoy visiting, especially people Harold and Annette wanted to be with.

And that, in fact, was the point: utilizing the great benefits of his wealth to enhance the richness of his relationships with friends. The Arkansas property was a wonderful retreat.

Annette had changed him profoundly, Harold knew, guiding him and encouraging him to do so much more than just hold his own in a social gathering. The very process of social interaction had become another personal renaissance, and he was thoroughly enjoying getting to know the wide array of people around them, men and women whose lives and stories would have remained unknown to him in the years before Annette, when his world was encompassed only by work and family.

Their Arkansas weekends, in fact, had become a predictable, controllable way to add to the scope of those friendships, and those who accompanied them to Fort Smith always seemed appreciative and responsive—as well as amazed at how much beauty he'd enshrined in all the manicuring his caretaker had done over the years.

"We have these four-wheelers," Harold was explaining as they sat and talked in the observation tower a few hours later, each of them nursing one of Harold's special homemade margaritas. "Tomorrow morning, after breakfast, we'll get one for each of you and go on a tour of the place. We've got deer, wild turkey, bears, elk, several lakes, waterfalls, Indian burial grounds, and all kinds of things to show you. We're also going to do a little fishing, and I guarantee you, you will catch fish, because we've got the lakes well stocked. We've also got Davy Joe and Delmer, who'll clean whatever we catch. Then, around noon, we'll have a little picnic lunch."

"This ... this whole expanse, Harold, looks like some incredible state park," one of the women said, eliciting a smile from her host.

"Well, that's kind of the idea, and we've got several picnic places and tables and White Oak Creek and a lot of pathways, so it's designed to be like a park."

"It's truly beautiful," one of the men remarked.

"Thanks," Harold replied, trying not to beam too broadly, his eyes drawn back to the edge of the woods where a solitary buck had paused to test the air, looking in their direction as if he could hear their voices. "I really do love this place."

There was a lull in the conversation as the assembled group drank in the lengthening shadows and ruddy hues of sundown, triggering a brief anthology of good memories in Harold's mind. There had been so many fun trips over the years up here with the girls, and now with Amy and Andy and his family as well. Of course, the McKinney, Texas, ranch was the most accessible family retreat, sitting less than a half hour by road from his North Dallas office, but Arkansas was still the most satisfying.

He was, in fact, growing very fond of the McKinney ranch as well, and he was seriously considering Annette's suggestion that they should build a second house there. He'd originally bought the McKinney land so that Serena and Amy would have a place to ride horses, but the ranch was growing into a true family retreat.

"Harold, did you hear me?" Annette's soft voice interrupted his reverie.

"Sorry?"

"I think our guests are running dry. We need more margaritas." She stared at him a few seconds. "Where were you just then?"

He smiled and squeezed her hand. "Somewhere between here and paradise, I guess," he replied, getting to his feet to work on a new batch of margaritas. "Which, from where we are, is a really short distance."

When he returned to the group, the conversation had drifted to the subject of charitable giving. One of his guests, a physician, was relaying welcome news about the deep research into arthritis already resulting from the many millions of dollars Harold was donating to the University of Texas Southwestern Medical School for that purpose.

"You've already done a tremendous amount of good," the doctor was saying.

"Well, that's exactly the sort of thing I want to accomplish. I really intend to leave the majority of what I've amassed to good causes. I've made adequate provisions for my daughters and grandchildren, and have trained my daughters to continue our family philanthropy."

"Harold, you know what I really admire about you?" the doctor asked. "I admire your humility, and the fact that you don't go around wearing your success on your sleeve and expecting everyone to salute. In fact, if I didn't already know you, I'd suspect you were successful, but I'd never suspect you were rich."

Annette was nodding. "You ought to hear Courtney Henderson, Harold's tennis pro, on the same subject," she said with a chuckle. "Harold and Courtney have been playing tennis for years, and one day a couple of years ago, Harold invited him to one of the Cowboys' games. The day was terrible—wet and stormy and miserable in the stands at Texas Stadium. Well, when Harold went to pick up Courtney to take him to our Skybox, he came out bringing a big blanket and big boots."

Annette continued, "He was expecting to sit in the stands and suffer like everyone else . . . and Courtney couldn't figure out why Harold was dressed up nice with no storm gear in sight. You know, he figured that Harold was going to get soaked. Courtney's known him for all these years, and yet he had no idea he's wealthy, and no idea he has a private box."

"I thought everybody had a private box," Harold teased.

The next year, Harold treated Courtney and his wife to a European cruise.

"My point is, and one of the reasons I love him . . . is just what you said," Annette explained. "Having all this hasn't changed him. He's still the same."

"Look over there," Harold interrupted, pointing toward the western horizon. "I never get tired of watching that ruddy glow blend into the cobalt blue of the darkening sky, and right now the terminator is just descending."

"The what?" someone asked.

"Terminator. The dividing band between day and night that the astronauts can see so clearly from space. In fact, when they're in orbit, they see it eighteen times per day."

As the others suspended their conversations and turned to watch the final vestiges of the sunset, Annette's previous words evoked in Harold a warm memory of Golden, Texas. He thought of Glenn, his brother, who was equally fond of saying that he hadn't changed, as were some of his other lifelong friends from Golden.

Harold made a mental note to call Johnny Dowell the following week. The annual Sweet Potato Festival was coming up, and he would make the trek with cash in hand to drop about $5,000 buying a few cases of sweet potatoes to support the Golden area. Undoubtedly, Johnny would be there, and he looked forward to seeing him.

CHAPTER 49

DALLAS LOVE FIELD, DALLAS, TEXAS: 1989

J. Landis Martin—veteran corporate attorney and the new president of NL Industries—left the plane that had carried him from Denver and charged into the familiar surroundings of the DFW terminal, organizing his thoughts for the day ahead. He paused long enough to check his watch. The flight had been late, and he was already behind schedule.

He passed a newsstand and quickly doubled back to buy a copy of the *Dallas Morning News,* eager to see the front page of the business section. As expected, a headline above the fold proclaimed the news of yesterday afternoon: "Georgia Gulf Turns Down Simmons Bid." Lanny stuffed the paper under his arm and headed for the exit in search of his waiting car. Georgia Gulf was not a problem. Either Contran would end up selling the stock for a substantial profit, or would end up owning the billion-dollar company for a fraction of its true value.

But it wasn't Georgia Gulf that was occupying his thoughts.

With the move of NL headquarters from New York to Houston complete, planning had begun for what would probably prove to be the biggest battle of Harold's career: his impending attempt to take control of Lockheed, one of the nation's largest aerospace defense contractors.

Yet it had been the tremendous flow of dollars into defense under the Reagan Administration, Lanny knew, that had caused existing management of some defense companies to get lazy, a mesmerized state which had begun to crumble with Soviet perestroika, and thirteen days before, on November 9, the collapse of the Berlin Wall.

The copy of the *Morning News* was filled with follow-up articles and references to the historic event and the continuous unraveling of Soviet influence. For all practical purposes, the cold war was ending, and in the misguided euphoria of the moment, there were wags and writers all over America eagerly anticipating the end of any significant need for a standing U.S. military. Huge anticipated cutbacks in defense spending were depressing Lockheed's stock and forcing Harold to act. Lockheed had been diversifying into industries it didn't understand, diluting its value and performance, and with the world changing, its survival—and the viability of Harold's investment—depended on Lockheed's changing its corporate strategy and becoming much more efficient.

Lanny lowered the paper and watched the North Dallas landscape sliding by. So far, Harold seemed pleased with his performance as head of NL, and he was enjoying the pace and the challenge, though the sheer volume of decision-making on a daily basis was somewhat akin to drinking out of a fire hose. Most of the restructuring of NL was now complete, however, and that was a relief. The host of complex transactions Harold had directed had gone smoothly, and it was now obvious that the decision to spin off Baroid, the drilling services company, as a separate entity flush with a new stock offering had been a brilliant call. Contran was still the largest, controlling shareholder of Baroid at 45 percent, but the move had helped NL's balance sheet substantially, ridding it of the previous losses from the temporary collapse of the oilfield supply business.

A new office building under construction near Northwest Highway and Preston Road caught his attention as they whisked north up the tollway. The building was festooned with cranes and activity as Dallas began to shake off the disastrous mid-'80s crash in real estate. While the so-called traveling crane atop the new high-rise was no longer jokingly called the "official bird of North Texas," the economy was collectively daring to hope again. This time around, however, there was a substantial hole in the Texas business landscape where a host of previously strong Texas banks had once ruled.

For decades, all the major Dallas banking institutions, including Republic, First International Bancshares, and the Mercantile, had been overly exuberant in providing loans to the oil and real estate industries. But in the middle of the 1980s, almost all were fire-sold to out-of-state banking corporations to prevent bankruptcy, as the final collapse of the domestic oil patch destroyed billions of dollars of equity. It was fascinating, Lanny thought, how dramatically things had changed. When he'd first met him, Harold was still struggling to arrange bank loans through local institutions and was working hard to keep them happy. Now he had international bankers from literally all over the world making pilgrimages to North Dallas trying to convince him to borrow their money. It was an exciting time to be one of Harold Simmons' inner circle.

And now Lockheed.

Harold had begun buying Lockheed stock on the open market when it fell below $33 per share in late spring. They had filed the required notifications to Lockheed that he was buying, and they had triggered the predictable response.

"Lanny, look what these guys have done," Harold had said several months back one morning in his office. "They already had that thirty percent poison pill, and now they've reduced the trigger point to twenty percent." He'd plopped the notification on the edge of his desk for Lanny to see.

Harold had become very passionate on the subject of poison pills for a reason Lanny understood well: The widespread adoption of poison pills was essentially destroying his capabilities to acquire undervalued companies. Poison pills, by their nature, gave an entrenched management a nearly foolproof way to retain control regardless of poor past performance or lack of personal ownership. And despite Harold's stunning defeat of the NL poison pill, corporate lawyers all over the country had been working overtime to construct better, more impregnable versions that could not be defeated by a so-called "raider," each of them fully understanding that ultimately the fate of the poison pill defense rested with the Supreme Court of Delaware, where most major American companies were incorporated. If the court ultimately ruled that the poison pill provisions being passed by thousands of Delaware corporations were illegal as a concept, the game would be over, and Harold would have a clear track once again.

And how could they rule otherwise? Poison pills essentially operated by cutting the value of an "unauthorized" purchaser's holdings in half for the offense of having bought too many shares on the open market. The provisions essentially destroyed the open-market concept and called into serious question whether or not a purchaser of common stock was actually purchasing anything of real value, since ultimate control of a company was to be determined solely by that company's management and board, the only entities that could suspend the operation of a poison pill. Harold Simmons wasn't the only one who felt strongly that the poison pill defense was immoral and illegal and flatly wrong, nor was he the only one who predicted that even the management-friendly Delaware Supreme Court would not be brave enough to uphold the poison pill concept.

But to the utter amazement of sophisticated investors, corporate lawyers, and Harold Simmons, the Delaware court did uphold the poison pill, handing entrenched managements everywhere an incredible victory, and all but destroying the very process that had permitted Harold to rise from being the owner of only one drugstore to owning a billion-dollar empire—a process that had forced many a management to become far more efficient and responsive to its stockholders, lest Harold turn his attentions on them.

"Poison pills are devastatingly simple in their basic form," Lanny had explained on numerous occasions. "If the pill kicks in at twenty percent and someone tries to buy more than that without management approval, *all* the stockholders except the outsider get to buy more shares for half-price, essentially cutting the value of the outsider's shares in half. Harold believes it's a totally illegal confiscation of property."

Lanny shook himself back to the present. They were approaching the intersection of Dallas North Tollway and LBJ Freeway, where Contran's offices were located in a modern, high-rise complex known as Lincoln Center. What would probably end up being a running gun battle with Daniel Tellup, chairman of Lockheed out in Calabasas, California, was already under way, and since it was technically NL Industries trying to do the acquisition, Lanny would be deeply involved in every decision.

He checked the papers he'd been examining and stuffed them back in his briefcase. There was a war to plan, and he wanted to be ready.

■　　■　　■

Within thirty days the battle lines were clearly drawn. Harold

Simmons, through NL Industries, had acquired just under 20 percent of Lockheed, and based on the mediocre financial performance of Lockheed, losses in the previous year due to defense contract cancelations and other write-downs, Harold had asked for six seats on the board. His prime intention for seeking board membership was to help guide the company back to profitability, whether he ultimately controlled the corporation or not. In fact, the stock price was going down, trapping him in the investment and creating a clear and strong incentive for him to contribute his considerable management and financial skills to helping Lockheed improve.

But Dan Tellup, Lockheed's chief, flatly refused to give Harold Simmons or his appointees even one board seat and publicly said that a mere 20 percent ownership of the company did not justify any seats on *his* board of directors. The statement was puzzling, Harold thought, coming from a management team who together owned less than one percent of the stock, yet believed themselves to be entitled to iron-clad control of the company and its board.

Harold increased the pressure on Tellup by publicly recommending major changes, including the sale of a few divisions Lockheed had begun which had little, if anything, to do with their main business of designing and producing cutting-edge aircraft such as the F-117 Stealth fighter, or the highly successful Lockheed C-130 transport. But by January, with no hope of forcing the removal of the poison pill, either by court action or negotiation, Harold saw his investment of over $500 million sink from $44 a share back to the low thirties. Major changes were clearly needed, yet Lockheed management was determined to squander as much as $8 million to defend its control.

With Lockheed's poison pill firmly in place, acquiring the corporation without Tellup's permission would be financially impossible, and Tellup had no intention of even listening to Harold Simmons, let alone selling more stock to him. All the finely honed skills and methods Harold had developed over the previous two decades—the sophisticated and repeatedly successful approach to corporate acquisition that had earned him over a billion dollars in net worth and significantly improved the values of the companies he had acquired—had been neutralized by the lethal combination of the corporate poison pill resolution and the Delaware Supreme Court.

There was, however, one other way to go about gaining control.

Instead of taking over by the brute force of majority ownership, there was still the possibility of winning a proxy contest—cajoling the support of enough shareholders to form a majority and sweep the old board of directors of Lockheed away in favor of one appointed by Harold. Proxy contests were nothing new, but their use had been eclipsed for decades by the fancy financing methods Wall Street had developed during the late seventies and eighties (including the advent of so-called "junk bonds," which had financed a decade of leveraged buyouts for other raiders, some responsible, some not).

By February 1990, Contran and NL had hired a proxy-solicitation firm named D.F. King to prepare for the proxy battle. One of the first acts of stage-setting recommended by the firm was a rapid alteration of Harold's public image.

CHAPTER 50

DALLAS, TEXAS: 1990

"I already have a PR guy," Harold had replied to the suggestion.

"Yes, sir, but he hasn't succeeded in changing the basic image that Harold Simmons is a corporate raider ready to rape, pillage, and plunder Lockheed. That's what they're going to be playing on. If they can scare the shareholders, institutions and individuals, they win."

Within weeks, Harold sat before a video camera in an interview-style format discussing his philosophies and intentions for Lockheed. "The name 'corporate raider' suggests a destructive intent," he said at one point, when asked if his methods were similar to other corporate raiders. "That's not my record at all. I'm a builder."

The videotape was only one part of D.F. King's strategy, however. In addition to the video and reams of printed materials, Harold himself was needed to personally win over the institutional stockholders, many of whom were in New York.

It began to feel like a political campaign, Harold remarked, and one which demanded he engage in one of his least favorite activities: public speaking.

With Annette aboard, Harold piloted the Fanjet Falcon to New York in early February. They settled into a suite in the Plaza Hotel, but there was little time to enjoy it. While Annette spent the days shopping for furnishings for the company's various properties, Harold began a two-week campaign. He was whisked away in the morning by a hired car, briefed on the way about the people with whom he'd be talking, and prepped on how best to explain why a Lockheed run by Harold Simmons with a hand-picked Simmons board would stand a significantly better chance of increasing Lockheed's profits and future worth.

It was an uphill battle. Many of the stockholders, who were otherwise dissatisfied with Lockheed's dismal performance, nevertheless remained on the fence, especially in the face of the equally impassioned pleas for loyalty by Daniel Tellup and his management team, who were also crisscrossing New York looking for votes. Deep within, Harold was nursing some serious doubts whether he could win the proxy vote, and the skeptical attitude of many of those he addressed did little to bolster confidence. Yet, there was no reason not to try—and try hard. He was committing more than $8 million to the campaign in order to protect a half-billion-dollar investment, and that was reasonable. Whether any amount of money and effort could convince hide-bound New Yorkers to trust his management skills and judgment was something else. In fact, the reception in several meetings was all but frosty, and on a particular morning at Foley Square in lower Manhattan, the response from the men and women who controlled the New York City workers' pension fund was openly hostile.

While Tellup and the Lockheed management were working hard to paint Harold Simmons as a corporate-raiding devil intent on breaking up and destroying Lockheed for personal gain, Harold—through NL Industries—took out an equal number of full-page *Wall Street Journal* and other industry ads countering Lockheed's incendiary statements, including several ads that gave not only the names of the board members Harold would install if NL won, but their pictures as well.

The alternate board was impressive. In order to neutralize concerns that a Simmons-controlled Lockheed would have trouble understanding the special nature of a major aerospace defense contractor, Harold had recruited the well-known former chief of naval operations, Admiral Elmo Zumwalt; Senator John Tower, a pillar of U.S. defense support in the Senate; former Air Force Secretary Hans Mark; an Air Force general; Southwest Airlines' co-creator Lamar Muse; and several other well-thought-of men, in addition to Harold himself, Fred Bartlit, Mike Snetzer, and Lanny Martin.

In fact, there was little concern among the fence-sitting stockholders and fund managers about NL's proposed board for Lockheed, but there was great hesitation about unseating Dan Tellup's experienced management team in favor of someone new. The hyperbole and invective heaped on Harold personally weighed heavily in their collective minds.

At the end of the second week, Harold and Annette flew back to Dallas. The moment of truth would be the upcoming stockholders' meeting set for May in California, and that gave them over two months to change all the minds they needed. Changes were already beginning to occur, as first one fund, and then another, reevaluated what Harold had been saying.

Lockheed had also hired a proxy solicitation firm, and their first and most important bit of paid advice was an urgent recommendation to move up the date of the shareholders meeting from May to March to thwart the Simmons-NL assault. "The more time they have to work on your shareholders," officials of the Georgeson Company told Tellup's team, "the closer they get to success."

Tellup and his board immediately changed the date from May 30 to March 30, catching Harold and his team by surprise. NL formally challenged the date change, but the challenge was to the existing board, which was clearly uninterested in cooperation. Lockheed also created a 20 percent block of stock by issuing corporate treasury stock to a newly formed ESOP (employee stock ownership plan). The company's management would vote this stock, for which they paid nothing, thereby offsetting the 20 percent block owned by Harold.

As the showdown neared, the activity in and around Harold's office in Dallas increased. Pam Phillips, his secretary and gatekeeper, had been struck from the first by the calm and sedate manner in which business was conducted by Harold and those around him, and while the current pace as seen by any outsider would have been indistinguishable from the same sedate and steady methodology, she could feel the difference on a day-by-day basis. The office was the command bridge of a corporate ship in the middle of a war, and the definitive battle was just ahead.

"What we're facing if we lose," Contran Vice President Steve Watson explained, "has nothing to do with going bankrupt or anything terrible, but it has everything to do with controlling the investment. With the stock down so far, we don't want to sell it and realize a huge loss when it will someday go back up. But in the meantime we've got a half-billion dollars trapped in Lockheed with no way to force them to reform."

Dueling full-page ads in the *Wall Street Journal* heralded the intensity of the fight:

"Don't risk your investment on NL's promises," trumpeted Tellup's ad on March 26.

"Who will best serve Lockheed?" NL's ad shot back from an adjacent page.

Toward the end of March, the extremely nervous Lockheed senior management team began to understand that their hopes for a unified show of loyalty among the shareholders was a pipe dream, not only because of their previous lackluster financial performance but because many of the proposals made by Harold Simmons and NL were excellent ideas which made sound business sense. The proposals were becoming popular with some of the other shareholders, and threatening Tellup's control. Several days before the stockholders' meeting, Tellup surprised everyone by announcing that he and his board would support several key recommendations, including the NL proposal to oppose ever paying "greenmail" to rid Lockheed of a raider. He also held out the possibility of creating more board seats to represent members of the institutional shareholders' ranks, as long as the name Harold Simmons was not on the list. The unexpected concessions made under the gun were enough to win back several key investment groups and significantly bolster Dan Tellup's optimism.

On March 30, the day of the stockholder meeting, Lanny Martin and Harold knew that, despite their previous confidence, they were facing an almost impossible task. The NL ballots were green, the Lockheed ballots were blue, and even though there were some Lockheed employees sporting "Vote Green" and "We're with Harold" signs, as some 4,000 stockholders filed into a huge Lockheed hangar at Burbank's airport, the prognosis for the green forces prevailing was not good.

Tellup knew better than to freeze the Simmons team out at the meeting. He was dealing with enough investor distrust as it was. Instead, he conducted the meeting in gentlemanly fashion, giving Harold time to speak, and recognizing as well one of Harold's recommended board members, Admiral Bud Zumwalt. The admiral approached the microphone and gave a brief but moving tribute to the chairman of Contran and NL. "I think you all know me," the former chief of naval operations said, aware that the Lockheed people knew him very well from navy days. "I think you also know that I've been called the toughest outside director in America, because I'm not a pushover. I think, then, you'll understand that I would not be on Harold Simmons' team if I didn't have the highest regard for Harold. If he tells you he's going to do something, he's going to do it, and that includes all the excellent plans he has for this company. You need not worry about some hidden agenda. Harold Simmons is a man of his word."

Admiral Zumwalt was applauded as he sat down, but when the day had ended, those who voted for NL's slate of directors failed to crest 40 percent, leaving Dan Tellup in complete control.

On April 16, Tellup briefly reconvened the annual meeting to formally place on the record the final tally of the proxy voting, and afterward, Tellup and several of his senior officers had lunch with Harold and Lanny, who presented the Lockheed victors with a five-page letter outlining the changes they wanted to see instituted at Lockheed as quickly as possible. It was understood that there was a penalty for failing to heed the advice. Tellup was well aware Harold would be quite capable of mounting another bruising proxy battle the following year, and if he had failed to perform by that time, many of the institutional votes he'd just received might evaporate. In addition, Harold made it clear that he considered Tellup's voting of the employee stock ownership plan shares to have been fraudulent, and that a new vote should be held—a suggestion everyone knew would be immediately rejected.

During the proxy contest, Harold had authorized and announced a federal lawsuit against Lockheed, seeking an injunction to prevent management from manipulation of the employee ballots, and the creation of the ESOP plan's 20 percent vote. Tellup snorted in public that the suit was groundless and nothing but "pure harassment." Harold's team knew otherwise, but the California federal judge whose court landed the case decided to push it to the back burner and essentially ignore all NL's requests for quick relief.

While the financial media reported Tellup's victory nationwide, Harold returned to Dallas with a firm resolve to keep on fighting to boost Lockheed's worth, a position bolstered by a continued pledge of support from most of the investors who had stood with him. He had few other reasonable options. The stock was too depressed to sell without taking a mammoth and unnecessary loss, which meant that like it or not, his investment was essentially at the mercy of Tellup and his team.

The prospect of mounting an even more energetic proxy contest in

1991 was one option, and, in the meantime, the invested money would be safe. Lockheed was not about to collapse. In fact, the company was still an extremely valuable company and paid a consistent dividend. Harold and Lanny knew that Dan Tellup would be working harder than he had in years to improve things in the following year using the same ideas Harold had publicly recommended, in the hopes that another proxy contest wouldn't be necessary.

■   ■   ■

While intense research and discussions continued in Dallas, there was other business to attend to, not the least of which was Georgia Gulf, where matters came to a head in May.

Harold had decided Georgia Gulf could be potentially worth hundreds of millions in profit if he could acquire control. But in late spring, a recognized investment guru with no apparent connection to the company flew to Santa Barbara to convince Harold not to try. Hard times were ahead for the chemical manufacturer, the man counseled, and it wasn't the gold mine it appeared to be.

Harold mulled it over and decided to sell, making a $16 million profit. The fact that ownership of Georgia Gulf would have ultimately netted a profit of nearly a billion dollars would not be known for nearly a decade, but the end of the acquisition attempt left him free to concentrate on Lockheed, whose stock had refused to rebound.

Help, however, came from an unexpected and wholly unwanted quarter: Iraqi dictator Sadaam Hussein began his brutal invasion of Kuwait in August of 1990 and triggered Operations Desert Shield and Desert Storm, and, in the process, sent Lockheed stock and that of most defense contractors soaring again—especially when it appeared that the Lockheed-built Stealth Fighter, the F-117, was going to end up being one of the stars of the impending war.

Five months had elapsed since the loss in Burbank, but Lockheed's board had made one small concession to Harold's suggestion that the company drop its poison pill defense: Any stockholder who wanted to tender for 100 percent of Lockheed's outstanding stock, the board said, could do so exempt from the poison pill. It was going to be all or nothing, and with the stock price going up again, there was a now-or-never trigger point approaching, above which the cost of purchase of the whole company would be too great.

Harold and Lanny had quietly arranged heavyweight European financing to make up the difference between the extra half-billion dollars in cash that NL (and Contran) could contribute to a complete buy-out, and the $600 million more that Harold figured would be needed. The resulting Lockheed debt would not be unmanageable, but Harold knew that Tellup would seize on it as an excuse not to sell.

There were many sound reasons why a successful acquisition could eventually double or triple Contran's overall net value after taking the company private, but there would also be risks in trying to swallow the Lockheed elephant with far more debt in the deal than Harold had ever used before. On one hand, the market value of the stock was recovering toward the half-billion mark again, as Lockheed's stock price inched back up with good promise of rising further. On the other hand, there was still much that Tellup had refused to do to fix Lockheed, and the actions he was stubbornly refusing to take could mean the difference between moderate profits and marginal stability versus great profits and firm stability.

In the final analysis, however, the gamble, if it was a gamble, was clearly worth it, and supported by the hard assets of the company.

In November, NL Industries, through Lanny Martin, announced an offer to purchase all of the shares of Lockheed NL did not already own for $40 per share, which would price the company at a total value of $1.6 billion and make each shareholder a considerable profit.

Dan Tellup curtly responded that Lockheed would study the offer in due course, and by December 3 it was formally rejected. The flimsy grounds cited by the Lockheed chairman were that the Lockheed board was worried the Simmons forces might eventually be unable to raise the rest of the purchase money, ignoring the reality that $500 million had already been spent on the existing NL stock, and another half billion was available in cash. Unlike highly leveraged buyouts of the mid-eighties, less than half the purchase price would be from new debt. Tellup went so far as to suggest that Harold's bid was insincere, and merely an excuse to mount a new proxy contest. But while the offer was completely serious, Tellup's rejection of it made a renewed proxy war all but unavoidable.

There was, however, a new problem blocking Harold by early

spring of 1991. The changes Lockheed had made under the pressure he had mounted, along with very careful accounting to yield the most attractive year-end statement, had succeeded in producing a year-end profit much more in line with what Harold had said Lockheed could achieve, and since the recovery had come under Tellup's leadership, the underlying investor unrest that had sent so many institutions into Harold's camp the year before began to dissipate. Coupled with the abandonment of a major European stockholder who had pledged to stay on Harold's side, but instead had switched without warning, it was becoming increasingly obvious by the end of January that a proxy victory was even less likely than before. In addition, the federal court in California was dragging its feet on the suit against Lockheed's use of employee and ESOP proxies, which meant Tellup would probably use the very same method he had used before to skew the results.

And finally, Lockheed's stock itself had recovered to $44 per share.

On March 18, Harold decided that the improved stock price and the new international tensions, which could positively impact Lockheed, had changed the odds. The new equation convinced him to sell out. Harold gave the order and in one trade liquidated all but 500,000 shares of NL's holdings, locking in an approximate $50 million paper loss as he also withdrew the recommended alternate slate of directors.

The fight was over, and Lockheed's management had won.

In the perception of the public and the press, Harold Simmons had been badly defeated in the Lockheed battle, but there were plenty of participants and observers who knew better. In fact, the loss was completely offset by the dividends received and by a court award of $30 million to NL for Lockheed's improper maneuvers with the employee stock fund. And in a broader sense, Harold's two-year battle had indirectly benefited almost everyone, including the interests of the United States in maintaining strong and capable defense contractors. As one Lockheed insider later stated off the record, "Harold Simmons was the best thing to ever happen to Lockheed. It got Tellup off his duff and forced him to start managing for profit and for the shareholders, and made us produce better products. We ought to have a statue of Harold erected in the lobby for saving the company."

In Dallas, the unsuccessful fight was seen as little more than an interlude in Harold's remarkable career, but in fact, it marked the end of an era. Thanks to the Delaware Supreme Court and the survival of the poison pill, and thanks to a rising stock market that was beginning to translate far more careful analyses of corporate worth into more realistic prices, "business as usual" at Contran was no longer possible. While hidden value corporate bargains might still be lurking out there, Harold knew, most of them would remain inaccessible, and it became apparent that it was time to turn more to managing the incredible wealth he'd built than focusing all his professional attention on the next deal.

Then, too, in the aftermath of Lockheed, he found himself turning his attention to matters that had seemed relatively back-burner during the previous decades, including the shattering discovery that Serena, at the tender age of twenty-one, had developed a rare form of cancer.

CHAPTER 51

DALLAS, TEXAS: 1991

*T*he headaches had been accompanied by occasional hearing loss, and the symptoms Serena was suffering were beginning to alarm her and her father and stepmother. Repeated trips to doctors in Dallas had turned up little in the way of answers, until an MRI was ordered. Within a few days, Harold and Annette were sitting with his youngest daughter in a physician's office listening to the chilling news that Serena had a cancerous mass growing internally in the area between her eyes and nose. The only good news was that it had not invaded her brain.

More tests were ordered immediately at the Southwestern Medical Center, and the word finally passed that perhaps the best authorities on that type of cancer were in California at Stanford.

Harold and Annette flew Serena out immediately. Surgery was not recommended, but a serious bombardment of radiation was, and Harold arranged for the regimen. At the end of the long summer of treatment, the good news was confirmed that the tumor had shrunk measurably, and the prognosis was good. Serena returned to Dallas essentially cancer-free, her bond with her father even stronger.

"I know I'm alive only because I'm Harold Simmons' daughter," she openly told friends. "That's partly because of the money, but the money would be immaterial if he didn't care so much. I'm alive because of who he is."

With the challenge of Serena's physical battle, perhaps the last thing Harold was thinking about in 1991 as he passed his sixtieth birth-day was his own death. But his lawyers had been worried about the issue for some time, especially as it might affect the Harold Simmons trust after his demise. In fact, if his estate (as owned by the trust) amounted to a billion dollars at death and something wasn't done to re-structure the trust, the Internal Revenue Service would be at the door demanding $550 million of it.

The estate tax problem originated with the way the trust had been drawn to give Harold almost total control of the assets. That level of control failed IRS tests, and subjected the proceeds of the trust to the full fury of the federal estate tax. In 1989 the attorneys working on the problem had recommended an intermediate step. If, they advised, the one large trust was broken into two separate trusts—one attributable to Harold's original contributions, the other to Sandra's—the succes-sor trust flowing from that original grant made by Sandra would be ex-empt from estate taxes when Harold died, and would thus cut the es-tate tax problem in half. And, since Sandra had never exercised con-trol over the trust either before or after their divorce, her death would bring no estate tax consequences.

The second trust, however, was still subject to massive estate taxes and would inevitably be reduced by hundreds of millions of dollars if something more wasn't done to shield it. The "something more" was a plan recommended by the tax lawyers in 1994: dissolve Harold's trust and use the proceeds to form a new charitable trust, which would never go to the girls but would be usable by them during their lives. Harold's four daughters would still share the proceeds of the "Sandra" trust when their father died, and, Harold reasoned, by having the charitable trust there to pay the daughters an additional healthy management fee that would employ them for life, giving the rest away to charity would end up a win-win solution. With his net worth (through the trusts) already topping $1.6 billion, each daughter stood to receive at least $200 million from the Sandra trust alone—a considerable fortune by anyone's standards.

The first step was fairly straightforward: secure each daughter's ap-proval in the form of a simple document in which each daughter was to formally forswear and release her status as a beneficiary of the "Harold" trust. Once all four had agreed and signed the releases, Harold would become the grantor of the new charitable trust. The method required the formal filing of a court action naming all the potential beneficiaries, including the grandchildren, but from the first, there was no question that without unanimous agreement among the daughters and the grandchildren, the plan would fail. One dissenting vote would kill the idea and waste all the money expended on legal fees to set up the "giveback" legal action.

Harold discussed the matter with Lisa, who was now a full-time employee and the executive director of the Harold Simmons Foundation, the charitable giving arm of Contran that had already made headlines with major gifts to medical research and education in Dallas and elsewhere. Armed with Lisa's approval, Harold waited for an opportunity to talk with the other three.

Taking his daughters to lunch several times a month in Dallas had become a pleasant habit for Harold. There was seldom anything expensive involved, just father and daughters—usually Andrea and Serena and Lisa—getting together at Furr's Cafeteria or a similar establishment. With Andrea's moods swinging wildly and unpredictably between open expressions of love for her father and equally open expressions of hate and fury, Harold could never be sure whether the periodic lunches would end up being fun or agony. On a particular day in January 1996, however, Andrea arrived at Furr's Cafeteria in what appeared to be a suitably friendly frame of mind as she joined Serena and her father in line.

Harold had called his two daughters the day before. "I need to talk to you both," he'd said to Serena, "because my lawyers have come up with a way to eliminate the estate tax problem on the trust, but I'll need you to work with me to make it successful, and I need to explain it to you."

With the three of them around the table joking about how unusually bad and overcooked the food was that day, Harold changed the subject to that of the trust and the potentially ruinous taxes that would be paid on his death. There was a way, he explained, to avoid the problem if half of the trust money was returned to him. "What I'll do, then," Harold explained, "is form what's called a charitable remainder trust which will pay all the remaining funds to charity after all of you have died as well. In the meantime, the new trust can employ you at great salaries, and you can plan and direct how the eventual distribution will be done. What you need to do, however, is sign away your interest in half of the present trusts."

"And that will save the taxes?" Serena asked.

"It'll save literally hundreds of millions in taxes that otherwise would go to the government. This way that money will eventually benefit people directly."

Serena was clearly excited by the plan. Having graduated the year before with a degree in social work from the University of Texas at Arlington, Serena was working for the AIDS Interfaith Network. Embarrassed by her family's wealth in a world of poverty, yet sincerely appreciative of what her father and his money had been able to provide for her, Serena was devoted to charitable causes and well aware that it was only due to her father's largess that she could donate her own services on a full-time basis. The prospect of eventually helping to distribute hundreds of millions of dollars to needy human causes was a wonderful idea, and she told her father she would fully support signing away her interest in the trust in order to have it become a charitable remainder trust.

Andrea, however, was guarded and distracted while listening to her father, and openly skeptical afterward as Harold paid the bill and the two daughters walked out together.

"I think this is a great idea, Andrea. How about you?" Serena said.

At first there was no response.

"Andrea?"

"I don't know about this, Serena," Andrea said, obviously disturbed about the concept of signing away her rights to some of the money.

Harold returned to the office convinced he had three of the four required votes, and after obtaining what he thought was Scheryle's approval by phone, he authorized the legal staff to file the action, triggering the second step, the formal serving of the legal papers on the four prime beneficiaries and the grandchildren.

The fact that a uniformed officer had served the formal notice that the pro forma "lawsuit" had been filed did not bother Serena, even though the officer came to her office. But when Andrea received the same papers—one of them in the name of her infant son, Ryan—the event triggered a furious reaction.

"He's *suing* us, Serena! Don't you understand that? Harold is *suing* us!" Andrea snarled at her sister over the phone after Serena had called to see if Andrea was going to approve their dad's plan.

Serena was stunned. "Andrea, it's just a legal instrument. He's not suing us."

"Yes, he is! He's suing his grandson, and he's suing me!"

Serena ended the conversation with an all-too-familiar tightness in her stomach and a determination to report the call to her father, who had incorrectly assumed that everyone was on board.

Andrea, meanwhile, was consulting a lawyer, who in turn hired an expert in breaking large family trusts. Andrea personally authorized them to demand a full accounting of the trust, though later she would testify, under oath, that she knew next to nothing about the trust, a claim wholly contradicted by the evidence.

Harold was disturbed to hear that Andrea had reacted badly to the service of process, but Serena was even more disturbed by a subsequent conversation with her sister. Harold and Annette had been planning a summer trip to Germany with Serena, and Andrea had made sneering reference to it: "Better not count on that Germany thing," she said.

"What do you mean by that?" Serena had asked.

"Just don't count on it, that's all. Something may be coming up." Andrea had ended the call fully aware that she had already authorized her growing team of lawyers—all of whom were to be paid healthy contingency fees from any money they recovered from the trust—to file a lawsuit against her father for tens of millions of dollars in damages, and to have the trust dissolved and her share paid out immediately, demands that were later modified or dropped to make the suit appear less grasping before a jury.

In Tucson, meanwhile, Scheryle and her husband—with the aid of Andrea's calls and the assurances and representations of her own lawyers—had arrived at the same conclusion and rationale: All the money in the trusts belonged to them, not their father, and they should have it now. They could break his iron-willed reluctance to pay whatever they wanted by suing him back. After all, Andrea had wailed, "Harold" had sued first, a technicality that wholly ignored the fact that the action to dissolve the first trust required all four daughters' full agreement and was in no way a formal adverse litigation.

"I'm going to sue you, Harold!" Scheryle snarled at her father by phone one afternoon as he drove home from work, astounded at her acidic response. For the first time in a long time, Harold felt himself becoming angry.

"No, you won't, Scheryle."

"Yes, I will!" she insisted.

"Well, let me tell you something, young lady. If you file a lawsuit, it will be the biggest mistake you've ever made in your life."

There were other heated words exchanged before he terminated the call, almost quaking with anger over the stupidity of his daughter's words and attitude.

"She won't really do it," Harold assured Annette that evening as he related the infuriating call. Annette had been watching the gathering storm with great misgivings, fully expecting Andrea to go off the deep end and cause major troubles, but not necessarily expecting Scheryle to join her. Now, however, the schism was becoming all too clear. Andrea and Scheryle appeared grasping and insatiable and now seemed to have made up their minds that the money in the family trust was entirely theirs, and they wanted it immediately. Waiting for Harold to die was apparently too inconvenient.

Annette hesitated before coming to bed after the conversation. Harold had tried to reassure her and dismissed it for the night, but Annette stared out of the window for a few minutes, looking at the beauty of the backyard, where she had worked so hard to give Andrea the best possible wedding party just a few years before. There was little doubt in her mind that Harold was underestimating both of them. Annette had felt hate from them so many times before, and now that perceived hatefulness had allies with legal licenses and a major monetary incentive to destroy: the possibility of ransacking the enormously successful family trust.

She turned back toward the bed, fighting the growing kernel of fear in her middle.

CHAPTER 52

DALLAS, TEXAS: 1996

*F*rom the moment that Andrea Simmons Swanson retained a critical mass of lawyers whose income depended on breaking whatever trust was placed in their path, the chances of preventing Harold's mercurial third daughter from igniting a legal explosion diminished exponentially. Whatever Andrea's true motivation was in reacting with outrage to what her father had believed was a coordinated effort to reform the trusts, her enlistment of Scheryle Simmons Partigian in Tucson rapidly escalated into the filing of a genuine lawsuit, this one in a probate court in Dallas, seeking to remove Harold Simmons as trustee from both trusts and to gain the payment of tens of millions in alleged "damages" to the four daughters and the grandchildren who were technically the beneficiaries of the trusts.

In fact, the 1964 legal document that created the Harold Simmons trust contained all the language needed to find Scheryle and Andrea's arguments legally wrong and dispense with their attempt to wrest the trust from their father's control. The language of the original trust document itself clearly gave Harold unlimited rights to use the assets as he thought best, to buy or sell houses, planes, companies, stock, or anything else the trust owned without being second-guessed. Even in terms of compensation, there were no real limits to what Harold could pay himself as trustee over the years, although it was a fact that Harold had been extremely conservative and had never taken a dime from the corpus of the trust, despite his dizzying success as trustee, and the un-limited right he had as trustee to do so (the right of self-dealing). Even as the chief executive of the main company the trust owned, Contran Corporation, Harold had taken less than half the salary he would have been entitled to in any other corporation, and when the trust had been split into two parts, his salary and benefits had remained the same.

From Harold's point of view, and that of almost all those who knew him well, the lawsuit was an immediate family tragedy, blowing what should have been nothing more than a private disagreement into a mas-sive public fight in the courts complete with extensive and sometimes lurid media coverage. Unlike many corporate empire builders, Harold had never sought the limelight of public notoriety. Finding himself thrust once more onto the center stage of public attention at the hands of two of his four daughters—as well as being publicly accused of "mismanag-ing" a trust he had started with $33,000 and managed into $1.3 billion—was an extremely upsetting turn of fate. But with characteristic faith in his own assessment of right and wrong, he prepared Annette and himself for the fight, refusing to be forced into a settlement of a legal action which bore all the earmarks of an attempt at legal extortion. With the encouragement of daughters Lisa and Serena, both of whom flatly re-fused to join their respective sisters in the lawsuit, the extremely expen-sive process of depositions and discovery got under way, with the ironic footnote that Scheryle and Andrea were apparently expecting their fa-ther to pay all the legal bills for their attempt to disenfranchise him.

While Harold at first dismissed the possibility that Scheryle and Andrea could win and force him from control of the trusts, his legal team was less sanguine, and what lay in the balance was staggering in scope: the ownership and control of Contran Corporation, owned in full by the trusts, and containing the vast majority of everything Harold Simmons had built.

"He spent his whole life," Fred Bartlit, Harold's lead attorney in de-fending the suit, would later say in court, "[putting] every good idea he had for an investment, every investment he had, he put it in the trust for the girls. He didn't build his own private . . . estate for himself that he could con-trol and build . . . for him and his wife." Indeed, there had never been an expectation on Harold's part that the trust itself was anything more than an intelligent vessel for preserving and protecting the money he made so as to have an even larger estate for his girls when he died.

The key was his death. Never had there been a reason to worry that anyone in the family would misunderstand that intent. But the Simmons extended family now included two nonworking male spouses, Lance Partigian and Randell Swanson, neither of whom seemed satisfied with the houses Harold had purchased for them or the massive allowances they enjoyed through their respective wives. When that extended family suddenly included a cadre of lawyers hot on the trail of massive spoils, dubious claims were filed against Harold with the aim of forcing a fat settlement, of which the plaintiff lawyers would receive 20 percent. When attempts to force a settlement failed, the request for damages was dropped to avoid the appearance of avarice, and the apparent fiction adopted that Scheryle and Andrea were merely suing as a matter of principle. The fact that the agreement with the law firms representing Scheryle and Andrea called for them to receive 20 percent of any money broken free from the trust, and the outside possibility, however remote, that the total figure against which that 20 percent could be applied might be in the hundreds of millions, motivated the plaintiff legal team to fight hard with virtually no regard for the feelings or the reputation—or the honest intent—of Harold Simmons. It was, in fact, a mercenary war, and given the clever maneuvering of the girls' legal team and the fact that the case would be presented to a jury of people to whom a billion of anything was beyond unthinkable, a disturbingly real possibility began to emerge that a nightmare scenario might include Harold being deposed as trustee.

It would be difficult to underestimate the potential damage of such an occurrence to the basic value of the Contran stock, the asset that formed the basis of the Simmons fortune. Contran without Harold Simmons would have become a corporation without a rudder, full of highly capable senior executives thrown into deep and immediate uncertainty, and the resulting tumult would undoubtedly affect the stock values of every associated company. While ruinous wholesale liquidation of the company at the hands of a substitute trustee would have been highly unlikely, neither was there anyone else who understood how to nurture and improve the value and performance of the billion-dollar industrial collection Harold had created and placed in the trust.

In addition, the personal disaster would have been massive. Removal as trustee of all he had created would have, in practical terms, wiped out the material benefits and rewards of thirty years of hard work. The fact that the possibility existed at all was bad enough in the eyes of the legions of friends who sent supportive letters and stood with him, but the fact that such a demise could come at the hands of two daughters, who had been given almost everything life had to offer, triggered more than a few comparisons to Shakespeare's King Lear.

■　　■　　■

As the pretrial preparations dragged into the spring and summer of 1997 with embarrassing attendant publicity, Harold found himself in the rather strange position of being accused of bad faith, essentially for turning $33,000 into $1.3 billion in thirty years, apparently without having given enough of it in the meantime to Andrea and Scheryle.

The trial itself began in November of 1997 in a turn-of-the-century courthouse on the west end of downtown Dallas, a block from the infamous Texas School Book Depository. The aim of the plaintiffs' lawyers would be to portray Harold Simmons as just as greedy and duplicitous as Andrea and Scheryle and their husbands would look if their full motivation, as Harold perceived it, could be explained to the jury. Yet, trying to present both girls as being wholly disinterested in the very money they were trying to dislodge from their father's hands was a tall order, and the plaintiffs' teams were already expending millions of their own funds to accomplish just that. The fight wound its way through daily newspaper and television coverage as the attacking forces pulled out all the stops, excoriating the most routine and innocent of Harold's executive decisions for the trusts as if the original trust document had *not* permitted "self-dealing," which it clearly did.

Closing arguments finally began on the morning of December 11, but the jury took until the following Wednesday to decide that they were hopelessly deadlocked over whether or not hypertechnical violations of the Texas trust guidelines constituted sufficient grounds to ignore the $33,000-to-$1.3 billion reality that the trust's beneficiaries had been anything but hurt by Harold's management.

Facing the disheartening prospect of having to go through the six-week trial all over again, plus the bruising reality that the jury had actually considered Scheryle and Andrea's arguments, Harold authorized his legal team in the following days *to discuss* a settlement.

The trial had been brutal on both of them, but every day after the agony of being in the courtroom Annette had faxed a largely upbeat report to Jill Smith, who then faxed it in turn to a network of their close Dallas friends. She recalled the supportive letters they'd received from the same network and from others—amazingly warm notes of support and encouragement and solid friendship which had bolstered them considerably. Her lifelong friend, Paul Bass, had sat most days by her side in the courtroom. The support and kindness of such friends had been a bedrock for her strength, and she knew it had done wonders for Harold's spirits as well.

As Christmas approached, Steve Watson, an accomplished CPA and senior vice president of Contran, as well as one of Harold's trusted inner circle, was assigned the responsibility for working with the legal team on a possible settlement with Andrea and Scheryle's lawyers, all of whom were unwilling to walk away from the vicinity of $1.3 billion without a significant cut of the fortune.

The fact that Scheryle and Andrea's lawyers had been able to talk three members of the jury into voting against Harold meant that they might be able to do so again in a second trial. That reality lessened the wisdom of refusing to negotiate and opting to try the case again. Then, too, the attacking law firms had failed to win, and would receive nothing if they spent millions more in a second trial and failed to remove him a second time. Steve Watson and the rest of Harold's legal team were driving a hard bargain and refusing to discuss a large cash settlement without creation of new trusts to prevent Andrea and Scheryle from blowing any money they might receive. The negotiations were brutal, and as they continued after Christmas, Harold and Annette decided to head to Santa Barbara for a few days of rest and distance from the storm.

On January 11 they returned to Dallas feeling marginally better, both of them well aware that the negotiations that had begun with monumental clashes and outrageous demands were moving toward an agreement Harold could accept. Steve Watson had been in the thick of the battle, and was reporting progress, though the strain of dealing with the avaricious interests of the thwarted plaintiff attorneys was taking a toll on him.

■　　■　　■

On February 10, 1998—after nearly two months of intense negotiation by Steve Watson and a team of Contran lawyers and executives—Harold sat in his office and approved a five-paragraph statement for the media announcing the settlement of the lawsuit.

I am very pleased with the settlement that Judge DeShazo approved today, which ends the trust lawsuit brought by two of my four daughters against me.

Under the settlement, I will remain trustee of the Simmons Family Trusts, which are worth more than $1 billion. I will also retain all the positions I hold with the companies owned by the Trusts.

The two daughters who sued will no longer be Trust beneficiaries and will have no rights to the Trusts. Trust assets totaling approximately $50 million for each [of the two] daughters [who sued] will be used to fund separate trusts for them and their children, and to pay legal bills. My two other daughters (and their children) will become the only beneficiaries of the Trusts.

This lawsuit was a sad event for my family. I have spent my career building the value of the Trusts for all my daughters' benefit. I believe this lawsuit and the attacks were wrong.

As I said, I am very pleased with the terms of this settlement, and am glad to end this matter.

CHAPTER 53

DALLAS LOVE FIELD, DALLAS, TEXAS: 2000

"*F*alcon November One Five Alpha Sierra cleared ILS approach, Runway One Three Left, maintain two thousand feet until established on localizer, contact Love Field tower now one-twenty-three-seven." Mike Bonnell relaxed his right index finger, letting the radio transmit rocker switch on the control yoke return to neutral as his boss, Harold Simmons, banked the Falcon left slightly and prepared to intercept the final course.

"One-twenty-three-seven," Harold echoed in confirmation, his hands on the controls, his mind partly on the pleasing fact that the day had gone so well.

There were several crates of East Texas sweet potatoes in the baggage compartment of N15AS, each of which he had purchased for thousands of dollars in order to donate money through the Sweet Potato Festival to the residents of his hometown of Golden.

But this was the second year he'd invited Cleta (Worley) Mitchell, Thomasine (Champion) Hamrick, Johnnie Bill (Gilbert) Trussels, and Bobbie Nell (Cathey) Wright along in the Falcon to fly from Dallas to Golden and back, and it had been a mutual delight.

Behind him in the plush cabin, four former girlfriends and classmates of one of the richest men in the world sat in the luxurious swivel chairs of his private jet and watched the frenetic complexity of North Dallas draw closer as they descended for landing. The years had robbed each of them of their husbands now, but the bonds that had been formed in the tiny community of Golden some sixty years before had remained unbroken. There was no shared agony of things they didn't have growing up, but instead a shared respect for the journey and for each other, as well as a shared pride in the fact that all four of them had managed to navigate life with more success than failure.

The talk on that day had been varied, enthusiastic, routine, focusing on children and grandchildren, plans and problems, and shared memories. The previous year's trip to Golden with Harold had broken the ice, and now they could luxuriate happily in the pretended routine of it all, as if for one day a year they could live like Harold lived.

But there was a strong, underlying current of pride in far more than just the business and monetary success of their former classmate, sitting unseen in the captain's seat of the cockpit some twenty feet away. There was a pride in the fact that he'd never become anything other than the steady and handsome young man they remembered from their childhood. There were no barriers in talking to him, no distance born of privilege or the caution of the rich man reacting to the all-too-common enmity of the jealous and the entreaties of the supplicant. Harold was Harold, year in and year out, and the same occasionally hilarious dry sense of humor had only sharpened with time.

All four of them had followed his business career over the decades and the travails of the daughter trial, faithfully clipping infuriatingly neutral newspaper articles written by reporters trying to be balanced in the face of horrid allegations against their friend. All four wished *they* could be called upon to tell the jury themselves what an incredibly good man Harold really was, and more to the point, how glad they were that now, more than ever, he really seemed to be enjoying life, as well as sharing some of those moments with the friends he never forgot.

"Okay," one of the four had said, "so we're your cheerleaders." But the pride ran deep, and what Harold C. had accomplished enriched them all in ways money could never affect. It was a validation of the worth of their community and their values, and a validation of their characters forged together in the small world they had shared so long ago.

■   ■   ■

By the summer of 2001, it was more than comfortable for Harold to leave the corporate ship sailing steadily without his daily presence. The superlative staff he had assembled—a staff whose metal had been forged in the fires of corporate combat from NL Industries through Lockheed—let him do what he did best: think, and apply his strategic talents where necessary. He had no intention of retiring, of course. Even the daily challenges of running a far-flung conglomerate empire were just too interesting to permit a master financier and an accomplished business leader to disconnect. But with the administrative prowess of his brother Glenn and the steady professionalism of men like Steve Watson (now president of the corporation), Contran could be overseen by its chairman through telephone, fax, and the daily FedEx dispatch from Dallas or wherever in the world he wanted to be.

And the world *had* opened up to his interest and his presence as he and Annette took, and planned, more trips. With the decade-long rise of stock values, and corporate stock prices reaching insane levels based on nothing more than wild, unprincipled speculation, even previously undervalued industries were seeing their public valuation soar beyond the boundaries of sanity. There were few corporations trading publicly that came close to fitting Harold's traditional tests, and even with the collapse of the dot-com corporations—stocks inflated beyond all vestiges of reality often for companies that had never made a profit—the bargains were few and far between.

Even where there might be a viable undervalued target, there were the laws of the State of Delaware, the friend of the entrenched. As long as the state refused to change or ameliorate their statutes permitting poison pills and other scorched-earth management defenses, Harold's well-honed ability to find hidden values in public companies was all but useless, and a relic of another time. Certainly, Contran had continued to explore new businesses under his careful direction, including investment in a company processing nuclear waste in an untapped market. But even that had become a hostage of political ambition and shifting laws, as governors and bureaucrats alike stalled the basic issue of where to dispose of the nation's nuclear power waste in favor of wallowing in regulations and mindless delays.

With the stock market sinking back toward some semblance of reality, Harold watched and waited, possessed of the assets to be a formidable force on the acquisition trail when the prices, and the values, were right.

In the meantime, there was still a world out there he had yet to fully experience, and he was going to take advantage of the opportunity. In the late spring of 2001, he and Annette boarded N15AS along with Mike Bonnell and Al DiNiro—his two professional pilots—to begin a multi-week trip to Australia and New Zealand. On return, what had become an annual "move" to Santa Barbara began, with Harold looking forward to playing golf in the balmy temperatures of the California coast while Dallas roasted in hundred-degree heat.

Golf had become a passion for Harold, an invigorating battle with himself. He'd been very good at tennis, an intense and capable player, but he'd been increasingly hampered by what the rigors of the game were doing to his back, and eventually it was time to quit. Golf had been the substitute, and he'd attacked it with his usual dedication to detail and precision, just as he had flying, enjoying the ability to overcome the normal obstacles and improve with every round. He was loving golf, and golfing in the Montecito area was a daily joy.

A small host of pleasant routines had taken hold of them at Piranhurst, routines that soothed and enervated him at the same time. Breakfasts and lunches were an example, usually prepared and served on the various patios or poolside garden lanai by Gilles and Francoise Bellanger, the French husband and wife team who took care of their home year round. The evenings were often social, with the two of them driving down their tree-lined driveway to have dinner with friends or attend a local party, if not hosting many of the same friends at Piranhurst.

And in the late afternoons, Annette and Harold had become fond of walking through their own grounds and down the surrounding lanes of Montecito, enjoying each other and holding hands, walking quietly, sometimes stopping to pick a ripe orange off one of their trees. Both were continually amazed that such an estate could be theirs.

"I never feel as if I own this place," Harold had said more than once. "I feel like we've just been allowed to borrow it for a while."

Montecito and Santa Barbara had become almost as much their home as Dallas, and when two of their closest local friends found a well-known and well-loved national celebrity on their doorstep one day in June 2001, Harold and Annette were among the first to hear about it.

"Oprah? You're kidding!"

"No," was the laughing reply on the other end of the phone. "She's been shopping for a place in the Santa Barbara area and she wants to buy ours."

"But, you're not selling, are you?"

"We weren't," Marlene said. "But when she offered Bob fifty million dollars, he decided he was too much of a businessman not to accept."

With the Montecito area abuzz about the arrival of the most successful woman in American entertainment history, Annette had decided to invite their new neighbor to dinner in early July, an invitation quickly and graciously accepted. A thorough veteran of countless parties and dinners and social events, Annette still found herself smiling somewhat uncontrollably over the upcoming party, a small betrayal of the internal excitement they both felt. On the shelf in the den of Piranhurst's west wing sat a picture of Harold and Annette with Burt Reynolds and Loni Anderson from a single evening years before, when the two Hollywood luminaries had been their "new best friends for the night." It was a fun memory, just as Harold's friendship with actor Michael Douglas was an added delight.

And now the opportunities afforded by being good at what you did in America meant a chance to meet, and entertain, and get to know a woman whose reputation for graciousness and genuine warmth preceded her. Both Harold and Annette were far beyond fawning over a celebrity, but the ability to feel excitement in the presence of a major public figure was yet another validation that the two kids from East Texas who had found each other so belatedly in life were still there, their personalities unaffected and unspoiled by their achievements and their wealth—as a dizzying array of friends could attest.

And life itself was getting progressively better, especially in the absence of the continuous torture Andrea and Scheryle had always imposed. The two estranged daughters were blocked by terms of the settlement from making contact, and that, Annette thought, had been a hidden gift. If they had simply won the daughter trial outright, Andrea and Scheryle would still be out there, ready, willing, and able to make their lives miserable to infinity. Now, thanks to the hung jury and the resulting settlement, they were gone, validating the premise that the agony had turned out for the best, despite the intense pain it had imposed.

CHAPTER 54

DALLAS, TEXAS: 2001

*E*lizabeth Woolverton looked up from her desk outside Harold Simmons' office and smiled at the procession of familiar faces parading out of a Friday afternoon meeting. She had come aboard as Harold's secretary when Pam Phillips retired years before, and knew each of the men well: Glenn Simmons, Bill Lindquist, and Steve Watson. They were all touching base before Harold departed for a weekend at the 400-acre McKinney farm just north of Dallas.

"How're you doing?" Glenn asked her, exchanging small talk as they pushed through the door to the hallway and she moved into Harold's office.

"Mr. Simmons? Serena wanted to talk with you before you leave."

"Okay," he said, a big smile spreading across his face at the mention of his youngest daughter's name. She and her husband would be coming to lunch at the farm later in the weekend. "She's still in her office?" he asked.

"Yes, sir. I think she and Lisa are meeting about something."

The thought of his two daughters—the two "good daughters" as they were now unofficially known in the family—working together in the company environment he had created pleased him greatly, as did the closeness that he and Serena Simmons Connelly had developed again following the "divorce" from Andrea. Even Annette was feeling the warmth of the acceptance of Harold's youngest, whose personality was that of the perennial healer. Where her older sister had pressured her to reject Annette, Serena, left to her own impulses, had embraced her father's third wife warmly, and she had developed a habit of thanking her father in small notes every now and then, notes that meant more to Harold than he'd ever admit.

Lisa Simmons Epstein, too, had grown closer. They were together in the beautiful glass tower that housed the offices Harold had built, and when he was gone, it would be Lisa, the head of the Simmons Foundation dedicated to giving away money to worthy causes, and Serena, who had always been uncomfortable with the incredible wealth of her family and anxious to share it, who would inherit over $1.5 billion worth of corporate value. It was their father's desire that they give most of that wealth away in a manner that did society the most good, and neither daughter would be inclined to disappoint him.

"I'll see you on Monday," Harold told his secretary as he signed the last document she'd prepared for him and slipped out through the meeting room side and made his way down the carpeted hallway, a definite spring in his step as he turned into his daughter's office.

■　　■　　■

The family sat down to Sunday lunch in the home Annette had designed and decorated. Serena and her husband Tom sat on the left, now friends with Annette's daughter Amy, Annette's son Andy, his wife, Kammy, Lisa, her husband, James, and all the grandchildren settled into chairs near the other end of the table, as Annette placed another serving dish in the middle and took her chair next to her husband.

Harold had been waiting to say grace, and he began now, bowing his head and holding hands with his loved ones as the family did likewise, thanking his Maker for the food, for their good health, and their love for each other, ending the prayer with the heartfelt words, "Thank you, thank you, thank you."

A moment of silence passed and the family prepared to open their eyes and raise their heads, as Harold suddenly continued, his eyes tightly shut, his heart welling.

"God, please," he said quietly, "don't let us ever forget . . . how very, very blessed we are!"

Harold Simmons
Family Album

High School Senior Harold Simmons

Harold at age one.

Parents Leon and Fairess Simmons.

Harold and Glenn with their mother,
Fairess Simmons, circa 1939.

Harold at eleven, Glenn at fourteen.

Leon Simmons (father), circa 1949-50.

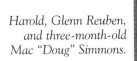

*Harold, Glenn Reuben,
and three-month-old
Mac "Doug" Simmons.*

Harold and daughters
Andrea and Serena.

Harold Simmons.

Opening of Ward's Drug.

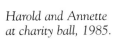

*Harold and Annette
at charity ball, 1985.*

*At Serena's wedding,
October 7, 1995.*

Christmas, 1999.

Natalie, Serena and Tom's baby,
with Harold (2000).

Lisa (holding baby Harrison),
Harold and Serena.

Tom Connelly, Serena Connelly, Harold and Annette Simmons,
Lisa Epstein (holding Harrison), and James Epstein.

The Arkansas farm.

On the McKinney farm.

Harold's sixtieth birthday.

Harold's seventieth birthday with Glen Campbell.

Harold and Annette with Larry Hagman.

Harold with Tom Landry.

Harold and Annette at Deloache.

Deloache Garden.

Oprah Winfrey and
Harold Simmons, 2003.

Harold and Annette
in Montecito, 2001.

Harold's friends from high school.

Sweet Potato Festival in Golden, Texas.

The family, 1989.

The family, Thanksgiving 1999. From left: Andy Fleck, Adrienne Fleck, with Austin and Kammy Fleck in front, Serena Connelly (holding Harrison Epstein), Lisa Epstein, Annette and Harold Simmons, Tom Connelly, and Amy Weber. (Not pictured: James Epstein.)